AF568110

ENV BOOKS SERIES

HEAVY METALS AND METALLOIDS IN BIOSPHERE

IMPACTS AND ASSESSMENT

Editors

Dr. Avnish Chauhan
Associate Professor
Phonics Group of Institutions
Roorkee (Uttarakhand)
(INDIA)

Dr. Sandeep Gupta
Assistant Professor
Department of Applied Science & Humanities
Ajay Kumar Garg Engineering College
Adhyatmik Nagar, Ghaziabad (UP)
(INDIA)

Dr. Pawan Kumar 'Bharti'
Vice President
Society for Environment, Health, Awareness of Nutrition & Toxicology (SEHAT)
1775, Sohan Ganj, Near Clock Tower
Delhi - 110 007
(INDIA)
E-mail: gurupawanbharti@gmail.com

DISCOVERY PUBLISHING HOUSE PVT. LTD.
INDIA

Published by:

Namit Wasan

DISCOVERY PUBLISHING HOUSE PVT. LTD.
4383/4B, Ansari Road, Darya Ganj
New Delhi-110 002 (India)
Phone : +91-11-23279245, 43596064-65
Fax : +91-11-23253475
E-mail : discoverypublishinghouse@gmail.com
namitwasan9@gmail.com
sales@discoverypublishinggroup.com
website: www.discoverypublishinggroup.com

First Edition: 2017

ISBN: 978-93-5056-860-6

Heavy Metals and Metalloids in Biosphere
Impacts and Assessment

Printed at:
Infinity Imaging Systems
Delhi

ENV Books Series, (India)

Calls lengthy and error free chapters for further volumes of books on various environmental issues. (Send your manuscripts to envbooks@gmail.com)

Founding Editor (Editor-in-Chief)

Dr. Pawan Kumar 'Bharti'

Society for Environment, Health, Awareness of Nutrition & Toxicology (SEHAT-India)
1775, Sohanganj, Near Clock Tower, Delhi-7, (India)
E-mail:*gurupawanbharti@rediffmail.com*

Other Titles by Editor-in-Chief:

1. **Advances in Biotechnology and Ecological Sciences**
   Bharti, P.K., Chauhan, A. and Ray, J. (eds.)
   (ISBN: 978-93-5056-358-8).
2. **Advances in Agriculture and Ecology**
   Bharti, P.K.; Chauhan, A. and Ezeaku Peter Ikemefuna (eds.)
   (ISBN: 978-93-5056-362-5).
3. **Agriculture and Environmental Biotechnology**
   Bharti, P.K. and Chauhan, A. (eds.)
   (ISBN: 978-93-5056-479-0).
4. **Agriculture Development and Sustainable Environment**
   Ray, J. and Bharti, P.K. (eds.)
   (ISBN: 978-93-5056-759-3).
5. **Agriculture Ecology and Environment**
   Bharti, P.K. and Olubukola O. Babalola (eds.)
   (ISBN: 978-93-5056-480-6).
6. **Agriculture Ecology, Sustainable Development and Agribusiness Management**
   Mehta Piyush; Sharma Pankaj; and 'Bharti' P.K. (eds.)
   (ISBN: 978-93-5056-851-4).
7. **Agriculture, Environment and Nano-science**
   Bharti, Pawan K. (ed.)
   (ISBN: 978-93-5056-760-5).

8. **Agricultural Practices and Crop Disease Control**
Chauhan Alka and Sharma Anubhuti (eds.)
(ISBN: 978-93-5056-859-0).

9. **Agro-biodiversity:** ***Conservation and Sustainable Development***
Sharma, Pankaj; Singh, Narayan; and Bharti, P.K. (eds.)
(ISBN: 978-93-505-782-1).

10. **Agro-forestry and Climate Change**
Bharti, Pawan K. and Singh, Narayan (eds.)
(ISBN: 978-93-5056-514-8).

11. **Agro-forestry and Sustainable Agriculture**
Sharma, Pankaj; Bharti, P.K. (eds.)
(ISBN: 978-93-5056-786-9).

12. **Aquaculture and Fisheries Environment**
Gupta, S.K. and Pawan K. Bharti (eds.)
(ISBN: 978-93-5056-408-0).

13. **Aquatic Biodiversity and Pollution**
Bharti, P.K.; Chauhan, A. and Kaoud, H.A.H. (eds.)
(ISBN: 978-93-5056-359-5).

14. **Aquatic Ecology and Biotechnology**
Bharti, P.K. and Zaki, M.S.A. (eds.)
(ISBN: 978-93-5056-451-6).

15. **Aquatic Environment and Toxicology**
Bharti, Pawan K. (ed.)
(ISBN: 978-93-5056-236-9).

16. **Biodiversity, Biotechnology and Environmental Conservation**
Bharti, P.K. and Bhandari, G. (eds.)
(ISBN: 978-93-5056-750-0).

17. **Biodiversity of Aquatic Ecosystem:** ***Significance, Threat and Conservation*** **(2013)**
Bharti, P.K. and Kaoud, H.A.H. (eds.)
(ISBN: 978-93-5056-297-0).

18. **Biological Diversity and Ecology**
Arya, M.K.; Bharti, P.K. and Ritesh Joshi (eds.)
(ISBN: 978-93-5056-785-2).

19. **Bioremediation and Microbial Biotechnology**
Gupta, Sandeep; and Bharti, P.K. (eds.)
(ISBN: 978-93-5056-783-8).

20. **Biotechnological Approaches and Water Ecosystem**
Zaki, M.S.A.; and Bharti, P.K. (eds.)
(ISBN: 978-93-5056-779-1).

21. **Biotechnology, Agro-ecology and Environment**
Chauhan, Avnish and Bharti, P.K. (eds.)
(ISBN: 978-93-5056-757-9).
22. **Biotechnology and Environmental Management**
Arya Arun; Raaz K. Maheswari and P.K. Bharti (eds.)
(ISBN: 978-93-5056-862-0).
23. **Clean Technologies and Environmental Protection**
Chauhan, A.; Sharma, S. and Bharti, P.K. (eds.)
(ISBN: 978-93-5056-731-9).
24. **Climate Change and Agriculture**
Bharti, P.K. and Chauhan, Avnish (eds.)
(ISBN: 978-93-5056-148-5).
25. **Climate Change and Biodiversity**
Bharti, P.K. and Chauhan, Avnish (eds.)
(ISBN: 978-93-5056-360-1).
26. **Climate Change, Disaster Management and Environment**
Chauhan, Alka; Bharti, P.K. (eds.)
(ISBN: 978-93-5056-784-5).
27. **Conservation and Cultivation of Medicinal Plants**
Bharti, P.K. and Singh Narayan (eds.)
(ISBN: 978-93-5056-740-1).
28. **Crop Productivity and Plant Disease Management**
Chauhan, Alka; Bharti, P.K. and Sadana, Deepti (eds.)
(ISBN: 978-93-5056-791-3).
29. **Eco-toxicology and Eco-technology**
Bharti, P.K. and Zaki, M. (eds.)
(ISBN: 978-93-5056-313-7).
30. **Environmental Biotechnology and Application**
Bharti, P.K. and Chauhan, Avnish (eds.)
(ISBN: 978-93-5056-262-8).
31. **Environmental Conservation and Biotechnology**
Chauhan, A. and P.K. Bharti (eds.)
(ISBN: 978-93-5056-512-4).
32. **Environmental Health and Problems**
Bharti, P.K. and Gajananda, Kh. (eds.)
(ISBN: 978-93-5056-263-5).
33. **Environmental Pollution and Biodiversity**
Bharti, P.K.; Chauhan, Avnish and Kumar, P. (eds.)
(ISBN: 978-93-5056-149-2).
34. **Farming Techniques and Crop Production**
Chauhan Alka; Sharma Anubhuti; Ray Jaswant and 'Bharti' P.K. (eds.)
(ISBN: 978-93-5056-855-2).

35. **Fisheries and Toxicology**
    Zaki, M.S.A.; Bharti, P.K. and Chauhan, A. (eds.)
    (ISBN: 978-93-5056-452-3).
36. **Fish Habitat and Aquaculture**
    Bharti, P.K.; Gupta Kr. Sanjay (eds.)
    (ISBN: 978-93-5056-744-9).
37. **Food Processing, Management and Nanotechnology**
    Chauhan, Avnish; Bharti, P.K. (eds.)
    (ISBN: 978-93-5056-796-8).
38. **Freshwater Ecosystem and Xenobiotics**
    Bharti, P.K.; Zaki, M. and Chauhan, A. (eds.)
    (ISBN: 978-93-5056-299-4).
39. **Limnology and Aquatic Science**
    Sharma, S. and Bharti, P.K. (eds.)
    (ISBN: 978-93-5056-735-7).
40. **Medicinal Plants:** ***Distribution, Utilization and Significance***
    Sharma, P.; Bharti, P.K. and Narayan Singh (eds.)
    (ISBN: 978-93-5056-734-0).
41. **Microbial Applications and Environment**
    Bharti, Pawan K. (ed.)
    (ISBN: 978-93-5056-515-5).
42. **Microbial Ecology and Habitat**
    Bharti, Pawan K. (ed.)
    (ISBN: 978-93-5056-514-8).
43. **Microbial Environment and Bioremediation**
    Chauhan Alka; K. Rathoure Ashok; and K Maheshwari Raaz (eds.)
    (ISBN: 978-93-5056-856-9).
44. **Natural Ecosystem and Climate Change**
    Bharti, P.K., and Kh. Gajananda (ed.)
    (ISBN: 978-93-5056-745-6).
45. **Pest Management and Agro-Techniques**
    Biswas, Asim; Bharti, P.K., Chauhan, Avnish (eds.)
    (ISBN: 978-93-5056-794-4).
46. **Prakriti me Aushadhi (*in Hindi*)**
    Singh, J.R.; Bharti, P.K. and Bharti, B.
    (ISBN: 978-93-5056-200-0).
47. **Seed Technology, Plant Growth and Cropping System**
    Tyagi, P.K. and Bharti, P.K. (eds.)
    (ISBN: 978-93-5056-738-8).

48. **Seed Treatment, Plant Heath and Agro-technology**
Chauhan, A. and Bharti, P.K. (eds.)
(ISBN: 978-93-5056-810-1).
49. **Soil Characteristics and Agro-ecology**
Avnish Chauhan and Bharti, P.K. (eds.)
(ISBN: 978-93-5056-758-6).
50. **Soil Contamination and Conservation**
Ezeaku, P.I. and Bharti, P.K. (eds.)
(ISBN: 978-93-5056-737-1).
51. **Soil Quality and Contamination**
Bharti, P.K. and Chauhan, Avnish (eds.)
(ISBN: 978-93-5056-361-8).
52. **Sustainable Aquaculture Management**
Gupta, S.K.; Bharti, P.K (eds.)
(ISBN: 978-93-5056-797-5).
53. **Waste Disposal and Management**
Bharti, P.K.; Tabassum, B. and Bajaj, P. (eds.)
(ISBN: 978-93-5056-729-6).
54. **Waste Generation and Utilization**
Bajaj Priya; Tabassum, B., and Bharti, P.K. (eds.)
(ISBN: 978-93-5056-792-0).
55. **Waste Management and Environmental Health**
Tabassum, B., Bajaj Priya, and Bharti, P.K. (eds.)
(ISBN: 978-93-5056-777-7).
56. **Water Resources and Agriculture**
Bharti, P.K. and Ezeaku Peter Ikemefuna (eds.)
(ISBN: 978-93-5056-481-3).
57. **Water Resources:** ***Mapping, Monitoring and Management***
Tyagi P.K; Chauhan Avnish and Bharti P.K. (eds.)
(ISBN: 978-93-5056-861-3).
58. **Waste Resources Management:** ***Monitoring and Assessment***
Gupta, Sandeep and Bharti, P.K. (eds.)
(ISBN: 978-93-5056-799-9).

Preface

The earth's surface and near surface regions are dominated by interfaces among solids, liquids, and gases. Such interfaces, particularly those between natural solids and aqueous solutions, play an enormously important role in a number of geological and geochemical processes. For example, 'water-rock' interactions over geologic time have been major contributors to both the rock cycle and the geochemical cycling of elements. In an environmental context, interfacial processes such as: mineral dissolution, mineral precipitation, and the sorption and desorption of chemical species are responsible for the release and/or sequestration of heavy metals that may eventually become pollutants in soils and groundwater.

Such processes range from dissolution of mineral particles in soils, which can release natural contaminants into pore waters, to the binding or sorption of metals and organic ligands to mineral surfaces, which can effectively immobilize contaminants and reduce their bioavailability. Precipitation is another common means of sequestering a heavy metal if the precipitated phase is relatively insoluble. Some heavy metal contaminants such as: lead normally exist in minerals in one dominant oxidation state, whereas others such as: arsenic and selenium can exist in several oxidation states and can undergo oxidation or reduction when they interact with mineral surfaces or organic compounds, which act as oxidants or reductants. Microorganisms and plants can have a profound influence on chemical reactions involving contaminants. Thus, mineral weathering rates and the solubility of mineral elements and anthropogenic contaminants are generally greater in surface soils, where plant and microbial activity are higher than in deeper parts of the soil and geologic column.

Ultimately, the impact of heavy metals and other environmental contaminants on humans and other organisms depends on their concentration levels, toxicity, and bioavailability, *i.e.*, the extent to which they are absorbed by the blood or stored in internal organs. The toxicity and bioavailability of a heavy metal, in turn, depend in part on reactivity and solubility, which are determined by the speciation or chemical form of the element.

Pollution induced by heavy metals and metalloids in soils is a serious environmental problem because, in comparison with the atmosphere and water, the soil environment has a much lower ability to recover from toxic effects. In soil, trace elements potentially toxic to plants and other living organisms are involved in chemical and biological reactions such as: solution and surface complexation, precipitation, sorption-desorption, and oxidation-reduction. These elements interact with a series of clay minerals, humic substances, metal oxides, microorganisms, extracellular enzymes, biopolymers, and other organic and inorganic ligands. Their behaviour depends on chemical and physicochemical as well as biological processes and their interactions with microbial activities. These physicochemical-biological interactions would influence the transfer of these elements from the inorganic and organic soil constituents to the soil solution and to plants and contaminate the terrestrial food chain, thus endangering human and animal health. Biogeochemical processes operating in soil environments that affect the fate, behaviour, and bioavailability of metals and metalloids are currently an area of active research.

The present book updates the subject content of environmental sciences, mineralogy, soil biochemistry, soil microbiology, related to understanding the biophysico-chemical processes of these metallic pollutants in environments.

Thanks are due to publisher and contributors from different institutions. The book will be helpful for the researchers, academia working in the field of metal and mineralogy, soil biochemistry, soil microbiology, Heavy metals and metalloids as related to understanding the biophysico-chemical processes of these pollutants in environments.

– Editors
(envbooks@gmail.com)

Contents

Pages 1-24

HEAVY METALS AND METALLOIDS IN BIOSPHERE: *IMPACTS AND ASSESSMENT*
***Edited by* : Dr. Avnish Chauhan; Dr. Sandeep Gupta & Dr. Pawan Kumar Bharti**
***Edition* : 2017**
ISBN : 978-93-5056-860-6
***Published by* : Discovery Publishing House Pvt. Ltd., New Delhi (India)**

Heavy Metals in Aquatic Ecosystem

Pawan Kumar Bharti

ABSTRACT

The present chapter deals with the water quality status of Sahastradhara stream by evaluating the solid waste-generation and the assessment of heavy metals along with the river stretch. A study on Heavy Metals assessment in the water of Sahastradhara hill-stream was conducted with different five sites at significant differences. Heavy Metals were found in fluctuated trend from first upstream to last downstream. The values of almost all Heavy Metals were found in increasing manner especially after the fourth sampling site. After the third sampling station, a solid waste dump site was found. So, there may be a doubt on relation between Heavy Metals in stream water and solid waste dumping site. Concentrations of all Heavy Metals at fourth and fifth sampling site were found very high in comparison to rest of the sampling sites.

***Keywords*:** water quality, river ecology, heavy metal, solid waste dumping site, aquatic ecosystem.

INTRODUCTION

Metals that are naturally introduced into the water bodies come primarily from such sources as rock weathering, soil erosion, or the dissolution of water-soluble salts. Naturally occurring metals move through aquatic environments independently of human activities, usually without any detrimental effects.

Humans consume metallic elements through both water and food. Some metals such as: sodium, potassium, magnesium, calcium, and iron are found in living tissue and are essential to human life. Probably less well known is that

Vice President, Society for Environment, Health, Awareness of Nutrition and Toxicology (SEHAT), 1775, Sohan Ganj, Near Clock Tower, Delhi - 110 007, India.

currently no less than six other heavy metals including: molybdenum, manganese, cobalt, copper, and zinc, have been linked to human growth, development, achievement, and reproduction (Vahrenkamp, 1979). Even these metals, however, can become toxic or aesthetically undesirable when their concentrations are too great. Several heavy metals, like: cadmium, lead, and mercury, are highly toxic at relatively low concentrations, can accumulate in body tissues over long periods of time, and are nonessential for human health.

The toxic heavy metals entering the ecosystem may lead to geo-accumulation, bioaccumulation and biomagnifications. Heavy metals like: Fe, Cu, Zn, Ni and other trace elements are important for proper functioning of biological systems and their deficiency or excess could lead to a number of disorders. Food chain contamination by heavy metals has become a burning issue in recent years because of their potential accumulation in biosystems through contaminated water, soil and air.

Therefore, a better understanding of heavy metal sources, their accumulation in the soil and the effect of their presence in water and soil on plant systems seem to be particularly important issues of present-day research on risk assessments (Lokeshwari and Chandrappa, 2006).

Water is an important substance required by all living organisms and for all anthropogenic activities. The problem of environmental pollution due to toxic metals has begun to cause concern now in most major metropolitan cities (Bharti, 2007a). Most of our water resources are gradually becoming polluted due to the addition of foreign materials from the surroundings. These include organic matter origin from plant and animal, land surface washing, Industrial and sewage effluents. In some tourist hilly regions, there are not any more industrial pollution, but tourist's anthropogenic activities may alter the water quality and the water quality of lakes of some tourist spot may affect the water quality of that water body.

Metals that are naturally introduced into the water body come primarily from such sources as rock weathering, soil erosion, or the dissolution of water-soluble salts. Naturally occurring metals move through aquatic environments independently of human activities, usually without any detrimental effects. Humans consume metallic elements through both water and food. Some metals such as: sodium, potassium, magnesium, calcium, and iron are found in living tissue and are essential to human life-biological anomalies arise when they are depleted or removed. Probably less well known is that currently no less than six other heavy metals including molybdenum, manganese, cobalt, copper, and zinc, have been linked to human growth, development, achievement, and reproduction (Friberg *et al.* 1979). Even these metals, however, can become toxic or aesthetically undesirable when their concentrations are too great. Several heavy metals, like: cadmium, lead, and mercury, are highly toxic at relatively low concentrations, can accumulate in body tissues over long periods of time, and are nonessential for human health.

Heavy Metal

Following Heavy Metals were selected for the evaluation in water of Sahastradhara hill-stream:

- Cadmium.
- Copper.
- Iron.
- Lead.
- Manganese.
- Nickel.
- Zinc.

Copper (Cu)

Copper in the natural waters also results in higher concentration due to pollution. It is used with sulphate as a pesticides and also separately as an algicide. Although, it passes such as: through the body but there is evidence of accumulation of trace quantities in liver. The limits of it in the standards are not due to its toxic effects but are due to its taste producing capacity.

Preparation of 1000 Cu (µg/ml) standard: Dissolve 1 gm of Cu in 50 ml of 6N of HNO_3 and dilute to 1 L to give 1000 µg/ml Cu.

Cadmium (Cd)

Cadmium is fairy dense silver white malleable and most toxic metal, which melts at 320.9°C. Cadmium is used for dye and paint pigment production, batteries, ceramic industries, wooden industries and plastic production. The Cd found in a sample of Ca is likely in a inorganic form and may be relatively less toxic to plants and animals, while same amount of Cd when present in zinc or phosphates may be highly toxic to plants and animals, especially when there is calcium deficiency in soil or livestock rations.

Preparation of 1000 Cd (µg/ml) standard: Dissolve 1 gm of Cd Metal in 20 ml of 5N HCl containing 0.5 ml of concentrated HNO_3 and dilute to 1 L to give 1000 µg/ml Cd.

Iron (Fe)

Iron is one of the most abundant elements of the rocks and soil, ranking fourth by weight. All kinds of waters including ground water have appreciable quantities of iron. Iron has more solubility at acidic pH, therefore large quantities of iron are leached out from the soils by acidic waters. In the alkaline medium iron remain comparatively low in soluble phase.

Preparation of 1000 Fe (µg/ml) standard, dissolve 1.000 g of iron wire in 50 ml of (1+1) HNO_3 and dilute to 1 liter with deionized water to give 1000 µg/ml Fe.

Manganese (Mn)

Although not a toxic metal, Mn imparts objectionable and tenacious stains to laundry plumbing fixtures and clothing. It occurs in domestic waste water, industrial effluents, acid mine drainage and receiving strums and thereby enters water bodies. Mn is relatively non-toxic to animals, but toxic to plants at higher levels.

Preparation of 1000 Mn (μg/ml) standard: Dissolve 1 gm of Mn in 50 ml of 6N of HNO_3 and dilute to 1 L to give 1000 μg/ml Mn.

Nickel (Ni)

At high concentrations, nickel has toxic properties. Aquatic organisms have varying sensitivities to nickel salts depending on the water's pH, hardness, alkalinity and type of nickel compound under consideration. Nickel as a metal is a carcinogen.

Preparation of 1000 Ni (μg/ml) standard: Dissolve 1 gm of Ni metal in 50 ml of 6N of HNO_3 and dilute to 1 L to give 1000 μg/ml Ni.

Lead (Pb)

It is a dense soft metal and is quite resistant to corrosion. It has melting point of 327°C. Major source of lead is PbS (Galena). Lead is used for pipes, solders, electrodes, batteries, newsprint, and pigments in paints. Lead is also used in insecticides, beverages, ointments and synthetic dyes. The chemical form of lead determines its solubility in water and biological fluids, the extent of its fixation on soil and type of chemical reactions occurring in atmospheric, aquatic as well as soil environment.

Preparation of 1000 Pb (μg/ml) standard: Dissolve 1 gm of Pb metal in 20 ml of 6N of HNO_3 and dilute to 1 L to give 1000 μg/ml Pb.

Zinc (Zn)

Zinc is present in high concentrations in the wastes from pharmaceuticals, paint, galvanizing, cosmetics, dyes and pigments, etc., and their discharge increases its concentration in appreciable amounts in the waters. Zinc is very essential micronutrient in human beings and only at very high concentration it may cause some toxic effects. Zinc salts produce an undesirable taste to the water and causes water to appear milky and on boiling, a greasy surface scum may also form in the water (Mani *et al.* 2005).

Preparation of 1000 Zn (μg/ml) standard: Dissolve 1 gm of Zn metal in 40 ml of 5N HCl and dilute to 1 L to give 1000 μg/ml Zn.

Historical Resume

According to *Hippocrates* (460 B.C. - 345 B.C.), the father of medicine, 'water contributes much to health' and averted the rainwater should be used for drinking purpose after boiling and filtering, otherwise it would smell bed and cause harshness. The importance of water reveals from the beginning of civilization always took place near the water sources. Life can't exist without water it is a universal truths. This review includes some of the important contribution made from various parts of world. Various workers discussed the various aspects of water quality time to time from India and abroad nationally or internationally.

Pande and Mishra (2000) studied on the water quality of two fresh waters of Dehradun (Sahastradhara stream and Mussoorie lake).

Bharti (2004) described the limnological aspects and physico-chemical characteristics of Sahastradhara hill stream in Doon valley.

Malik and Bharti (2005a); Malik and Bharti (2005b); Malik and Bharti (2005c) described the nutrient dynamics, plankton diversity and primary productivity respectively in the water of stream Sahastradhara at Dehradun. Bharti and Malik (2005a) highlighted the Significance of rivers in Vedic literature. Bharti and Malik (2005b) elaborated the suitable fish habitats at different places of Sahastradhara river.

Malik and Bharti (2006) highlighted the recreational and tourism value of stream fishes in Sahastradhara. Malik and Bharti (2007a) made a note on the conservation of water resources in Indian ancient literature. Malik and Bharti (2007b) explored the use of benthos as a indicator of pollution in a river. Malik and Bharti (2007d) described the ecology of Sahastradhara Hill-stream at Dehradun (Uttaranchal).

Bharti (2007a) evaluated the heavy metal pathway in aquatic system of an industrial area at Panipat. Bharti (2007c) highlighted the effects of anthropogenic activities on the health of river Lalita. Bharti *et al.* (2008) studied on the influence of Heavy Metals on Abundance of Cyanophyceae Members in Three Spring-fed Lake in Kempty, Dehradun.

Bharti (2008) explained the status of water quality and ecotourism enhancement in Sahastradhara stream at Dehradun. Malik *et al.* (2009) explained the role of aquatic macrophytes in the remediation of metal pollutants in aquatic ecosystem. Malik *et al.* (2009) elaborated the distribution of Metals in Water of an Artificial Lake at Mussoorie, Uttarakhand.

Bharti (2010) explained the eutrophication problems of aquatic ecosystems. Malik and Bharti (2010) described the heavy metal route in an industrial environment. Bharti (2012) explored the physico-chemical, heavy metal and biological aspects of hill-stream Sahastradhara. Bharti *et al.* (2013); Bharti *et al.* (2014); Bharti and Niyogi (2015); Bharti *et al.* (2016) also emphasized on heavy metal quantification in various aquatic ecosystems in different geographical regions.

River and Tourism

Rivers always attract to the people especially nature lovers since the ancient times. People feel harmony, peace and internal satisfaction near the springs, streams or rivers. In the recent time, rivers are the part of tourisms. Many tourist places are established near or very closed to the rivers. Rivers or streams have a very old relation with tourisms not only in India but abroad.

A river basin is made up of a mosaic of contrasting and often competing biophysical, economic and social circumstances, and community interests. Only along limited reaches of a river basin is it possible to identify much commonality of attitude or purpose by the inhabitants. More typically, the segmentation of natural and human components of the basin is reflected in conflicting attitudes towards the single unifying element present – the river system.

Those living upstream tend to value the riverine environment primarily for its aesthetic appeal and perhaps its recreational role, rather than its economic function. Further downstream, the value of water for economic purposes becomes paramount to service agricultural, urban and industrial needs. The emphasis is on maximising the quantity of water available, with some level of biophysical degradation acceptable as a trade-off against economic viability and regional development. In the lower reaches of the basin, the riverine environment is degraded further from contaminated effluent, so that aquatic life, wetlands, estuaries, and the coastal zone, are frequently compromised by eutrophication and sedimentation.

Tourism and associated anthropogenic activities may cause effects on water ecosystem and can alter the water quality of that river or stream in many ways. The direct addition or dumping the waste material directly into river water can change many physico-chemical parameters of river water, so that the water quality can degrade drastically after increment in such type of activities and ultimately the entire aquatic ecosystem may disturb. The ecology of river water especially the living organisms of water column may realise the changes in their surrounding environment settings and few of them can show few indication to support or oppose the increasing pollution in the ecosystem. These few species are commonly called as biological indicators of pollution.

During the time of tourist activities especially at hot tourist spots, awareness for environment protection should be increased. Strict rule and regulations should be adopted for all individuals. Anthropogenic activities, which accelerated the rate of pollution or environmental degradation, should be avoided or banned or appropriate alternate should be adopted in those cases.

Anthropogenic Activities

Water is an important substance required by all living organisms and for all anthropogenic activities. The problem of environmental pollution due to toxic metals has begun to cause concern now in most major metropolitan cities (Bharti, 2007a). Most of our water resources are gradually becoming polluted due to the addition of foreign materials from the surroundings. These include: organic matter origin from plant and animal, land surface washing, Industrial and sewage effluents.

In some tourist hilly regions, there are not any more industrial pollution, but tourist's anthropogenic activities may alter the water quality and the water quality of lakes of some tourist spot may affect the water quality of that water body.

These are the major human activities which were observed during the study period in Sahastradhara region:

- Mass bathing.
- Addition of food materials directly into stream water.
- Clothes washing.
- Development of a solid waste dumping site near fourth site.
- Vehicle movement.
- Interference with vegetation composition.
- Dispersion of Polythene wrappers.
- Generation of feacal material.

Solid Waste Generation

Sahastradhara hill-stream is a fast developing tourist spot of north India. Many restaurants, shops, Dhabas and hotels are developed for the needs of tourists. Hotels and restaurants are increasing their number in a tremendous way. Due to the hotels, Dhaba and restaurants, a huge amount of solid waste is generated and dumped near fourth sampling site (very closed to Buddha temple).

The manual study of solid waste generated at this site was carried out on the basis of percentage composition of materials in solid waste.

Table 1.1: Percent composition of solid waste for various category waste materials

S.N.	Material	% Composition
1.	Wood products and woody toys	20
2.	Plastic and polythene	22
3.	Cartoons and papers	28
4.	Leaves and straw	8
5.	Waste Food materials	10
6.	Hairs and bones	5
7.	Glass and metals	3
8.	Ash	2
9.	Others	2

So, the major degradable material was wood products, papers, leaves, waste food and ash and the contribution of degradable materials into total solid waste is 68 per cent. The degradable material will never create a problem in near future, but rest 32 per cent of non-degradable solid waste will certainly harmful for the health of Sahastradhara stream and its water quality also.

Table 1.2: Percent composition of solid waste

S.N.	Material	% Composition
1.	Degradable	68
2.	Non-degradable	32

Besides the solid waste, the amount of sewage is increasing day-by-day due to the increasing number of tourist in Sahastradhara region. The major source of drinking water is the Sahastradhara stream and the sewage ultimately going dumped into the same water body into downstream. Increasing amount of waste may creates many negative impacts to the aquatic ecosystem of stream.

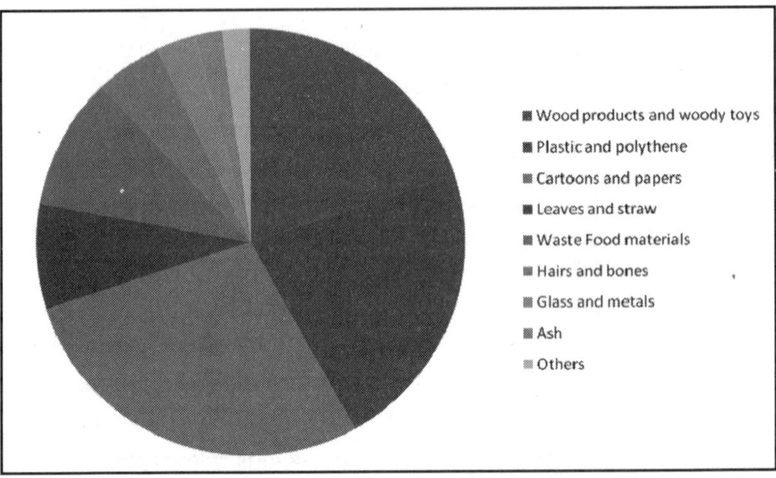

Fig. 1.1: **Percent composition of solid waste**

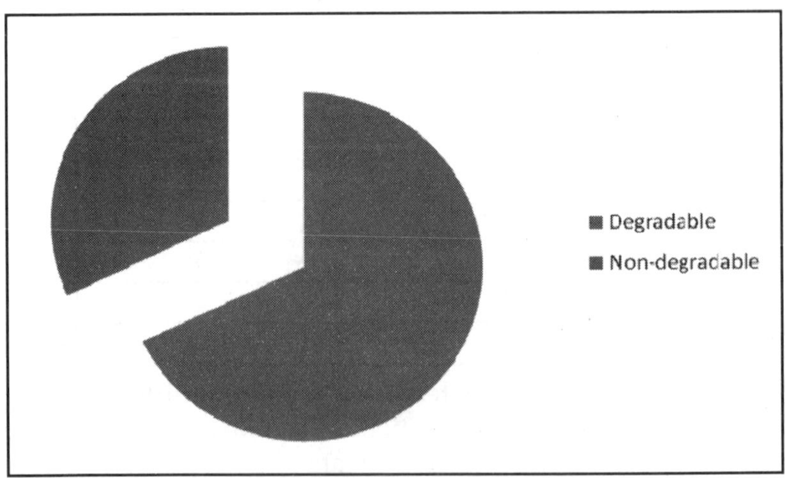

Fig. 1.2: **Percent degradability of solid waste**

Fig. 1.3: **A scene of mass bathing in Sahastradhara hill-stream**

Traffic Density

The study area is a fast developing tourist place near Dehradun. A large number of tourists are visited here throughout the year, and this number is going increase every year. Tourists, generally used the bus service, but sometimes, they prefer their vehicle for their comfortableness. So, the numbers of vehicle are also increasing day-by-day.

Vehicle plays an important role in this fast going era, so that every person uses the vehicle and contributes to traffic volume density. Expensive and luxury vehicles are the mark of prestigious in the fashionable time. So, few persons are using vehicle only for the purpose.

Vehicle volume is season dependable. A study was conducted for the evaluation of traffic load in Dun valley during the day times and nighttime in winter, summer and rainy seasons. A two days based survey was carried out for the assessment of traffic volume density in Sahastradhara Valley. Season-wise data is given for all type of vehicles (Bharti, 2012).

Table 1.3: Traffic Volume density in daytime (6.00AM to 6.00 PM)

S.N.	Vehicle Type	Winter	Summer	Rainy
1.	Trucks and tankers	10	15	8
2.	Buses	10	12	9
3.	Tractors and trailers	8	11	6
4.	JCBs and Earth Moving	5	6	2
5.	Jeeps and Sumo type	10	17	4
6.	Three wheeler	6	11	3
7.	Bikes and scooter	15	23	5
8.	Bicycle	4	7	2

Fig. 1.4 (A-F): Few anthropogenic activities near Sahastradhara hill-stream

Table 1.4: Traffic Volume density in nighttime (6.00 PM to 6.00 AM)

S.N.	Vehicle Type	Winter	Summer	Rainy
1.	Trucks and tankers	1	3	0
2.	Buses	0	1	0
3.	Tractors and trailers	0	2	0
4.	JCBs and Earth Moving	0	1	2
5.	Jeeps and Sumo type	1	2	0
6.	Three wheeler	0	1	0
7.	Bikes and scooter	1	6	0
8.	Bicycle	0	1	0

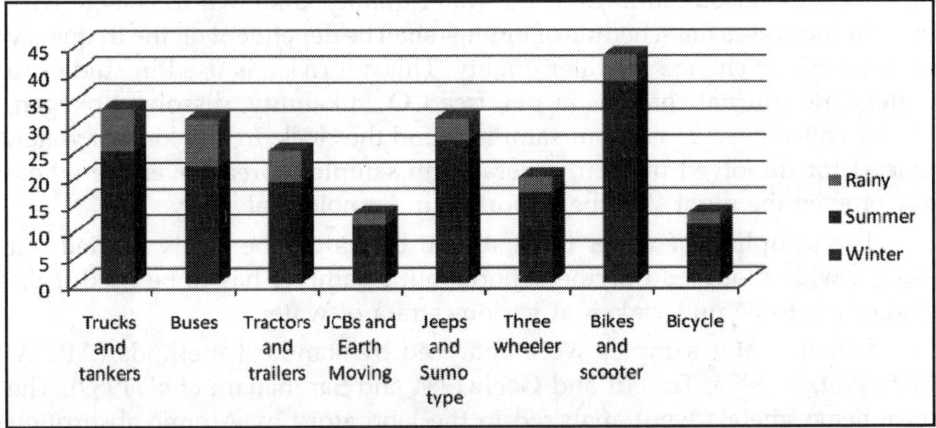

Fig. 1.5: **Traffic density in day hours**

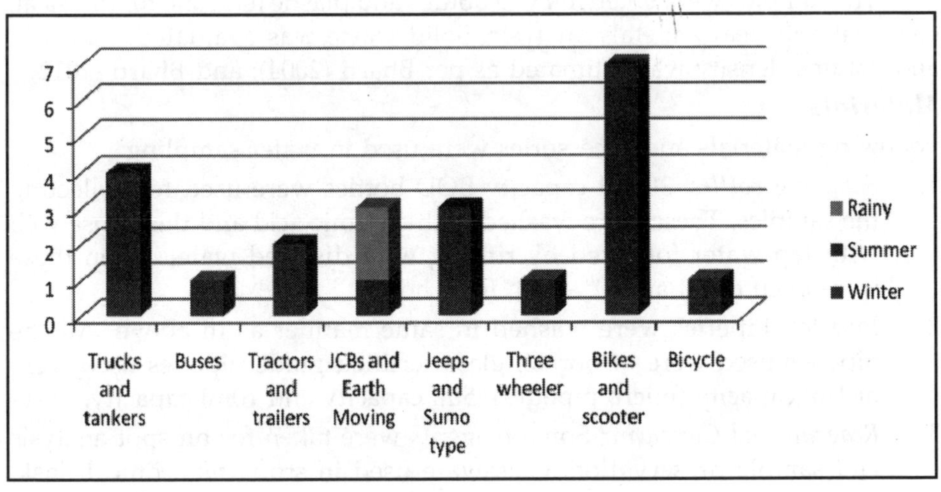

Fig. 1.6: **Traffic density in night hours**

Material and Methods

To assess the water quality of Sahastradhara hill-stream, five sampling stations were selected. Water samples were collected in plastic jericanes and analyzed according to APHA (1995) and Trivedi and Goel (1984) with the help of Atomic absorption spectrophotometer. The details of materials and methods are given below:

Sampling Methods

Grab sampling was generally applied during the sampling. A grab sample is an ordinary sample which is taken from a particular place representing the whole water quality. This type of sample is valid only when it is certain that the water quality is not changing in a short time and effluent discharges, if any, are fairy regular. It is advisable to collect and analyse the grab samples separately at various timings, if the water quality is known to change with time. In such cases the schedule of timings shall be dependent on the frequency of discharge or change in water quality. This approach is used in studies to understand diurnal changes in pH, free CO_2, alkalinity, dissolved oxygen, etc., by collecting a 2 or 3 hour sample round the clock. In any kind of water, at least for dissolved oxygen, several grab samples spread over the whole day or even the night shall be important in limnological study.

The sampling of water from stream banks can be easily carried out using a wide mouthed polythene bottle but a sampler has to be used if the studies are to be undertaken at various strata of water.

Stream water samples were analyzed by standard methods (APHA, 1995; Wetzel, 1975; Trivedi and Goel, 1984 and Santhanam *et al.* 1989). The trace heavy metals were analyzed in the laboratory by Atomic absorption spectrophotometer *AAS 4129 model* (APHA, 1995; ECIL Manual, 2004).

The samples were taken in BOD bottles and plastic Jeri cane for physical, chemical and heavy metals analysis. Solid waste was evaluated manually and volume density was estimated as per Bharti (2004); and Bharti (2012).

Materials

Following materials and accessories were used in water sampling:

1. *Sampling bottles*: 300ml capacity BOD bottles were used for collecting the samples. These were washed with chromic acid and then rinse well with tap water followed by rinsing with distilled water. Then these were oven dried at 160° - 180° for 3 hours.
2. *Pipettes:* Pipettes were washed in same manner as in above. All the pipettes used were of Borosil glass certified grade pipettes used were of 1ml capacity (micro pipettes), 5ml capacity and 10ml capacity.
3. *Reagents and Glassware*: Some reagents were taken for on spot analysis and sample preservation. Glassware used in study *viz;* conical flask, beaker, burettes etc., were of Borosil glass certified grade. All the

glassware were washed with chromic acid and then rinsed well with tap water and then with distilled water.

4. *Jeri canes:* Jeri cane used for carrying the samples from sampling sites to laboratories. Jeri cane made of plastic and washed well with water and then rinsed well with distilled water.
5. *Chemical bottles:* Some small chemical bottles were used for transporting some necessary chemical urgently required during the sampling for immediately analysis for selected parameters.
6. *Bag:* A bag of large carrying capacity was taken during the sampling for the collection of all water, soil and sediment samples.
7. *Thermometer:* Mercury thermometer was used for on spot measurement of the soil and water samples.
8. *pH meter:* A handy pen pH meter was used for on spot evaluation of the pH of surface water.

Digestion and dilution

Samples were collected in Borosil BOD bottles and some Jeri canes for laboratory experiments. Some parameters were determined immediately on sampling sites, for rest parameters and heavy metals; samples were stored in refrigerator at 4°C. Heavy metals may be analyzed in the 6 months period from the preservation date.

Samples were taken in Jeri canes for determination of the parameters like: conductivity, total solids, pH (hydrogen ion concentration), COD, free CO_2, total alkalinity, total hardness Ca/Mg, chlorides, lead, manganese, zinc, calcium and magnesium. Caps of cans were closed tightly after filling up of cane.

For dissolved oxygen/biochemical oxygen demand, samples were collected in sterilized 300 ml capacity BOD bottles. The bottles were filled completely with sample water up to the rim and stopper was placed only avoiding any kind of air bubble inside it. DO was immediately fixed by adding 2 ml each of alkaline potassium iodide and manganese sulphate ($MnSO_4$) at sampling spot. While the sample for BOD was incubated for 5 days in BOD incubator at 20°C.

Collected, preserved, diluted water samples were prepared for the evaluation of metal concentrations with the help of AAS 4129.

Metals enter in the surface water ecosystem through the disposing of waste materials and various. For every metal a standard was required and concentration may be detected by AAS. Diluted and completely digested samples were required for metal detection by AAS 4129. Metal elements were determined with the help of Atomic absorption spectrophotometer (Model AAS 4129). Alan Walsh first developed the technique of atomic absorption spectrophotometry in 1955, and since then it has emerged as a powerful tool in quantitative analysis of more than 70 metals. The major advantages of the method are that it is free from any kind of interferences and very small concentrations are possible to be measured (De, 2002). The AAS is based on the principle that atoms of elements, which normally remain in ground state under flame condition, absorb energy when subjected to radiation of specific wavelength. The absorption of radiation is proportional to the concentration of atoms of the element. The absorption of radiation by the atoms is independent of the wavelength of absorption and temperature of the atoms. These to feature provide AAS a distinct advantage over flame spectroscopy.

About AAS

ECIL's Atomic Absorption Spectrophotometer, AAS 4129 is a PC based instrument for absorption and emission analysis. It is used for quantitative elemental analysis mainly like: Copper, Iron, Zinc, Lead etc., by measuring the absorbance of a sample atomized in a flame. Some of the metals like: Sodium, Potassium, Calcium, and Lithium are analyzed by emission method. PC does the data processing and partial control of the instrument.

The liquid sample is nebulised (reduce to a spray) by the support gas. The fuel gas is mixed and burnt over the burner head. A modulated light from Hollow Cathode lamp of a pre-selected element travels through the flame and enters the monochromator. The monochromator selects the appropriate resonance line of the selected element and directs it on to the PMT. The DC signal generated by the flame emission is rejected by FE compensation circuit and the original signal of the lamp is amplified, phase sensitively rectified averaged by an integrator to obtain sample signal. A computer processes the sample signal for photometric computations (% T, ABS or CONC). Instrument controls like: wavelength, lamp current, gain, etc., are achieved and maintained by PC.

The cathode material of Hollow Cathode Lamp corresponds to the element of interest. ECIL's Atomic Absorption Spectrophotometer covers the complete range of Atomic Absorption applications. It incorporates State-of-the-art electronics, safety and operational convenience ensuring reliable and accurate analytical performance.

The data analysis and report making is done by the PC including selection of instrument parameters like: wavelength, lamp current selection, and EHT to PMT at various wavelength. The software is user-friendly window based GUI interface using menus, function key, prompts, error messages, enabling ease of operation. Information is presented in easy read menus. In most cases recommended values are filled.

The instrument was calibrated using regression techniques of linear and quadratic methods against standard solutions and concentration of unknown samples can be quantified. Instrument parameters and calibration parameters can be stored, as applications, which can be retrieved as and when, required. A hard copy of the results can be taken with the aid of a printer connected to one of the parallel ports of the PC.

Standard and calibration

Whenever, possible metals and metals oxides are to be preferred in the preparation of standards. This enables the analyst to dissolve them that samples and standards will contain identical elements and hence minimizes any chemical or physical interference effects.

Only concentrated standards (above 1000 μg/ml) should be held in storage. Working standards should be diluted from standards stock solutions only when needed. At low concentrations (less than 10 μg/ml) solutions have been found to deteriorate quite quickly because of the absorption on the walls of the container. Similar standard addition solutions can be prepared containing all of the required elements. This will avoid multiple splitting of the sample for individual elements and reduce the amount of time spent in preparing standards.

Before weighting, standards materials should be treated to ensure that they are in a standard state.

- *Metals*: Wash with acetone and ether to remove any oil layers. Remove any oxide coating by abrasion with emery cloth or by acid pickling and drying.
- *Oxides*: Dry at 110°C for two hours. If necessary, heat to evaluated temperatures to remove bound water.
- *Compounds*: Equilibration at constant water content, or drying at 110°C for two hours to remove any water.

Standards of known concentrations were prepared and evaluated the concentration of metal in water/soil digested sample. Every metal has some specific properties and atomic weight, so for every metal different condition of standard and calibration was applied for every metal (ECIL manual, 2004).

Table 1.5: Standard criteria for analyzing heavy metals by Atomic Absorption Spectrophotometer (AAS)

S. N.	Name	Symbol	Wave Length nm	Flame Gases	Instrument detection limits Mg/l	Sensitivity Mg/l	Optimum Concentration Range Mg/l
1.	Cadmium	Cd	228.8	A-Ac	0.002	0.025	0.05-2
2.	Copper	Cu	324.7	A-Ac	0.01	0.1	0.02-10
3.	Lead*	Pb	279.5	A-Ac	0.01	0.05	0.1-10
4.	Manganese	Mn	232.0	A-Ac	0.02	0.15	0.3-10
5.	Nickel	Ni	283.3	A-Ac	0.05	0.5	1-20
6.	Zinc	Zn	213.9	A-Ac	0.005	0.02	0.05-2
7.	Iron	Fe	248.3	A-Ac	0.02	0.12	0.3-10

A-Ac = Air-acetylene.

* The more sensitive 217.0 nm wavelength is recommended for instruments with background correction capabilities (APHA, 2005).

Table 1.6: Periodic position and relevant information of selected heavy metals

S.N.	Name	Symbol	Atomic Number	Atomic Weight	Shale Value (mg/kg)
1.	Cadmium	Cd	48	112.411	0.3
2.	Copper	Cu	29	63.546	45
3.	Lead	Pb	82	207.2	20
4.	Manganese	Mn	25	54.93805	850
5.	Nickel	Ni	28	58.6934	68
6.	Zinc	Zn	30	65.39	95
7.	Iron	Fe	26	55.845	47200

Source: IUPAC, 1994.

Significance of Heavy Metal

Many effects of Cd action results from interactions of various micro and macro elements as it antagonizes to Cu, Zn and Fe and also interferes with Ca absorption. Cadmium found in a sample of Ca is likely in an inorganic form and may be relatively less toxic to flora and fauna, while same amount of Cd when present in zinc or phosphates may be highly toxic to plants and animals, especially in calcium deficiency in soil. The use of contaminated water into irrigation may be increase the cadmium status in agricultural soil (Mani *et al.* 2005).

Copper is sometimes found in insufficient quantity in soil (Miller and Turk, 2002) but it may be added in to soil system by some anthropogenic activities. Copper may accumulate in living organisms and their various body parts. High amount if heavy metals like cu and Zn may harm to living organism of existing ecosystem (Aslam *et al.* 2004).

Iron has more solubility at acidic pH, therefore large quantities of iron are leached out from the soils by acidic waters. In the alkaline medium iron remain comparatively low in soluble phase. Excess calcium can reduced the activity of iron in soil and soil aeration may influence the availability of iron to plants (Miller and Turk, 2002).

Mathess (1974) reported that fresh ground water constitutes 0.00-0.007 ppm cadmium, WHO (1984) recommended Cd concentration should not exceed maximum of 0.01 ppm in raw drinking water supply, 0.5 ppm in irrigation water. USEPA (1990) recommended maximum permissible Cd concentration as 0.04 and 0.02 ppm to protect aquatic life including fish. Hart (1982) reported a concentration range of Pb 0.0003-0.03 ppm in natural fresh water.

Nickel is one of the second trace elements of the present study after cadmium. As it is very toxic to plants and animals in low concentrations and has a tendency to accumulate in body parts. However Ni was presented in very minor concentrations.

The presence of heavy metals in the aquatic environment has been of great concern to scientists and engineers because of their increased discharge, toxic nature, and other adverse effects on receiving waters (Singh, 2006).

In heavy metals analysis, the total concentrations of the metals are often determined. However, total concentration of trace metals provides no information concerning the fate of the metal in the terms of its interaction with sediments, its mobility, bioavailability, or resultant toxicity (Christie, 1995). It is now widely accepted that measuring total metal concentrations cannot fully assess the role of aquatic sediments as a sink or as a source of pollutants. In addition, determination of total elements does not given an accurate estimate of the likely environmental impact. Instead, it is desirable to have information on the potential availability of metals (whether toxic or essential) to biota under various environmental conditions. Since the mobility of heavy metals, as well as their bioavailability and related eco-toxicity to plants, critically depends upon chemical forms in which, a metal is present in the sediment, considerable interest exists in trace element speciation (Davidson *et al.* 1994).

Heavy metals are introduced into aquatic system from various anthropogenic sources. Heavy metals constitute a special group of contaminants of aquatic systems and deserve special attention. Since metals are not removed by natural degradation processes, they may become enriched in sediments over time. Metal contamination of sediments is an issue of growing concerns worldwide. Both natural processes and anthropogenic activities are responsible for introducing metals in to the aquatic system (Bharti, 2007a). Many contaminants discharged into surface waters rapidly become associated with the particulate matter and incorporated in sediments. Metals in aquatic systems become part of the water-sediment system and their distribution is controlled by a dynamic set of physical-chemical interactions and equilibrium, largely governed by pH and type of legends and chelating agents, oxidation state of the mineral components and the redox conditions of the system. Metal contaminated sediments may release heavy metals back to the overlying water column and, thus, pose risk to aquatic life and ecosystems. Due to their particle reactivity, heavy metals tend to accumulate in sediment as a result may persist in the environment long after their primary sources have been removed (Forstner and Wittman, 1981).

Heavy metals travel from one level to another in the ecological system due to the accumulation in abiotic and biotic components. Heavy metals have a tendency to accumulate and store in a component or trophic levels. The storage of heavy metals has created harmful effects for biotic components. The heavy metals accumulated in sediment and percolated down in to ground water known as bio-accumulation of metal. From ground water, heavy metals may turn into two ways; one is though irrigation and second is through drinking by human beings. The accumulation of heavy metals through the food chain is called the biomagnifications. The concentrations of metal increased at every next trophic level, whereas metals can cause various harmful effects on irrigated agricultural soil, human beings and livestock by alteration in some biochemical reaction in body cells (De, 2002).

Results and Discussion

Heavy metals in the water of Sahastradhara hill-stream were detected in very low concentration while upper sites has water free with some metallic contents due to the absence of anthropological activities. However, the area is free from industrial pollution, but due to the increasing tourist activities the water quality is going deteriorate since last few years in a tremendous way. Heavy Metals concentrations are given in Table 1.7 and the increasing trend of Heavy Metals concentrations is indicated by the Fig. 1.7.

Table. 1.7: Heavy Metals at all five locations at Sahastradhara stream (ppm)

S.N.	Parameter	Site-I	Site-II	Site-III	Site-IV	Site-V
1.	Cadmium	0.00	0.00	0.00	0.00	0.01
2.	Copper	0.00	0.00	0.00	0.01	0.01
3.	Iron	0.65	0.69	0.72	0.85	1.00
4.	Lead	0.00	0.00	0.01	0.02	0.03
5.	Manganese	0.04	0.06	0.08	0.16	0.21
6.	Zinc	0.01	0.01	0.02	0.03	0.05

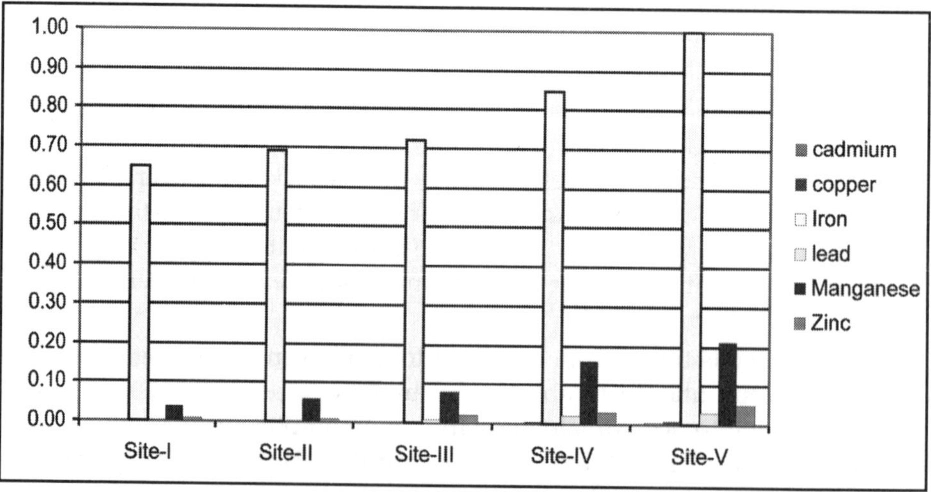

Fig. 1.7: **Showing the Heavy Metals concentrations at various sampling stations**

Heavy Metals were found almost nil or in very low concentrations at all selected site. Heavy Metals like: Cadmium, copper, lead were not found in high concentration at all sites during the study period. Cadmium, copper and lead were absolutely absent in upstreams, while Manganese, Zinc and Iron concentrations were found within the limit in upstream samples. The concentration of iron was maximum observed 1.0 mg/l at fifth station. Lead was found maximum 0.03 mg/l at last downstream site and Zinc concentration was 0.05 mg/l. Malik *et al.* (2009) described the role of Heavy Metals in the surface water of north India. The results of Bharti *et al.* (2010) were also indicated the relation of Heavy Metals with some biological agents in a north Indian water body.

Pollutant sources especially non-point sources of lotic systems are hard to control because they derive, often in small amounts, over a very wide area and enter the system at many locations along its length. Agricultural fields often deliver large quantities of sediments, nutrients, and chemicals like various pesticides to nearby streams and rivers. Urban and residential areas can also add to this pollution when contaminants are accumulated on impervious surfaces such as: roads and parking lots that then drain into the system. Elevated nutrient concentrations, especially nitrogen and phosphorus which are key components of fertilizers, can increase periphyton growth, which can be particularly dangerous in slow moving streams. Another pollutant, acid rain, forms from sulfur dioxide and nitrous oxide emitted from factories and power stations. These substances readily dissolve in atmospheric moisture and enter lotic systems through precipitation. This can lower the pH of these sites, affecting all trophic levels from algae to vertebrates. Mean species richness and total species numbers within a system decrease with decreasing pH. While direct pollution of lotic systems has been greatly reduced in the United States under the government's Clean Water Act, contaminants from diffuse, non-point sources, remain a large problem.

Beside these, few other anthropogenic activities like dams construction alter the flow, temperature, and sediment regime of lotic systems. Additionally, many rivers are dammed at multiple locations, amplifying the impact. Dams can cause enhanced clarity and reduced variability in stream flow, which in turn cause an increase in periphyton abundance. Invertebrates immediately below a dam can show reductions in species richness due to an overall reduction in habitat heterogeneity. Also, thermal changes can affect insect development, with abnormally warm winter temperatures obscuring cues to break egg diapause and overly cool summer temperatures leaving too few acceptable days to complete growth. Finally, dams fragment river systems, isolating previously continuous populations, and preventing the migrations of anadromous and catadromous species.

Control and Conservation

A huge quantity of solid waste is generated at any tourist place and the study area is not an exceptional case. It has been noticed and examined that the entire quantity of solid waste-generated at Sahastradhara is being dumped near the stream in a very rough manner. This dumped solid waste can cause various environment health hazards. So, the disposal practises for the solid waste should be proper and managed. Even the solid waste should be dumped anywhere very far from the stream basin. It should be keep in the mind that the leaching of pollutants from solid waste dumping site can also impacts on stream environment. Analytical results of the river water samples indicating that solid waste site is significantly contributing to increased the heavy metals concentration in aquatic ecosystem. Increasing tourist activities can impart to deteriorate the aquatic environment (Bharti, 2008).

Awareness for environment protection should be increased during the time of tourist activities especially at hot tourist spots. Strict rule and regulations should be adopted for all individuals. Anthropogenic activities, which accelerated the rate of pollution or environmental degradation, should be avoided or banned or appropriate alternate should be adopted in those cases.

DOs and Don't DOs

For the protection and conservation of natural habitat and vicinity of Sahastradhara hill-stream tourist place, everyone has to adopt and follow the regulations regarding pollution control. The contribution should be made at every level. Few important recommendations are given below:

- Don't dump biodegradable as well as non-degradable materials in stream.
- Don't drain community sewage and other liquid waste of hotel shops etc., directly in to stream.
- Pollution load should be minimized at personal level too.
- Ban on huge hotel buildings in close vicinity of natural water bodies.
- The water quality should be monitor regularly and emphasised to maintain the better survival of all biotic communities in term of biological productivity.
- Nutrients dynamics and heavy and toxic metal levels should be assessed after a specific period of time.
- Any disturbance must be prohibited in natural habitat of stream especially regarding bottom structure, biodiversity and macrophytes.
- Different varieties of colored and game fish should be kept for recreation of tourists in the stretch dams of Sahastradhara main spot.

- The endemic fish diversity should be conserved 'in situ' for enhancement the fish angling practices on the upper and lower stretches of Sahastradhara stream.
- Sahastradhara hill-stream should be promoted as 'Pollution free aquatic zone' by Government of Uttarakhand state and necessary initiative steps regarding conservation and management of natural springs should be taken on the basis of holistic sustainable aquatic resource management.
- Ecotourism should be based on sustainable resource utilization and management practices.
- The awareness programme about 'How to conserve and use the natural water bodies for recreations' should be promoted on the spot by Youth conservator groups.
- *Tal Mitra* or *Sarovar Mitra* should be appointed by the Government of Uttarakhand for the protection and conservation of water bodies in different regions.
- Tourist's numbers should be increased in sustainable way with minimum pollution potential.

Conclusion

The present chapter described the various pollution sources especially due to the tourist activities and other anthropogenic activities and their effects on the environment in a tourist place. Quantity of solid waste generated at tourist places, traffic density in different seasons, the degradation of organic matter and many other things can contribute to environment pollution significantly. Water quality alterations at various stations especially heavy metals of Sahastradhara stream have already been discussed in previous section. These activities can alter the physico-chemical parameters, planktonic and benthic diversity, heavy metal concentration and many other basic characteristics of a natural hill-stream. The diversity of river water may also change their population size, distribution, density and behaviour.

The rate of pollution due to the tourist's activities or other anthropogenic activities should be minimized in an integrated and sustainable manner. Currently, Tourism is one of the hottest industries in India also. On the other hand, environment is also important. So, the pollution abatement should be on top preferences and all the steps should be of eco-friendly manners. Tourisms should be promoted in all regions, but environment conservation is the first priority and above the all aspects.

Both the things can be managed easily with the help of strict regulations and appropriate management practices in the tourisms industry and that is the only way for sustainable development and the protection of aquatic environment.

REFERENCES

APHA, (1995). Standard Methods for Examination of Water and Waste Water. *American Public Health Association*, 19th edition. Inc, New York, pp. 1170.

Arjariya, Amita (2003). Physico-chemical Profile and Plankton Diversity of Ranital Lake, Chhatarpur, M.P., *Nature Env. Poll. Tech.*, 2(3): 327-328.

Aslam, M.M.; Baig, M.A.; Hassan, I.; Qazi, I.A.; Malik, M. and Saeed, H. (2004). Textile Waste Water Characterization and Reduction of its COD and BOD by Oxidation, *Electron. J. Environ. Agri. Food Chem.*, 3(6): 804-811.

Bharti, P.K. (2004). Limnological Study of Sahastradhara Hill-stream, Dehradun, *Dissertation, Gurukula Kangri University, Hardwar*, pp. 102.

Bharti, P.K. (2007a). Effect of Textile Industrial Effluents on Ground Water and Soil Quality at Panipat (Haryana). *Ph.D. Thesis submitted to Gurukula Kangri University, Haridwar*, pp. 191.

Bharti, P.K. (2007c). Any means to save Lalita river?, *Down To Earth*, 15(17): 3.

Bharti, P.K. (2008). 'Status of Water Quality and Ecotourism Enhancement in Sahastradhara Stream at Dehradun' in Third Uttarakhand State Science Congress organised by UCOST, Dehradun held on 10-11 November, 2008 at IIT, Roorkee.

Bharti, P.K. (2010). Sandushan - (Eutrophication), *Vigyan Pragati*, January 2010, pp. 29-31.

Bharti, P.K. (2012). Hill-stream Ecology, *Biotech Books*, pp. 246.

Bharti, P.K. and Malik, D.S. (2005a). Significance of Rivers in Vedic Literature, *Gurukula Shodha Bharti*, Vol. 4, pp. 217-221.

Bharti, P.K. and Malik, D.S. (2005b). Sahastradhara Nadi ke vibhinna sthhano par machhliyon ke anukool vaas sthhano ke liye upyukt dashaayen, in proceedings of (in Hindi) National Symposium: Uttaranchal me Maatyasyki ki bhaavi sambhaavnaye' organized by Department of Zoology, H.N.B. Garhwal University, Srinagar on 28-29 October 2005, pp. 84-87.

Bharti, P.K.; Malik, D.S. and Yadav, R. (2008). Influence of Heavy Metals on Abundance of Cyanophyceae Members in Three Spring-fed Lake in Kempty, Dehradun, *Journal of Ecology and Fisheries*, 1(1): 35-38.

Bharti, P.K.; Malik, D.S. and Yadav, R. (2010). Influence of Heavy Metals on Abundance of Cyanophyceae Members in Three Spring-fed Lake in Kempty, Dehradun, In: 'Advances in Aquatic Ecology, Vol. III' ed. by V.B. Sakhare, *Daya Publishing House, New Delhi*, pp. 107-111.

Bharti, P.K., Kumar, P. and Singh, V. (2013). Impact of Industrial Effluents on Ground Water and Soil Quality in the Vicinity of Industrial Area of Panipat city, India. *J. of Applied and Natural Sciences*, 5(1): 132-136.

Bharti, Pawan K.; Tyagi, P.K. and Singh, V. (2014). Assessment of Heavy Metals in the Water of Sahastradhara Hill Stream at Dehradun, India. *International Journal of Environment*. 3(3): 164-172.

Bharti, P.K. and Niyogi, U.K. (2015). Assessment of Pollution in a Freshwater Lake at Fisher Island, Larsemann Hills Over East Antarctica. Science International, 3(1): 25-30.

Bharti, P.K., Enn Kaup, Bhupesh Sharma and A.K. Tyagi (2016). Occurrence of Various Ingredients in the Lake Environments at Stornes Peninsula, Ingrid Christenson Coast, East Antarctica, *American Journal of Environmental Science and Technology*, 1(1): 1-10.

Christie, S.L. (1995). Speciation, In: Fitfield, F.W., Haines. P.J. (Eds). *Environmental Analytical Chemistry*, Chapman and Hall, UK, pp. 245-273.

Dagaonkar, A. and Saksena, D.N. (1992). Physico-chemical and Biological Characterization on Tample Tank, Kaila Sagar, Gwalior, *J. Hydrobiology,* 8: 11-19.

Davidson, C.M., Thomas R.P., McVey, S.E., Perala, R., Littlejohn, D. and Ure, A.M. (1994). Evaluation of a Sequential Extraction Procedure for the Speciation of Heavy Metals in Sediments. *Anal.Chim. Acta.,* 291: 277-286.

De, A.K. (2002). Environmental Chemistry, *New Age International (P) Limited Publishers,* pp. 392.

ECIL manual (2004) Methods Manual, Atomic Absorption Spectrophotometer, AAS 4129, *Electronic Corporation of India Limited,* Hyderabad - 500 062, pp. 85.

Forstner, U. and Wittman, G.T.W. (1981). Metal Pollution in the Aquatic Environment, Second ed. *Springer, Berlin,* pp. 486.

Friberg, L., Nordberg, G.F., and Vouk, V.B. (Eds.) (1979). *Handbook on the Toxicology of Metals.* Elsevier/North–Holland Biomedical Press, Amsterdam, pp. 709.

Hart, B.T. (1982). Trace Metals in Natural Waters, *Speciation Chem. Australian,* 49: 260-265.

IUPAC (1994). Atomic Weights of the Elements, 1993, *International Union of Pure and Applied* Chemistry, *Pure Appl. Chem.,* 66: 2423.

Lokeshwari, H. and Chandrappa, G.T. (2006). Impact of Heavy Metal Contamination of Bellandur Lake on Soil and Cultivated Vegetation, *Current Science,* 91(9): 622-627.

Malik, D.S. and Bharti, P.K. (2005a). Nutrient Dynamics in Rhithron zone of Shivalik Himalayan stream Sahastradhara, Dehradun (Uttaranchal), *Env. Cons. J.* 6 (2): 63-68.

Malik, D.S. and Bharti, P.K. (2005b). Fluctuation in Planktonic Population of Sahastradhara Hill-Stream at Dehradun (Uttaranchal), *Aquacult.* 6 (2): 191-198.

Malik, D.S. and Bharti, P.K. (2005c). Primary Production Efficiency of Sahstradhara Hill-stream, Dehradun, *Env. Cons. J.* 6 (3): 117-121.

Malik, D.S. and Bharti, P.K. (2007a). Water Resources Conservation in Vedas, *Gurukula Shodha Bharati,* Vol. 7, pp. 231-235.

Malik, D.S. and Bharti, P.K. (2007b). Macro-zoobanthos as Pollution Indicator in River Saung at Dehradun (Uttaranchal), *J. Exp. Zool. India,* 10 (1): 221-222.

Malik, D.S. and Bharti, P.K. (2007d). Ecology of Sahastradhara Hill-stream at Dehradun (Uttaranchal), In: 'Advances in Aquatic Ecology, Vol. I' ed. by V.B. Sakhare, *Daya Publishing House, New Delhi,* pp. 1-11.

Malik, D.S.; Yadav, R. and Bharti, P.K. (2009). Role of Aquatic Macrophytes in the Remediation of Metal Pollutants, In: 'Aquatic Ecology II', *Narendra Publishing House,* New Delhi, pp. 145-158.

Malik, D.S.; Bharti, P.K.; Negi, K.S. and Yadav, R. (2009). Distribution of Metals in Water of An Artificial Lake at Mussoorie, Uttarakhand, In: 'Aquatic Biology and Aquaculture' edited by V.B. Sakhare, Ambajoagi, MS, *Manglam Publication, New Delhi,* pp. 77-95.

Malik, D.S. and Bharti, P.K. (2006). Sahastradhara me Matasya vinod evam paryatan, in Proceeding of National Seminar on 'Meethajal matsyiki' organized by Rashtriya matsya anuvanshik sansadhan bureau, Lucknow.

Malik, D.S.; Bharti, P.K.; Negi, K.S. and Yadav, R. (2009). Distribution of Metals in Water of An Artificial Lake at Mussoorie, Uttarakhand, In: 'Aquatic Biology and Aquaculture' edited by V.B. Sakhare, Ambajoagi, MS, *Manglam Publication, New Delhi,* pp. 77-95.

Mani, V.; Kaur, H. and Mohini, M. (2005). Toxic Metals and Environmental Pollution, *J. Ind. Poll. Cont.,* 21(1): 101-107.

Mathess, G. (1974). Heavy Metals as Trace Constituents in Natural and Polluted Ground Water, *Goel mijnbouw, New Jersy,* USA, 53: 149-155.

Millar, C.E. and Turk, L.M. (2002). Fundamentals of Soil Science, Biotech Books, Delhi 35, pp. 462.

Pande, R.K. and Mishra, A. (2000). Water Quality Study of Fresh Waters of Dehradun (Sahastradhara Stream and Mussoorie lake), *Aquacult*, 1(1): 57-62.

Santhanam, R.; Velayntham, P. and Jegatheesan, G; (1989). A Manual of Freshwater Ecology,. *Daya Publishing House Delhi* - 110 006: 3-17, 53-92.

Singh, A.K. (2006). Chemistry of arsenic in Ground Water of Genges-Brahmaputra River Basin, *Current Science*, 91 (5): 599-606.

Trivedi, R.K. and Goel, P.K. (1984). Chemical and Biological Methods for Water Pollution Studies Karad: *Environmental publication*, pp. 1-251.

USEPA (1990). Operation and Quality Control Manual, Environmental Protection Agency (EPA), Athens, GA 30613.

Vahrenkamp, H., (1979). Metalle in Lebensprozessen: Chemie in Unserer Zeit, 7: 97-105.

Wetzel, R.G. (1975). Limnology, *W.B. Saunders Co. Philadelphia*, pp. 743.

HEAVY METALS AND METALLOIDS IN BIOSPHERE: *IMPACTS AND ASSESSMENT*
Edited by : Dr. Avnish Chauhan; Dr. Sandeep Gupta & Dr. Pawan Kumar Bharti
Edition : 2017
ISBN : 978-93-5056-860-6
Published by : Discovery Publishing House Pvt. Ltd., New Delhi (India)

Study on Heavy Metal Accumulation in Fin Fishes from Industrially Crowded Area Around Hooghly River, West Bengal, India

Piyalee Sural[1]; A.K. Patra[1]
Indranil Ghosh[2*]; Anandamay Adak[3]
Satyendranath Maitra[4]

ABSTRACT

We have carried out Atomic Absorption Spectrophotometric analysis (Perkin-Elmer-5100) of two selective heavy metals (Cu and Pb), form four stations of Hooghly estuary (Zone-I) in three edible fin-fishes, viz; Setipinna phasa, Glossogobius giuris and Pseudapocryptes lanceolatus. The metal concentration in sediment and water from the four stations were also detected. Physico-chemical parameters like: dissolved oxygen, dissolved carbon di-oxide, pH and temperature were also recorded. The water flowing through this region is constantly receiving municipal wastes from twin-cities of Kolkata and Howrah, as well as industrial effluents from the industrial areas of Howrah and Hooghly districts. Higher concentration of Pb was found in water than that in sediment from all the stations. Pb concentrations were also high in skeletal parts of Setipinna phasa and Pseudapocryptes lanceolatusi which may signify the skeletal parts of these two fishes to be included in heavy metal pollution monitoring activities.

1. Department of Zoology, Utkal University, Bhubneswar, Orissa, India.
2. Department of Aquaculture, West Bengal University of Animal and Fishery Science, West Bengal, India.
3. Environmental Science Section, Bose Institute, Kolkata, West Bengal, India.
4. Department of Zoology, A.P.C. College, New Barrackpore, West Bengal India.

INTRODUCTION

Water is one of the most important natural resources on this planet for maintaining the life processes with its multidimensional usage, both externally and internally for each and every living organism above microbe level, and that demands a well thought technological knowledge for its sustainable management both for quality and quantity. More so in regard to the fresh water management as most of the higher forms of life depend upon the fresh water availability for various purposes. Particularly when man has exploited all sorts of fresh water resources available on this Globe within the last about eight to ten thousand years or so. Since the marine water and the fresh water both are impregnated with diversified live forms and interdependent on each other, it has become necessitated for a skillful management with judicious vision of our water bodies (both marine and fresh water) if they are to be used for diverse purposes as for sustainable domestic and industrial supply, crop irrigation, transport, recreation, commercial marine and fresh water fisheries and aquaculture, power generation, land drainage and waste disposal etc. The most important objectives of water management programme are the preservation of aquatic life, maintenance of life bearing water quality and the quantitative paradigm.

The greatest catastrophe of the twentieth century is the over-exploitation of natural resources together with injudicious usage of water severely and irrevocably strained their limited quantity in the only known (within this solar galaxy), life bearing planet – the Earth. One of the consequences of technological progress and industrial revolution has been the release of a large number of chemicals into the environment. Today's Environment had to evolve by means of intense interaction among the living and the nonliving factors through the ages of about two billion of years to be sustainably congenial to maintain several ecosystems to culminate in a well orcastrated interdependent processes to give rise to the only an unique Biosphere. Evidences suggest that the endurance of all the eco-systems to bear – stresses, put upon by Anthropogenic activities, has exceeded by manifold beyond limits as a consequence the interactive balance between the already existing ecosystems and newly evolved environment has been shattered within the last hundred years or so and there lies the actual problem for future existing of all the living organisms in general and the man in particular. Water pollution, like: other environmental concerns, has been the focus of widespread public interest for about four decades now. Aquatic pollution may be defined as Anthropogenic addition of varied types of highly toxic and deleterious materials intolerable to any organisms to the aquatic environment deteriorating water quality affecting fisheries, human health, agriculture and aquatic removable resources. Aquatic pollution is commonly associated with the man made discharge of effluents from sewers and sewage treatment plants, drains and factories.

The sources of water pollution may be broadly classified as:

(a) Domestic sewage.

(b) Soil erosion and sedimentation.

(c) Industrial organic and inorganic wastes.

(d) Agricultural wastes.

(e) Oil and oil dispersants.

(f) Radioactive wastes.

(g) Solid wastes (Datta and Das, 2005).

When we speak about pollution of aquatic resources, its effect on fish assumes foremost importance as it is the major source of animal protein in our diet. Fishes and allied edible aquatic products have been exposing to various xenobiotic onslaughts in the Natural domain. Being unable to change their habitat in time of distress in aquatic environment, fishes are the most vulnerable of all animals.

Heavy metals are recognised as an important group of industrial pollutant. On the basis of some toxicity tests, the absence of fish, mollusks and crustaceans was ascribed to the presence of toxic metals in the water. In many rivers, the effects of heavy metallic pollutions are compounded by substantial inputs of organic matter and other industrial pollutants (Carpenter, 1926). Heavy metal is an imprecise term that is generally taken to include the metallic elements with an atomic weight greater than 40, but excluding the alkaline earth metals, alkali metals, lanthanides and actinides. Heavy metals are known to be the natural ingredients of the earth's crust (Mandal, 2008). Metals are normally regarded as ones having atomic numbers 22-92 in all groups from period 3 to 7 in the periodic table (Waldichuk, 1974). The most important heavy metals from the view of water pollution are: zinc, copper, lead, cadmium, mercury, nickel and chromium. They are also regarded as toxic metals. Metals like zinc and copper are essential trace elements to living organisms but become toxic at higher concentration (Hellawell, 1986). Quite apart from industrial sources, domestic waste contain substantial quantities of metals because the water has been in prolonged contact with Copper, Zinc or Lead pipe works or tanks. Heavy metals may be listed in approximate order of decreasing toxicity as follows: Hg, Cd, Cu, Zn, Ni, Pb, Cr, Al, Co (Whitton and Say, 1975). The seriousness and persistence of heavy metals in water are compounded by the fact that they are generally water soluble, non-degradable, and strongly bonded to polypeptides and proteins (Datta and Das, 2005).

Davis *et al.* (1996) have opined that determining the metal bioavailability is critical in assessing the necessity to remediate contaminated sediments. Authors have recorded low bioaccumulation factors for As, Cr and Pb in sediment and concluded that sediments act to sequester metals rendering them non-bioavailable due to precipitation of solids and sorption of iron phases. Contamination of soils and waters with heavy metals may lead to toxemias in fishes and may result in biological accumulation and subtle changes in physiological functions leading to inability to survive (Post, 1987). Chronic toxicity of some metals may lead to loss of reproductive capabilities, body malformations and susceptibility to infectious organisms. Even if the fish do not die instantaneously, reports suggest there is high bioaccumulation of Manganese, Copper, Chromium and Lead in fish flesh causing disease in men who consume them. The heavy metals even below permissible levels may cause disorders in the aquatic ecosystem because of their toxicity, water solubility and non-degradable qualities (Agarwal, 1991). The natural sources, *i.e.,* mining and metal processing contribute to 21 per cent of the industrial output of metal pollution in India. Various water bodies in India have been reported to be increasingly polluted by toxic metals like: Mercury, Manganese, Molybdenum, Zinc, Vanadium, Selenium, Chromium and Lead (Krishnamurthi and Viswanathan, 1991).

Many heavy metals, whether organically complexed or not, are known to accumulate in plant and animal tissues to very high levels, posing a potential toxic hazard to the organisms themselves, or organisms higher in the food chains including: humans which may consume them (Abel, 1996). Heavy metal toxicity is the inherent capacity of the metal to affect adversely the biological activity. The adverse effect is due to non-degradation of metals leading to accumulation in tissues and an interaction of the metal with the protein or enzyme lead to changes in physiological and metabolic processes (Giesy *et al.* 1998). Among the shellfishes, the bivalve molluscs appear to have high capability for concentrating metals in their body along with other foreign materials found in their environment when they filter from food particles during feeding. Copper is an essential trace element required in minute quantities by freshwater fishes for their growth and development. This metal proved to be highly toxic to fishes even at fairly low concentrations and it results in death or sub-lethal pathology at different functional systems (Moore and Ramamurthy, 1984).

Heavy metal contents of the aquatic animals originate from two roots of intake. The free ions and simple compounds dissolved in the water are taken up directly through the epithelium of the skin, gills and alimentary track while others accumulated in food organisms are incorporated by nutrition (Solanki *et al.* 1982). Plankton which serves as natural food of the fish species has a tendency to accumulate metals in their system (Madamba and Pamulaklakin, 1994). The toxicity levels of heavy metals depend upon many factors like its oxidation state, ligand attached to the metal, pH of the medium, route through which it enters into the organism and the regulatory mechanism present in the organism. Metals in water bind the cell membrane in aquatic organisms affecting transport processes through the cell wall and the membrane. Heavy metallic ions have been found to precipitate the mucous secretion of the gills in fish. These precipitates occupy the interlamellar spaces of the gills arresting the movement of gill filaments and block their respiratory tract (Adhikari, 2001). Metals from water and soil phases gradually accumulate in biotic communities like: the plankton, benthos, hydrophytes and finally fishes through the processes of absorption, ingestion, digestion and assimilation.

Significant reduction in spermatogenetic activity may also be caused by Lead, as studied in *Colisa fasciatus*. Lead has also been shown to produce blood discracia and impairment of gills, liver, kidney and spleen in fish (Haider, 1964). Sources of Lead in water include: mining, coal, automobile, dyeing, petrochemicals, storage batteries, water pipes; that of Copper in water include electric goods, kitchen ware, algaecide, fungicide, pigments; sources of Zinc include phosphate fertilizers, distillery, pharmaceuticals, metal processing, dye industries; sources of Chromium including: leather, tannery, thermal power plants, mining, fertilizers, textile, photography, seed disinfection (Agarwal, 2006). Permissible limits of Pb, Cd, Zn and Cr in water according to World Health Organization are 50, 10, 5000 and 50µg/L respectively. Safe concentration of Cd in fishes is ≤0.001ppm, Cr ≤0.05ppm, Cu ≤0.015ppm, Pb ≤0.03ppm, Zn ≤0.05ppm and Hg ≤0.00005ppm (Bengt-Erik, 1975). Lead is considered as a cumulative poison and it gets deposited in the bones. The effects of a fifteen day exposure to sub-lethal concentration of Lead nitrate on *Heteropneustes fossilis* indicated a mark inhibition in the activity of carbohydrates (Sastry and Gupta, 1978). A concentration of 0.5ppm of Copper in water is lethal to many algae while most fish succumb to a very low concentration. Raingear and Sheila (1975) [adopted from Text Book on Fish and Fisheries of India by V.G. Hingham, 1991] observed that the activity of liver enzymes succinct dehydrogenate and malice dehydrogenate in *Tilapia Mozambican* declined when the fish was exposed to 70µg/L Copper Sulphate solution.

In many parts of the world, rivers have become contaminated with heavy metals such as: Zinc, Lead and Copper as a result of mining and associated activities (Abel, 1996). Heavy metal contamination has been a problem for fisheries only in the rivers especially at the point source of pollution. The Ganga river system constitutes the largest river system in India. The Ganga is a perennial river taking its origin from Gangotri in the snow bound Himalayas about 3,129 km above mean sea level. Gorging a distance of about 220 km in the Himalayas, it enters the plains at Haridwar and after meandering over a distance of about 2290 km in the Indo-gangetic plains in the states of Uttar Pradesh, Bihar and West Bengal, ultimately joins the Bay of Bengal (Jhingran, 1997). The stretch of 90 km between Tribeni and Batanagar near Calcutta is highly industrialized with various types of factories dealing with pulp and paper, distillery, tannery, textile (cotton and rayon), heavy chemicals, paints and varnishes, hydrogenated oil, matches, cycle rim, petroleum oil, tar, pigment, insecticides and fungicides and other miscellaneous products flanking on both sides of the river Hooghly. Of these, wastes from paper and pulp, distillery, heavy chemicals, textiles shellac and a number of domestic outfalls contribute substantially to the pollution complex. The Hooghly receives about 252 mgd of liquid wastes of which 77mgd are drained from industrial sources. Ghosh *et al.* (1973) have found that while 62.2 per cent of the total Biological Oxygen Demand load is from industrial wastes, the domestic and municipal wastes contribute 37.8 per cent of the BOD load. Seth and Bhaskaran (1950) while studying the industrial wastes disposal and the sanitary condition in the Hooghly observed the pollutional zone to extend 15 metres below the point where the Titagarh paper mill wastes are discharged. The middle stretch of river Ganga is found heavily polluted (Das *et al.* 2007). Content of Cr, Cu, Pb and Zn was found high in the sediment and fish samples collected from middle stretch of the river (Joshi, 1991). Due to greater dilution, metal content in a significant stretch of the estuarine zone were found lower than the middle stretch.

Ganga and its tributaries are the main source of agriculture, fisheries and power generation in many places along its banks. Ganga ecosystem has been a subject of intense enquiry and study in the recent years. The river which was used to be a symbol of purity is today a sick river due to overuse and abuse. Its recuperation capacity is limited and it has exhausted at many points (De, 1999). Both quality and quantity of water of this mighty river have gone down considerably due to rapid development of industries on its river banks, due to many fold increase in the discharge of domestic industrial and agricultural wastes into the river system. The resource value of Ganga is fast declining and its rich biological and genetic diversity is dwindling (Bilgrami, 1991). With the growing urbanization, 'Ganga' (Ganges) river receive a very high quantum of city sewage and discharge of effluents from various factories on its way. Such discharges of effluents, which are mostly untreated, have posed serious pollution problems, especially from heavy metals.

It is necessary to maintain within certain limits the many parameters which contribute to the chemical quality of water. Monitoring of an aquatic environment is immensely helpful in assessing the health of ecosystem. Bilgrami and Dutta Munshi (1979) found resident fishes to be very suitable for monitoring the toxic potentials of the effluents discharged in river Ganga from a tannery and a distillery at Mokama, Bihar. The central objective of scientific studies is to predict and prevent damage to natural systems so as to make it possible for life to exist on earth. Monitoring has many purposes, some of which, although in brief, have been discussed by Cairns (1995). The main purpose of biological monitoring is to protect and preserve the biological integrity of natural ecosystems, which include taking preventive measures. There exist thousands of potentially useful indicators of some aspects of environmental quality. The microorganisms, flora and fauna are affected by pollution in different ways, depending on the nature of pollutants, the environmental variables, as well as the resistance and adaptability of each population. A battery of different organisms from these groups has been widely used as a test system for monitoring pollution. Biological methods for assessing aquatic pollution range from floristic/faunistic studies by complex field surveys, community analyses and specific in situ or laboratory assays.

Fish are preferred for toxicity testing of industrial, thermal, pesticide, metallic, crude oil, domestic or any other kind of pollution because of their direct relevance to human beings. Toxicity testing through fish bioassay is a simple basic laboratory tool for the detection, evaluation and abatement of water pollution. The laboratory monitoring of the effects of effluent toxins on fish have been in use since the 1950s (McLeay, 1986). Fish have been widely acclaimed as a test species for evaluating the potency of toxicants to cause lethality (acute toxicity or any other sub lethal responses using behavioural, biochemical, physiological and haematological responses. Test for acute toxicity are conducted under regulated laboratory conditions following methodologies as laid down by: APHA, ASTM, OECD and USEPA (A.P.H.A, 1999; A.S.T.M., 1980; U.S.E.P.A., 1975) so that a uniform methodology is adopted all over the world to test the toxicity of xenobiotic chemicals.

Sarkar *et al.* (1994) have attempted to compile the information on fish toxicity testing. One way to measure lethal toxicity is to determine the concentration of the poison which will kill half of the sample of animals within a specific period such as: 4 days – this value is termed as the 96 hour median lethal concentration or 96h LC50. Procedures and the trend of research on the subject have received a thrust during the last decade in India. Different species from various levels of organisms can be employed using standard methods for monitoring surveillance and control of pollution.

Basu (1965) opined that the Hooghly estuary was less productive than the Matlah estuary, a component of Hooghly-Matlah estuarine system as the latter is free from pollution. Basu (1966) has further observed that the water quality around the outfall of pulp and paper mills is unsatisfactory for normal animal and plant life. This point was further investigated by Gopalakrishnan *et al.* (1970). Inspite of high dilution in the estuary, indirect adverse effects of pollutants on fisheries are becoming more and more apparent. There are evidences to show that spawning grounds, fish food, fish eggs and larvae are also being destroyed by the pollutants. In India, systematic information on metal contamination is lacking for the major systems except a few like: Ganga, Yamuna, Damodar and Hooghly estuary (Mukhopadhyay, 2002). In this present study, an attempt has been made to study the extent of heavy metal (Lead and Copper) concentration in water, sediment and in hard part and soft part of harvested edible finfishes (*Setipinna phasa, Glossogobius giuris* and *Pseudapocryptes lanceolatus*) at four different locations in the uppermost transitional zone of Hooghly estuary. The locations include Panihati on the eastern bank, and Belur, Uttarpara and Konnagar on the western bank of the river Hooghly.

Review of Some Literatures

In this section, an attempt has been made to describe the results of various investigations conducted in this direction, which provides a thorough understanding to carry out this present work. A perusal of available scientific literature has been made and on its basis the review can be distinguished into two broad heads:

- Assessment of heavy metal content in water and sediment of flowing and stagnant water bodies.
- Assessment of heavy metal accumulation in body of fishes and aquatic invertebrates.

Assessment of Heavy Metal Content in Water and Sediment of Flowing and Stagnant Water Bodies

In our country, much research has been done and reported in scientific literature on the concentration of metallic elements in water and sediment of rivers and lentic water bodies. Kamble and Patil (2000) undertook a study on the assessment of concentration of heavy metals in upstream and downstream of the Kanhan river in Nagpur. The study revealed that contamination of Cu, Pb, Zn, Ni, Co, Cd, Mn and Cr was more in Kanhan river downstream than upstream. But the concentration was lower than the permissible limits. The values were accordingly; Cu 11.0-15.0µg/L, Pb 10.0-25.0µg/L, Zn 11.0-24µg/L, Co 5.0-8.0µg/L, Cd 3.0-4.0µg/L and Cr 1.0-2.0µg/L.

Patil and Srivastava (2003) determined heavy metal content in soil and sediment samples of Tapti river basin in Khandesh region, Maharashtra. Concentration of Hg in sediment samples ranged from 1.54-3µg/g, Cr 2.86-5.58µg/g, Cu 1.0-2.10µg/g, Zn 10.1-40µg/g and Cd 0.58-1.0µg/g. In soil samples, concentration of Zn was found to be 0.64-1.32µg/g, Cd 0.21-0.40µg/g, Cu 0.90-1.72µg/g. Biswal *et al.* (1998) determined the concentration of heavy metals in water and sediment of Kusei river flowing through Daitari Iron Mining Area in Orissa state. In upstream region, concentration of Pb, Zn, Ni and Co in sediment were found to be 200±11.2, 122±18.3, 198±16.5 and 112±18.6µg/g respectively and in downstream, concentration of Pb, Zn, Ni and Co in sediment have been found to be 153±14.8, 119±10.5, 100±17.3 and 107±10.8µg/g respectively. In upstream region, concentration of Pb, Zn, Ni and Co in water has been recorded as 0.028, 0.005, 0.016 and 0.022 µg/ml respectively. In downstream region, concentration of Pb, Zn, Ni and Co in water has been recorded as 0.034, 0.006, 0.018 and 0.016 µg/ml respectively. Ganesan *et al.* (1991) conducted investigation on concentration of trace metals in water and sediment of river Khan and Kshipra in Ujjain, Madhya Pradesh.

Madhyastha *et al.* (1996) analysed water and sediment samples from Nethravati river basin for a period of 24 months for quantitative estimation of Cu, Fe, Mn, Zn, Pb and Ni. Dissolved Cu levels varied between 4.0-102.0 µg/L in Nethravati river downstream, 0-24.0 µg/L in upstream. Values of Mn were recorded as 4.6-37 µg/L in water and 38.6-99.4 µg/gm in sediment. Concentration of Zinc varied between 12.2-40.6 µg/gm in sediments, concentration of Lead ranged between 0-23.4 µg/L in water. Singh and Mahaveer (1998) evaluated the level of metal in soil sediment and water of river Ghagara, Uttar Pradesh. In soil sediments, concentration of Copper was found to vary from 10.75-23.05 µg/g, Cr 7.83-19.87 µg/g, Zn 31.84-346.30 µg/g, Pb 10.00-25.50 µg/g and Cd 1.85-5.83 µg/g. In water, authors recorded concentration of Cu as 0.70-33.40 µg/L, Cr trace, Zn 6.82-129.90 µg/L, Pb trace-30.0 µg/L and Cd 1.45-3.05 µg/L.

Kumar (1989) monitored the concentration of Cu, Mn, Pb, Cr and Ni in clay fraction of Gomti river sediments around Lucknow. Mean concentration of Cu was found to be 92 µg/g, Mn 974 µg/g, Zn 177 µg/g, Co 31 µg/g, Pb 49 µg/g, Ni 70 µg/g and Cr 86 µg/g. Harihar Polyfibre Company (HPF) and Gwalior Rayon Silk Manufacturing Company (GRASIM) discharges effluent in Tungabhadra river in Dharwad Dist., Karnataka. Joseph (1992) studied the extent of metal accumulation in fish and sediments in Tungabhadra river. At outfalls of GRASIM and HPF, concentration of Zn has been found to be 1.60-3.20 µg/ml and 1.20-2.26 µg/ml respectively. At the two stations, concentration of Cr was at below detection level and 0.04-0.08µg/ml respectively. Sediment samples contained 245-324 µg/g Zn at the outfall points. Cr content in sediment was found to lie between 1.3-15.9 µg/g.

In Yamuna river water, Jhingran and Joshi (1987) recorded 0-0.38 ppb Cd, 0-1.32 ppb Cr, 2.3-18 ppb Cu, 0.8-6.9 ppb Pb and 22-54.7 ppb Zn content. Krishnamurti and Bharat (1994) recorded 2-4 ppb Cd, 6-17 ppb Cr, 15-28 ppb Cu, 12-20 ppb Ni, 17-55 ppb Pb and 112-167 ppb Zn in water of Kali river, Karnataka. In water of Subarnarekha river, Dutta Munshi and Singh (1990) [complete reference not found] recorded 150-250 ppb Cr, 127-182 ppb Cu, 200-420 ppb Pb and 205-292 ppb Zn.

Guhathakurta and Kaviraj (2000) recorded 0.04-0.10 µg/ml Cd, 0-9.66 µg/ml Zn, 0.03-0.16 µg/ml Pb and 14.3-170 µg/ml Fe in water of brackishwater ponds of Sundarban mangrove system in India. Reddy and Prasad (1991) reported the presence of detectable amounts of metals, *viz;* Zn (1152 µg/L), Cu (105 µg/L), Fe (60 µg/L), Mn (82 µg/L), Cr (9.5 µg/L) and Pb (76 µg/L) in Banjara lake, Hyderabad. Kaushik *et al.* (1999) studied the heavy metal content in Motijheel Surajkhand Ranital reservoirs in Madhya Pradesh. In reservoir water, concentration of Cd recorded was 9-10 ppb, Cr 20-48 ppb, Cu 17-34 ppb, Ni 1-4 ppb, Pb 2-9 ppb and Zn 65-120 ppb. Prasad (2004) made a pre-liminary effort to study the heavy metal pollution of groundwater resources in Lote industrial area of Jamtara Dist., Jharkhand and analysed Mn, Cu, Fe and Zn concentration in natural spring water and dugwell water.

Assessment of Heavy Metal Accumulation in Body of Fishes and Aquatic Invertebrates

Many Indian workers did quantitative analysis of body tissues of fishes and aquatic invertebrates which indicated accumulation of toxic metals involved. Mitra and Chowdhury (1993a) estimated concentration of Zinc, Copper, Manganese, Iron, Cobalt, Nickel and Lead in the body tissues of gastropod *Nerita articulata* inhabiting the lower stretch of Hooghly estuary, West Bengal. Highest concentration of the metals was detected during the monsoon. Concentration of Zn ranged between 56.29-98.89 µg/g, Cu 9.33-29.85 µg/g, Mn 9.87-27.21 µg/g, Ni 4.11-7.65 µg/g and Pb 3.0-8.16 µg/g. Mitra and Chowdhury (1993b) undertook a study to understand the metal concentrations in the soft tissues of the oyster *Crassostrea cucullata* from the lower part of the estuary. During monsoon period, concentration of Zn in gill and mantle have been recorded as 1098 ppm and 1540 ppm respectively, concentration of Copper in gill and mantle was 80.45 ppm and 126.8 ppm respectively, concentration of Mn in gill and mantle was 22.80 ppm and 178.52 ppm respectively and that of Fe in gill and mantle was 196.45 ppm and 165.52 ppm respectively.

Ghosh I *et al.* (1996) found high Fe and Zn concentration in body tissues of *Neritina smithi wood* from Nayachar Island, Hooghly estuary, West Bengal.

Yazdandoost and Katdare (1999) studied the extent of heavy metal accumulation in *Notopterus notopterus* and *Channa marulius* in Mula, Mutha and Pauna rivers in Pune Dist., Maharasthra. In *N. notopterus,* bioconcentration of Cu was found in the range 0.827-3.33mg/kg, Zn 11.59-105.60mg/kg, Cd 0.19-0.80mg/kg and Cr 0.047-0.583mg/kg.

Gopal and Maheswari Devi (1991) made an attempt to find out the effect of sublethal concentration of Cu, Cd, Hg, and Pb on the absorption efficiency of *Channa striatus*. The results have indicated that food utilization efficiency of the fish has been affected by sublethal concentration (1/10th of LC50) of heavy metals. Guhathakurta and Kaviraj (2000) estimated 0.11-3.2 µg/g Cd, 7.3-4809.5 µg/g Zn, 22.9-42.1 µg/g Pb and 5.0-495 µg/g Fe in shrimp muscle in brackishwater ponds of Sundarban, West Bengal. In mullets, Cd was detected in the range 0.11-0.15 µg/g, Zn 1.4-272.2 µg/g, Pb 29.7-44.8 µg/g and Fe 185-215 µg/g.

Suryawanshi (2008) examined the distribution and seasonal variations Zn, Pb, Cd and Cu in *Meretrix meretrix* inhabiting Kalbadevi creek at Ratnagiri coast of Maharashtra. Soft body on dry weight basis showed more concentration of Zn (105.61-132.5 µg/g dry tissue), Pb (19.06-35.28 µg/g dry tissue) and Cu (1.34-1.59 µg/g dry tissue) during monsoon. Low level of Zn (80.04-98.07 µg/g dry tissue), Pb (17.80-22.63 µg/g dry tissue) and Cu (0.12

µg/g dry tissue) were observed in summer. Banerjee *et al.* (2006) made an attempt to determine the seasonal pattern of metal accumulation (Zn and Cu) in the edible crab *Scylla serrata* from Malancha region of Sundarban, West Bengal. Concentration of Zn has been found to lie in the range 311.37-648.29µg/g dry weight of body tissue and that of Cu 90.0-225.35µg/g dry weight of body tissue.

Joseph and Shrivastava (1992) estimated concentration of metals in muscle tissues of adult *Penaeus indicus* collected from Ennore estuary in Madras. Concentration of Pb was recorded as 2.2-4.7 µg/g, Cd 0.9-2.2 µg/g, Zn 87-130 µg/g, Cu 50.2-70.3 µg/g, Ni 1.2-2.2 µg/g and Cr 3.1-6.0 µg/g. Higher levels were observed during monsoon. Biswas and Santra (2000) did Atomic Absorption Spectroscopic analyses of accumulated residues of three heavy metals namely: Lead, Cadmium and Chromium in three fishes *Labeo rohita, Cirrhinus mrigala* and *Oreochromis mossambicus* collected from Kolkata city markets. Pb, Cd and Cr levels in *Labeo rohita* were 0.04-0.20, 0.02-0.14 and 0.09-0.42µg/kg respectively, the same in *Cirrhinus mrigala* were 0.72-1.3, 0.03-0.92 and 0.95-2.6µg/kg respectively. *Oreochromis mossambicus* showed 0.24-1.8µg/kg Pb, 0.16-1.2µg/kg Cd and 0.41-4.1µg/kg Cr.

Vinodhini and Narayanan (2008) determined the bioaccumulation of Cd, Pb, Ni and Cr in gill, liver, kidney and flesh tissues of *Cyprinus carpio* after exposing the fish to sub-lethal concentrations of the metals for 32 days. Concentration of Cr was recorded as 0.790±0.026 µg/g in gills, 0.863±0.015 µg/g in liver, 0.943±0.021 µg/g in kidney and 1.083±0.021 µg/g in flesh. Concentration of Cd was determined to be1.883±0.015 µg/g in gills, 1.693±0.015 µg/g in liver, 1.166±0.015 µg/g in kidney and 0.646±0.025 µg/g in flesh. Concentration of Lead was found to be 1.400±0.020 µg/g in gills, 2.000±0.017 µg/g in liver, 1.900±0.020 µg/g in kidney and 1.460±0.036 µg/g in flesh. Villareal *et al.* (1986) investigated on the bioaccumulation of Lead, Copper, Iron and Zinc by fish in a transect of the Santa Catarina river in Nuevo Leon, Mexico. Katze *et al.* (1999) have observed that both Copper and Zinc are present in elevated levels in Olifants river, South Africa as reflected in the bioaccumulation of these metals in the fishes *Oreochromis mossambicus* and *Clarias gariepinus*. Copper content in the organs and tissues indicated the following pattern: liver>gills>skin>muscle.

Panigrahi and Chakraborty (2002) assed the impact of tannery effluent on *Tilapia nilotica* by conducting a 90 day outdoor chronic test of tannery effluent on the fish. Cr is the main pollutant discharged from tannery effluent. Stunted growth, low fecundity was observed in the fishes. Roy and Dubey (2002) conducted a static bio assay test to determine the 24 hr, 48hr, 72hr and 96hr LC50 of Chromium Sulphate powder to *Heteropneustes fossilis*. Cr exposed experimental fish exhibited significant increase in blood glucose level. Change in blood glucose concentration is the most consistent response to stressors. Maruthanayagam *et al.* (2002) conducted an experiment for 9 days to find out the effects of sub lethal concentration of Cu on survival rate, behaviour and morphological changes in *Labeo rohita*. The LC50 value of Cu (0.04ppm) proved toxic for the fish. In 24hrs, in 0.04ppm of Copper treated fishes, nearly 50 per cent mortality was recorded.

Lokesh and Somasekhar (1989) observed that laboratory grown fungi *Trichoderma* sp., *Aspergilus* sp., *Sclerotium* sp., and *Macrophomina* sp., developed resistance to higher doses of Cu, Ni, Co and Cd. According to the authors, metal tolerant forms of fungi can be best made use of in monitoring metal pollution in aquatic environment. Rahamawati *et al.* (unpublished paper) investigated the depuration time for Copper and Lead in *Oreochromis mossambicus*. Authors have concluded that Copper depuration need time more than three days but Lead concentration in depuration process decreased significantly in three days.

Chandrasekhar *et al.* (2003) estimated the concentration of heavy metals such as: Zn, Cu, Fe and Mn in benthic organism foraminifera. Concentration of metals was high near the point of coal fly site. In all sites, Zn showed the concentration (325-382μg/g) followed by Fe (28-89μg/g), Mn (1.0-34μg/g) and Cu. Accumulation of metals in the Gangetic benthic organisms have been recorded for Zn (11.8-17.6mg/kg), Cr (1.8-3.4mg/kg) and As (1.2-2.8mg/kg). Maximum accumulation of metals was found in gastropods (Mukhopadhyay, 2002). Estimation of metals in various tissues of fishes from Ganga river system revealed Zn in the range of 1.6-25 μg/g, Cu 0.3-2.9 μg/g, Cd trace-0.76 μg/g, Hg ND-0.56 μg/g and Cr ND-0.56 μg/g.

Earlier workers (De, 1999; Bilgrami and Dutta Munshi, 1985; Singh 1992) have made a detailed investigation on the status of environment of river Ganga, its soil and physico-chemical characteristics, plankton profile and benthic population and the capture fishery. Several other workers (Saikia *et al.* 1988; Singh and Mahaveer, 1997; Vass *et al.* 1998; Kaunan *et al.* 1993; Mohammad *et al.* 1987; Subramanian, 1985; Mitra *et al.* 1996; Ramesh *et al.* 1999; Samanta *et al.* 2005; Prasad *et al.* 1989; Ghosh *et al.* 1983; Israili, 1991) have studied the heavy metal content in water, sediment and fish in different zones of the Ganga river and Hooghly estuary.

Materials and Methods

Study site

For the assessment of Copper and Lead content in water, sediment and finfishes *Setipinna phasa, Glossogobius giuris* and *Pseudapocryptes lanceolatus* of the uppermost transitional zone of Hooghly estuary, West Bengal, samples were collected in pre-monsoon, monsoon and monsoon from four locations:

(a) Panihati (on the eastern bank in North 24 Parganas District, 22.69°N 88.37°E).

(b) Belur (on the western bank in Howrah District, 13.1629°N 75.8571°E).

(c) Uttarpara (on the western bank in Hooghly District, 22.67°N 88.35°E).

(d) Konnagar (on the western bank in Hooghly District, 22.7°N 88.35°E).

Methodical processing of the samples for estimation of the metals was done. The water samples were collected separately from the sampling stations and analysed for the parameters like: temperature, pH, dissolved oxygen content and free carbon dioxide.

Hooghly estuary and its Features

The lower portion of the river Bhagirathi where the tidal impact is observed is known as Hooghly River or Hooghly estuary. Hooghly is the largest estuary in India covering a distance of about 295 km from the sea face (confluence point with Bay of Bengal) to Nabadwip in the District of Nadia, West Bengal. The estuary has been demarcated into three zones, each covering about 97 km. The freshwater zone is between Nabadwip and Barrackpore, transitional zone between Barrackpore and Falta and the lower saline zone from Falta to sea face. The main Hooghly is regarded as a positive estuary where the salinity ranges from fresh water condition (salinity even below 0.1 psu) to greater than 30 psu in different parts and during different seasons from the head of the estuary to the confluence point with the Bay of Bengal (Ghosh, 2008).

The estuary now needs a re-zonation. From the point of view of water salinity, the freshwater zone has now been extended to almost Diamond Harbour from Nabadwip and the transitional zone may be considered as has been shifted further below Diamond Harbour to Kakdwip, while the high saline zone is restricted to Sagar and Frasergunj-Bakkhali in the lowermost part of the estuary. Investigation conducted by CIFRI to evaluate the present status of fish diversity in a 12 km stretch between Bichallighat and Barrackpore revealed a shift of most of the brackish water fish species to further downstream.

Features of the Sampling Stations

According to Menon *et al.* (1972), the limit of freshwater zone of Hooghly estuary is from Nabadwip in the north to Barrackpore in the south, a distance of 95 km. Further southwards, transitional zone begins. The locations Konnagar (closest from Barrackpore, about 3 km), Uttarpara, Belur and Panihati (farthest from Barrackpore, about 9 km), situated on the bank of the estuary are at a distance of approximately 6 km on average from Barrackpore southwards, they fall in the transitional zone of the estuary. But according to new zonations described, the freshwater zone has now been extended to almost Diamond Harbour from Nabadwip and the transitional zone may be considered as has been shifted further below Diamond Harbour to Kakdwip. If this is considered, then the aforesaid four sampling stations will be included in the freshwater zone of the estuary.

Quite a few numbers of large and small scale industries and factories are situated in these four places and nearby regions. Effluents arising out of these factories drain into Hooghly estuary. Consequently, the estuary water gets contaminated with toxic and less-toxic metals and metallic compounds. Notable among the industries and factories include: Bengal Chemicals, Panihati, Hindal India Private Limited, Belur, Jindal Steel Industries, Belur, National Moulding Company Limited, Belur, Gun shell Factory, Cossipore, Hind motor automobile factory, Hindmotor, Panihati Paper mill, Panihati, Hindusthan Heavy Chemicals, Panihati, Indian oxygen, Panihati, National Iron and Steel Company, Belur, Mahadev Jute mill, Belur, Hanuman Jute mill, Badamtala, Ambica jute mill, Belur. Besides these, a brick kiln and beverage producing unit is situated at Uttarpara. Along with the effluents of industries and factories which drain into the estuary, metals like: Lead, Zinc, Copper, Manganese, Cobalt and Nickel is released and enters into estuarine water in considerable amount.

Systematic Position of the Finfishes Studied

(a) *Setipinna phasa*

Phylum : Chordata
Sub-phylum : Vertebrata
Class : Osteichthyes
Subclass : Actinopterygii
Order : Clupeiformes
Family : Engraulidae
Genus : Setipinna
Species : *Setipinna phasa* (Hamilton-Buchanan) (Locally called in 'Bengali' language as 'Phasa').

(b) *Glossogobius giuris*

Phylum : Chordata
Sub-phylum : Vertebrata
Class : Osteichthyes
Subclass : Actinopterygii
Order : Perciformes
Family : Gobiidae
Genus : Glossogobius
Species : *Glossogobius giuris* (Hamilton-Buchanan) (Locally called in 'Bengali' language as 'Bele').

(c) *Pseudapocryptes lanceolatus*

Phylum : Chordata
Sub-phylum : Vertebrata
Class : Osteichthyes
Subclass : Actinopterygii
Order : Perciformes
Family : Gobiidae
Genus : Pseudapocryptes
Species : *Pseudapocryptes lanceolatus* (Bloch and Schneider) (Locally called in 'Bengali' language as 'Guley').

Estimation of Water Quality Parameters

(a) Determination of pH of water sample was done by a portable pH meter (Hanna; Sensitivity ± 0.02).

(b) Determination of free carbon dioxide and dissolved oxygen content of water sample was done following the standard methods as described by APHA (1999).

Quantitative Estimation of Heavy Metals in Water Sample

Estimation of Copper and Lead in water samples collected from four stations in Hooghly estuary was done following the method as described by Kaviraj and Guhathakurta (2000). The following steps were followed:

(i) Water samples were filtered through Whatman filter paper No. 42 and then acidified with Nitric acid (1ml per litre of water sample).

(ii) Samples were stored in neutral polythene bottles previously washed in acid and preserved at -4°C until used for metal estimation.

(iii) Before analysis of metals, water samples were brought at room temperature. Sample was mixed well and 50 ml water sample was aliquoted and was taken in a Kjeldahl flask.

(iv) Five milliliter concentrated Nitric acid was added to the aliquot and the flask was gradually heated in a water bath.

(v) Heating was continued until the solution became almost transparent and was reduced to 10ml.

(vi) The solution was subsequently cooled, filtered under reduced pressure, diluted with deionised distilled water and stored in acid-washed glass bottles.

(vii) Concentration of metals in the filtered extracts was measured by Atomic Absorption Spectrophotometer (Perkin-Elmer Model 5100). Copper was measured at 324.7nm wave length and Lead at 217nm wave length.

Quantitative Estimation of Heavy Metals in Sediment Samples

Estimation of Copper and Lead in sediment samples collected from four stations in Hooghly estuary was done following the method as described by Kaviraj and Guhathakurta (2000). The following steps were followed:

(i) Sediment samples were collected at 10cm depth from the bank.

(ii) Each collected sample was packed separately in acid-soaked clean polythene packets and brought to the laboratory in ice buckets.

(iii) The sediment samples were dried at 105°C to constant weight.

(iv) The samples were grinded and the fraction was passed through 500μmt sieve and stored in clean polythene packets at -20°C.

(v) Sediment samples were digested with strong nitric acid and hydrochloric acid mixture following the method of Pinta (1975).

(vi) Extracted samples were filtered under reduced pressure through acid-soaked Qualigens filter paper and were stored in acid-washed glass bottles.

(vii) Concentration of metals in the filtered extracts was measured by Atomic Absorption Spectrophotometer (Perkin-Elmer Model 5100). Copper was measured at 324.7nm wave length and Lead at 217nm wavelength.

Quantitative Estimation of Heavy Metal Accumulation in Fishes

Accumulation of various metals like: copper, lead, zinc, and cadmium in the fish tissues (muscle, liver, kidney, scales, fins, gills and gonads) have been determined by Atomic Absorption Spectrophotometric method. The digestion of tissues was made according to the procedure described by Chernoff (1975). The following steps were followed:

(i) The fishes were collected in live condition from the sampling stations and the muscular part (soft part) and skeletal part (hard part) were separated using sterile scissors and sharp plastic scalpel. It was covered with aluminium foil.

(ii) Soft part and hard part were weighed accurately to 1gm and put in an acid washed hard glass test tube containing 5 ml of concentrated nitric acid.

(iii) Samples were kept overnight at room temperature.

(iv) After 24 hours, 3 ml of sulphuric acid and 2 ml of perchloric acid were added to the samples simultaneously.

(v) Samples were digested at 85±5°C temperature in regulated hot plate bath until the solution turned transparent.

(vi) The mixture was cooled and filtered through an acid-soaked Whatman filter paper and subsequently adjusted to the required volume with deionised distilled water.

(vii) The metallic concentration was detected in Atomic Absorption Spectrophotometer (Perkin Elmer Model 5100). The values were expressed in µg/g.

Results

The study was conducted in three seasons (pre-monsoon, monsoon, post-monsoon) in 2013 from the four stations, and the results are the mean value (shown in Tables 2.1 to 2.5). According to Menon *et al.* (1972), these four stations are included in the uppermost part of the freshwater zone of Hooghly estuary.

Dissolved Oxygen, Free Carbon Dioxide and pH of Water Samples

Water samples collected from four stations were analysed for the parameters like: dissolved oxygen, free carbon dioxide, pH and temperature and average values were calculated. Water samples collected from Konnagar, dissolved oxygen content was found to be 11.06 mg/L, free carbon dioxide 8.8 mg/L, pH 6.5 and water temperature was 20°C. In water samples collected from Belur, dissolved oxygen content was found to be 11.02 mg/L, free carbon dioxide 8.3 mg/L, pH 6.5 and water temperature was 19.4°C. In water samples collected from Panihati, dissolved oxygen content was found to be 11.06 mg/L, free carbon dioxide 8.7 mg/L, pH 6.5 and water temperature was 20°C. In water samples collected from Uttarpara, dissolved oxygen content was found to be 10.66 mg/L, free carbon dioxide 7.9 mg/L, pH 7.0 and water temperature was 18.8°C.

Contrasting situation was observed in the extent of concentration of metals (Pb and Cu) in water and sediment of Hooghly estuary (Table 2.1).

Concentration of metals in three fishes from four stations are shown in Table 2.2, Table 2.3, Table 2.4 and Table 2.5.

Table 2.1: Concentration of Lead and Copper determined in sediment and water samples collected from study sites

	Konnagar		Panihati		Uttarpara		Belur	
	Lead	Copper	Lead	Copper	Lead	Copper	Lead	Copper
In sediment (µg/g)	26.12-33.88	16.02-23.83	30.60-32.63	23.65-24.35	23.08-30.04	22.16-32.41	32.63-40.08	16.42-32.93
In water (µg/ml)	0.11-0.15	*BDL	0.11-0.16	BDL	BDL	BDL	BDL	BDL

*BDL= Below Detectable Level.

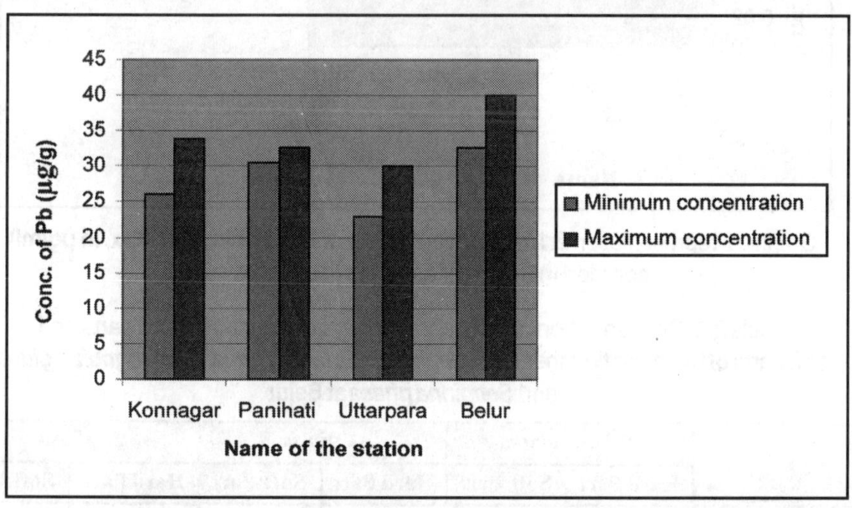

Graphical representation 2.1(a): **Concentration of Lead (min. and max. in µg/g) recorded in the sediment samples in the study sites**

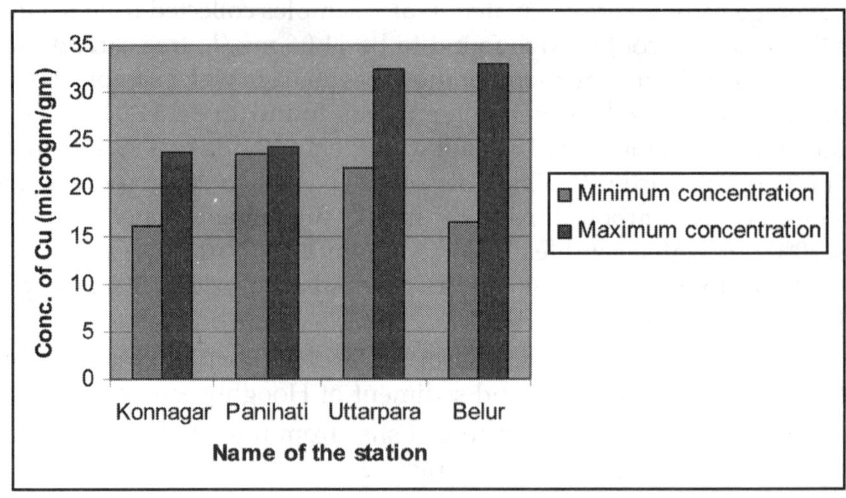

Graphical representation 2.1(b): **Concentration of Copper (min. and max. in µg/g) recorded in the sediment samples in the study sites**

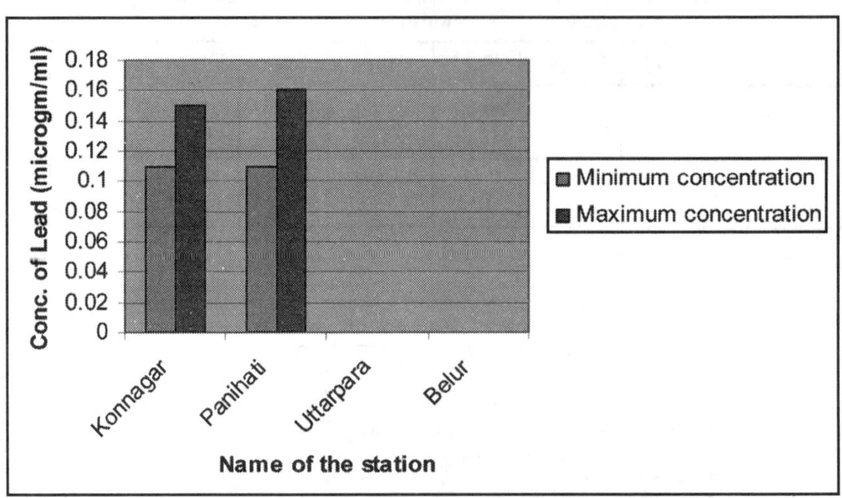

Graphical representation 2.1(c): **Concentration of Lead (min. and max. in µg/ml) recorded in the water samples in the study sites**

Table 2.2: Concentration of Lead and Copper determined in hard parts and soft parts of the three finfishes *Pseudapocryptes lanceolatus, Glossogobius giuris* and *Setipinna phasa* at Belur

	P. lanceolatus		*G. giuris*		*S. phasa*	
	Hard Part	**Soft Part**	**Hard Part**	**Soft Part**	**Hard Part**	**Soft Part**
Lead (µg/g)	74.85	9.49	BDL	12.10	61.57	10.21
Copper (µg/g)	50.56	2.77	0.86	2.84	7.38	4.08

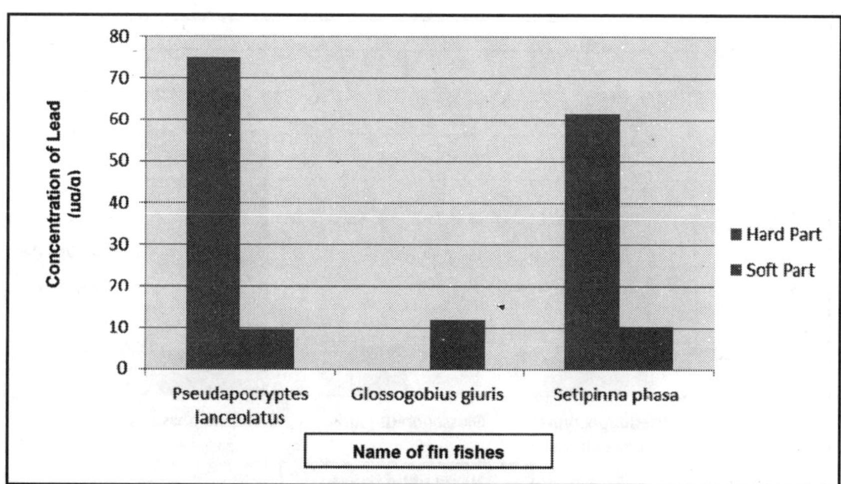

Graphical representation 2.2(a): **Concentration of Lead determined in hard parts and soft parts of the three finfishes *Pseudapocryptes lanceolatus, Glossogobius giuris* and *Setipinna phasa* at Belur**

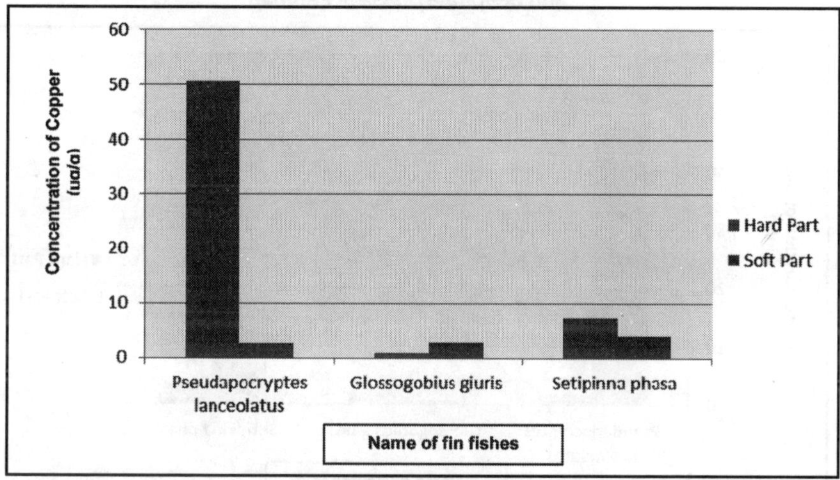

Graphical representation 2.2(b): **Concentration of Copper determined in hard parts and soft parts of the three finfishes *Pseudapocryptes lanceolatus, Glossogobius giuris* and *Setipinna phasa* at Belur**

Table 2.3: Concentration of Lead and Copper determined in hard parts and soft parts of the three finfishes *Pseudapocryptes lanceolatus, Glossogobius giuris* and *Setipinna phasa* at Panihati

	P. lanceolatus		*G. giuris*		*S. phasa*	
	Hard Part	**Soft Part**	**Hard Part**	**Soft Part**	**Hard Part**	**Soft Part**
Lead (µg/g)	70.50	9.34	BDL	11.07	58.78	10.23
Copper (µg/g)	47.88	1.99	0.71	2.72	6.99	3.98

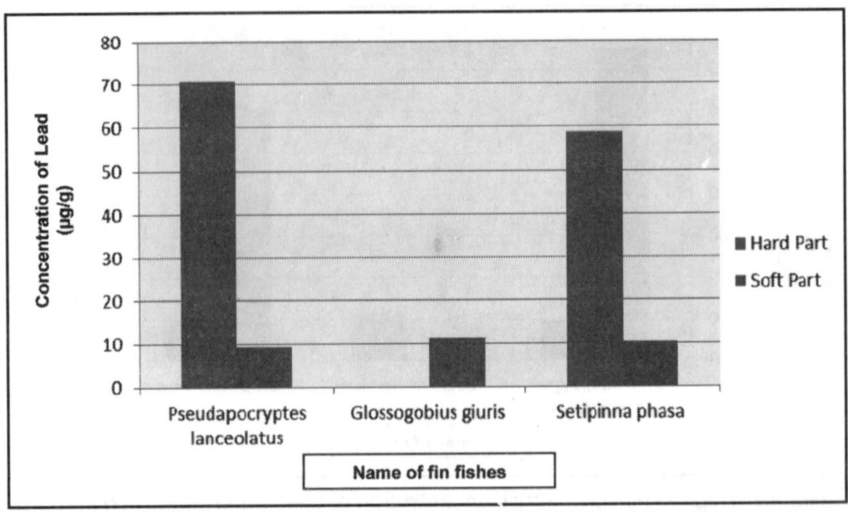

Graphical representation 2.3.a: **Concentration of Lead determined in hard parts and soft parts of the three finfishes *Pseudapocryptes lanceolatus, Glossogobius giuris* and *Setipinna phasa* at Panihati**

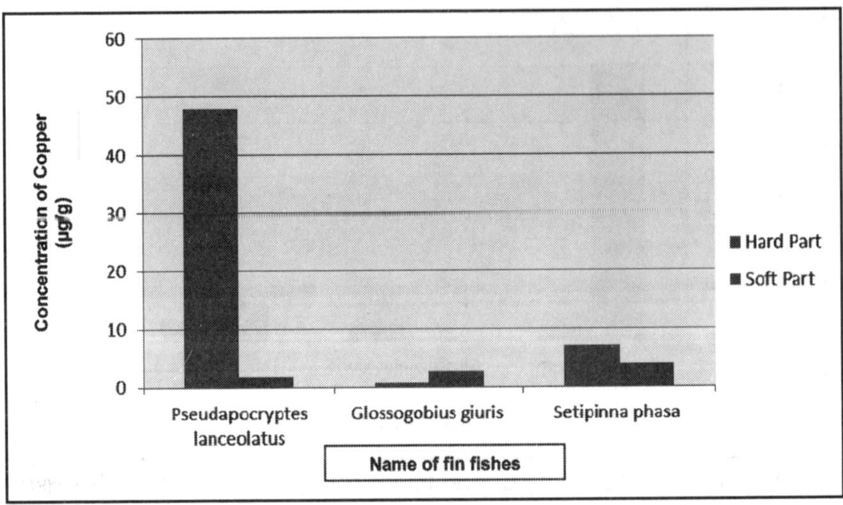

Graphical representation 2.3.b: **Concentration of Copper determined in hard parts and soft parts of the three finfishes *Pseudapocryptes lanceolatus, Glossogobius giuris* and *Setipinna phasa* at Panihati**

Table 2.4: Concentration of Lead and Copper determined in hard parts and soft parts of the three finfishes *Pseudapocryptes lanceolatus, Glossogobius giuris* and *Setipinna phasa* at Konnagar

	Hard Part	Soft Part	Hard Part	Soft Part	Hard Part	Soft Part
Lead (µg/g)	68.51	8.34	BDL	11.11	58.69	10.22
Copper (µg/g)	43.68	1.90	0.66	2.72	6.97	3.97

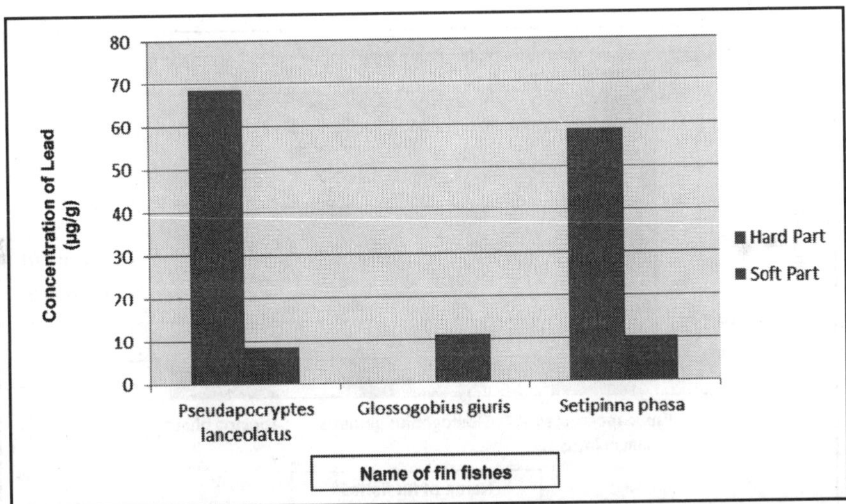

Graphical representation 2.4.a: **Concentration of Lead determined in hard parts and soft parts of the three finfishes *Pseudapocryptes lanceolatus, Glossogobius giuris* and *Setipinna phasa* at Konnagar**

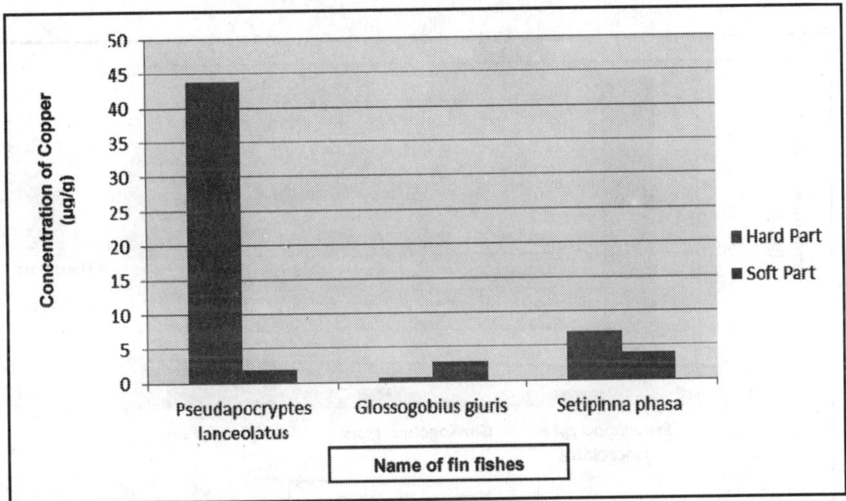

Graphical representation 2.4.b: **Concentration of Copper determined in hard parts and soft parts of the three finfishes *Pseudapocryptes lanceolatus, Glossogobius giuris* and *Setipinna phasa* at Konnagar**

Table 2.5: Concentration of Lead and Copper determined in hard parts and soft parts of the three finfishes *Pseudapocryptes lanceolatus, Glossogobius giuris* and *Setipinna phasa* at Uttarpara

	Hard Part	Soft Part	Hard Part	Soft Part	Hard Part	Soft Part
Lead (µg/g)	67.51	7.84	BDL	10.01	57.66	10.17
Copper (µg/g)	42.68	1.92	0.65	2.63	6.91	3.93

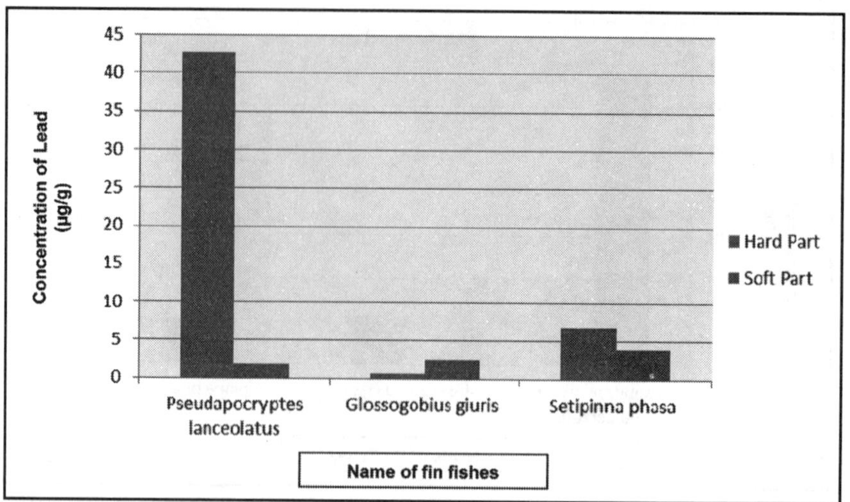

Graphical representation 2.5.a: **Concentration of Lead determined in hard parts and soft parts of the three finfishes *Pseudapocryptes lanceolatus, Glossogobius giuris* and *Setipinna phasa* at Uttarpara**

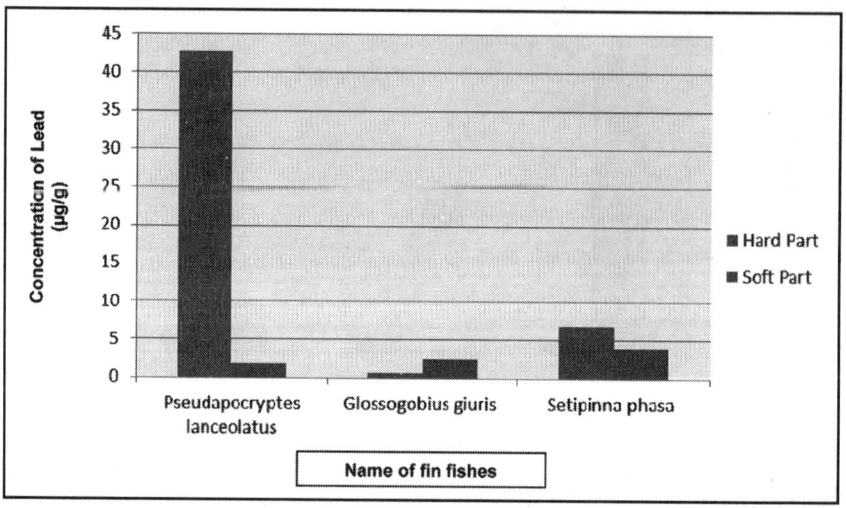

Graphical representation 2.5.b: **Concentration of Copper determined in hard parts and soft parts of the three finfishes *Pseudapocryptes lanceolatus, Glossogobius giuris* and *Setipinna phasa* at Uttarpara**

Discussion

Bioaccumulation is the ability that an organism has to concentrate an element or compound from food and water to a level higher than that of its environment (Villareal *et al.* 1986; Smith, 1988). It is the "Progressive increase in the amount of a substance in an organism or part of an organism which occurs because the rate of intake exceeds the organism's ability to remove the substance from the body." (International Union of Pure And Applied Chemistry, 1993).

In the present study, it has been observed that lead content is comparatively more in water and sediment than copper. Lead was detected in sediment from the four stations (Konnagar, Panihati, Uttarpara, and Belur.) contained quite high concentrations ranging between 23.08-40.08µg/g. The Lead content is detected in water ranging from 0.11-0.16 µg/g. Copper content was detected in the sediment is ranging from16.02-32.93 µg/g, where as the lead content in the water was ranging between 0.11-0.16 µg/g in Konnagar and Panihati. The lead content present in the sediment of Belur is relatively high than that of the other stations. On the other hand the lead content of the sediment was found to be in increasing order in the stations as follows:

Belur >Panihati >Konnagar > Uttarpara

This may due to be the presence of various industries like: textile, pharmaceutical industries, battery manufacturing units, jute mills, gun shell factory etc.

Heavy metal pollution can arise from many sources but most commonly arises from the purification of metals, *e.g.*, the smelting of copper and the preparation of nuclear fuels. Electroplating is the primary source of chromium and cadmium. Through precipitation of their compounds or by ion exchange into soil and mud, heavy metal pollutants can be localized and lay dormant to those places. Unlike organic pollutants, heavy metals do not decay and thus pose a different kind of challenge for remediation. Currently, plants or microorganisms are tentatively supposed to remove some heavy metals such as: mercury. Plants which exhibit hyper accumulation can be used to remove heavy metals from soils by concentrating them in their bio matter. Some treatment of mining tailings has occurred where the vegetation is then incinerated to recover the heavy metals.

Fish has capability to uptake Cu and Pb from the water to be bioacumulated. This process depends on several factors such as: the concentrations and time of exposure. Cu and Pb are lipophilic so can be easily bound in fatty tissue of fish even though fish has capacity to depurate (transfer or remove) the metal to surrounding environment (water) (EPA, 1996). Capability to accumulate the metal, especially Cu and Lead, has potential risk to upper tropic level such as: human. Higher Cu accumulation could affect human health such as: in homeostatic control (Harris, 1991). While Pb accumulation could effect gastric functions and accumulate in bone for 30-40 years (US EPA: 2004, Darmono: 1995).

In the present study it has been observed that the lead and copper have been accumulated more in the fish hard parts than the soft parts. Higher concentration of Pb in sketetal parts of *P. lanceolatus* and *S. phassa* suggest the suitability of the skeletal system of these two fishes to be used as indicators of Pb contamination. Trivedi S *et al.* (1995) reported similar type of observations in mud skipper, *Boleophthalmus boddaerti* from Nayachar Island, Hooghly estuary.

Singh *et al.* (1993) assessed the quantum of different metals in water and sediments in middle stretch of Ganga and also in flesh of *Cirrhinus reba* and *Puntius* sp. In water, concentration of Zn has been detected and found to lie within the range 12.7-48.6 µg/L, As 6.74-27.09 µg/L and Cr 0.48-1.91 µg/L. In flesh of *Cirrhinus reba*, concentration of Zn, As and Cr ranged between 14.87 µg/g, 1.84-4.50 µg/g and 0.98-6.84 µg/g respectively. In flesh of *Puntius* sp., concentration of Zn, As and Cr has been detected and found to lie in the range 12.86-28.92 µg/g, 0.98-3.96 µg/g and 1.76-3.84 µg/g. Concentration of Zn (60.58-96.82 µg/g), As (8.91-21.21 µg/g) and Cr (7.22-16.82 µg/g) was observed in the sediments.

Attempt has been made by Singh and Mahaveer (1997) to study the metal concentration in water and soil of river Ganga in seven different stations, *viz;* Sultanpur, Barauni, Munger, Bhagalpur, Kahalgaon, Manikchakghat and Farakka. In water, concentration of Cu ranged from 0-20 µg/L, Cr 2.6-28.38 µg/L, Cd trace-0.77 µg/L, Pb 15.5-61.12 µg/L and Zn 4.33-117 µg/L. In sediment, Concentration of Cu ranged from 4-32 µg/g, Cr 9-47.54 µg/g, Cd 1.39-1.85 µg/g, Pb 18.36-24.14 µg/g and Zn 30.3-783.9 µg/g. The same authors have also recorded concentration of Cr and Zn as 2.2-2.4ppb and 28-30ppb respectively in water of river Yamuna at Allahabad.

In Ganga water (upstream), concentrations of Cd, Cr, Cu, Ni, Pb and Zn have been recorded as 0-11, 0, 7-17, 12-50, 0 and 72-157ppb respectively (Saikia *et al.* 1988). Vass *et al.* (1998) estimated the metal concentration in Ganga water (midstream); the values recorded were 0-28ppb Cd, 3-119ppb Cr, 3-170ppb Cu, 1-10ppb Ni, 1-680ppb Pb and 1-311ppb Zn. In Hooghly estuary water, concentration of Cd, Cu, Pb and Zn were found to be 2-14ppb, 5-19ppb, 17-41ppb and 22-37ppb respectively (Samanta *et al.* 2005).

WBPCB (2004) undertook a study on "Monitoring of the effect of Devi Durga idol immersion in river Ganga and the change in chemical load therein'. At Babughat, following two days after idol immersion, concentration of Zn was recorded as 0.09-1.66mg/lit, whereas before the beginning of the festival, maximum concentration of Zn in the same position was 0.08mg/L.concentration of Pb had even increased after the process in Ganga water adjoining Babughat. On the opposite bank of the river at Shibpur crematory ghat, concentration of Zn after idol immersion was recorded as 0.05-0.49mg/L, whereas the maximum value recorded was 0.16mg/lit one month prior to the festival. Concentration of Zn recorded in a large confined water body at Dum, Kolkata on a day prior to Durga Puja festival was 0.01mg/L but after idol immersion, concentration of Zn had significantly increased and the value recorded was 0.10-0.22mg/L. Study on water samples collected from Babughat before and after Goddess Kali idol immersion has revealed that: concentration of Zn in Ganga river water was 0.04-0.08mg/L before immersion and the same after immersion was 0.05-0.83mg/L. Concentration of Cr in the mud lying beneath the shallow waters of idol immersion ghats did increased to some extent as a result of idol immersion.

Mukhopadhyay (2002) recorded the concentration of metals (Zn Cu, Cd and Pb) in water and sediment of Ganga river system at six stations, *viz;* Kanpur, Allahabad, Varanasi, Farakka, Tribeni and Rishra. In water, concentration of Zn has been found to lie in the range 0.03-0.09mg/L with a maximum 0.23mg/L at Allahabad, concentration of Cu 0.005-0.19mg/L, Cd 0.003-0.007mg/L and Pb 0.004-0.68mg/L. In soil (sediment), concentration of Zn has been found to lie between the range 50.0-249.0mg/kg, Cu 10.20-128.15mg/kg, Cd 2.25-9.95mg/kg and Pb 24.05-47.15mg/kg.

Estimation of metals in various tissues of fishes from Ganga river system revealed Zn in the range of 1.6-25 µg/g, Cu 0.3-2.9 µg/g, Cd trace-0.76 µg/g, Hg ND-0.56 µg/g and Cr ND-0.56 µg/g in four finfishes and *Labeo calbasu* and *Mystus gulio* had the highest metal concentrations (Mukhopadhyay, 2002).

In sediment of Ganga river (upstream), Cd has been found to accumulate in the range 0.8-29.4 µg/g, Cu 4.1-17.9 µg/g, Mn 107-226 µg/g, Ni 4.9-11.8 µg/g and Zn 26.3-48.3 µg/g (Saikia *et al.* 1988). In sediment of Ganga (midstream), Israili (1991) recorded 0.0-1.2 µg/g Cd, 3.0-51 µg/g Cr, 2.5-45 µg/g Cu, 70.9-511 µg/g Mn, 4.5-49 µg/g Ni, 1.2-16 µg/g Pb and 125-259 µg/g Zn. In the same region, in sediment, Kaunan *et al.* (1993) recorded 0.4-1 µg/g Cd, 12.8-20.9 µg/g Cr and 1.9-22 µg/g Pb.

In sediment of Hooghly estuary, Subramanian (1985) recorded 4.0-53.0 µg/g Cu, 250-800 µg/g Mn, 12-115 µg/g Pb and 12-611 µg/g Zn. In a separate study, Vass *et al.* (1998) recorded 2.5-7.7 µg/g Cd, 35.5-52.5 µg/g Cu, 24.0-36.4 µg/g Pb and 145.8-165.6 µg/g Zn in sediment of Hooghly estuary.

In sediment of Hooghly estuary mouth, Mitra *et al.* (1996) recorded 7.9-32.2 µg/g Cu, 53.6-286 µg/g Mn, 9.1-39 µg/g Ni, 3.0-27.4 µg/g Pb and 21.1-147.7 µg/g Zn. In the same area, Ramesh *et al.* (1999) recorded 0.4 µg/g Cd, 61.5 µg/g Cr, 37.5 µg/g Ni, 10.5 µg/g Pb and 64.4 µg/g Zn in sediment.

In sediments of rivers Hooghly and Haldi, Samanta *et al.* (2005) recorded 0.4-4.4 µg/g Cd, 3.9-80.4 µg/g Cu, 34.4-539.6 µg/g Mn, 0.5-79.4 µg/g Pb and 25-363.4 µg/g Zn.

Many toxic metals accumulate in fish tissues especially in liver, kidney, gill, heart, spleen and bone (Post, 1987). In the catfish *Rita rita* in Ganga river system, concentration of Zn in gills and kidney was found to be 30.60-287.60mg/kg and 59.44-1160.43mg/kg respectively, Cu in gills and kidney was found to be 3.12-80.84mg/kg and 38.12-241.88mg/kg respectively, Cd in gills and kidney was found to be 12.32-760mg/kg and 38.23-1410mg/kg respectively and Pb 56.42-1128mg/kg and 0.63-3296.28mg/kg respectively (Mukhopadhyay, 2002). Fish samples from Kanpur recorded lower metal levels in comparison to those of Rishra which falls within the industrially contaminated stretch of Hooghly estuary.

Kaviraj (1989) reported relatively high content of Zn in *Penaeus indicus* (135.6 µg/g) and in *Mastacembelus pancalus* (108.2 µg/g) in Hooghly estuary.

Nasreen (1991) reported the toxic level of Lead on *Tetrahymena pyriformes* on short exposure for 3.5hours. Sahgal (1987) reported Lead toxicity on *Lebistes reticulata* at a concentration 1.72ppm, which caused decreased swimming activity and increased opercular movement. Srivastava (1987) reported Lead toxicity on Colisa fasciatus at 1.5ppm on 96 hours exposure.

Radhakrishnaiah (1992) reported that Labeo rohita, on both short term and long term exposure to Copper showed increased blood glucose level and increased glycogen content in liver. Srivastava (1982) observed declining glycogen level in liver and muscle due to exposure to Copper.

The present study revealed that the lead and copper is accumulated more in the fish skeletal parts than soft tissues.

Even though fish has capacity to depurate copper and lead by replace it to the unpolluted water, further research should be conducted especially in field scale and find out water parameters such as: pH, hardness, combination pH-hardness or other combination of parameter that could effectively reduce Cu and Pb concentration in water and sediment as well as in fishes.

However it can also be conjectured that the regular monitoring of pollutants in the river Hooghly is needed, especially in the industrial belt where there is frequent discharge of toxic metals as well as other chemo toxic agents both from the industry and/or anthropogenic waste. The metal in some cases may be the favourable medium for some pathogenic microorganisms. Severe out break of diseases may occur with the increasing concentration of metal, which in turn may also lead to serious threat to the fish and other living organism dwelling in the river Hooghly; and subsequently may also be a threat to human health.

Hence the proper treatment may be necessary for the industrial and domestic waste products before they are being discharge into the river.

Conclusion

The holy river Gaga in the Indo-Gangetic delta is the fourth largest river in the world. But now-a-day's its water has become highly polluted due to rapid industrialization in conjunction with extreme human negligence allowing to discharge of industrial waste, domestic waste and municipal waste in the different places through its entire stretch of confluence. This survey regarding the heavy metal pollution in river Hooghly especially in the industrial belt (observed study area, Konnagar-Belur) indicates the presence of Lead and Copper content in the water, sediment as well as in fin fishes much above the tolerance level. In this case, in particular, two things are very significant which are: *(i)* differential Biomagnifications between the hard and soft parts of the fishes subjected for study here and *(ii)* the Bioaccumulation indices are also different for Lead and Copper. These facts could only be elucidated by further research in metabolic pathways regarding those metallic binding mechanism in soft as well as hard tissue. As regard to those Fishes being the Bioindicator, may be, some species of Fishes could serve the purpose that has to be rechecked and determined

REFERENCES

Abel, P.D. (1996). Water Pollution Biology 2nd Edition. Taylor and Francis Publication. 1-54 pp.

Adhikari, S. (2001). Heavy Metal Pollution in Aquaculture. In. *Nutrient and Environment Management in Aquaculture. CIFA (ICAR) Publication.* 49-52 pp.

Adhikari, S. and Pani, K.C. (2001). Methodologies of Water and Soil Analysis. In. *Nutrient and Environment Management in Aquaculture. CIFA (ICAR) Publication.* 57-63 pp.

APHA (1999). Standard Methods for the Examination of Water and Wastewater. *American Public Health Association; 20th edition* (January 1999).

Agarwal, K.C. (2006). Environmental Pollution; Causes, Effects and Controls. Narendra Publishing House, New Delhi. 61-93 pp.

Agarwal, S.K. (1991). Bioassay Evaluation of Acute Toxicity of Mercuric chloride to Air-breathing Fish *Channa punctatus* (Bloch); Mortality and Behaviour Study. *J. Environ. Biol.*, Vol. 12. 99-106 pp.

ASTM (1980). Standard Practice for Conducting Toxicity Tests with Fishes, Macro-invertebrates and Amphibians. Philadelphia, 1980.

Banerjee, K., Mitra, A., Chakraborty, R., Das, A. and Mukherjee, D. (2006). Heavy Metal Concentration in the edible crab *Scylla serrata* in the Malancha region of Indian Sundarbans. In. *A. Kumar Ed. Advanced Ecology.* Daya Publishing House, New Delhi. 288-293pp.

Basu, A.K. (1965). Observations the Probable Effects of Pollution on the Primary Productivity of the Hooghly and Matlah estuaries. *Hydrobiologia,* Vol. 25. 302-316pp.

Basu, A.K. (1966). Studies on the Effluents from Pulp and Papers Mills and its Role in Bringing the Physico-Chemical Changes Around the Several Discharge Points in the Hooghly River Estuary. *J. Instn. Engrs. India.* Vol. 46 No. 10. 108-116pp.

Bengt-Erik, B. (1975). Vertebral Damage in Fish Induced by Pollutants. In. *J.H. Koeman Ed. Sublethal Effects of Toxic Chemicals on Aquatic Animals. Elsevier Science Publication,* New York. 23-30 pp.

Bilgrami, K.S. and Dutta Munshi, J.S. (1979). Limnological Survey and Impact of Human Activities on the river Ganges. MAB Technical Report submitted to DST, Government of India. 1-91 pp.

Bilgrami, K.S. and Dutta Munshi J.S. (1985). Ecology of the River Ganga: Impact of Human Activities. Final Technical Report. 1-97pp.

Bilgrami, K.S. (1991). The Living Ganga. Narendra Publishing House, New Delhi. 17-22 pp.

Biswas, J.K. and Santra, S.C. (2000). Heavy Metal Levels in Marketable Vegetables and Fishes in Calcutta Metropolitan area. In. *B.B. Jana et al. Ed. Water Recycling and Resource Management in the Developing World. University of Kalyani,* West Bengal Publication. 371-376pp.

Biswal, D., Muralidhar, J. and Patra, C. (1998). Heavy Metal Concentration in Sediment and Water of River Kusei. *Indian Journal of Environmental Health,* Vol. 40, No. 4. 349-358pp.

Cairns, J. (1995). Chemical *vs.* Biological Pollution Monitoring.

Carpenter, K.E. (1926). On the Biological Factors Involved in the Destruction of River Fisheries by Pollution Due to Lead Mining. *Ann. Appl. Biol.,* Vol. 12. 1-13pp.

Chandrasekhar, N., Cherian, A., Gopinath, R. and Rajamanickam, M. (2003). Heavy Metals in Foraminifera from the Tuticorin Coastal Sediments. In. *Aquatic Environment and Toxicology.* Daya Publishing House, New Delhi. 336-339pp.

Chernoff, G.F. (1975). A Mouse Model of the Fetal Alcohol syndrome. *Teratology,* Vol. 11. 223-230pp.

Das, M.K., Samanta, S. and Saha, P.K. (2007). Riverine Health and Impact of Fisheries in India. *Policy Paper 1, CIFRI (ICAR) Publication.* 12-16pp.

Davis, A., Sellstone, C., Clough, S. and Barrick, R. (1996). Bioaccumulation of Arsenic, Copper and Lead: Constraints Imposed by Sediment Geochemistry. *Applied Geochemistry,* Vol. 11, No. 3. 409-423pp.

Datta, S. and Das, R.C. (2005). Conservation of Aquatic Environment. *CIFE (Deemed University) Kolkata Centre Publication.* 1-17pp.

De, D.K. (1999). The River Ganga-Environment and Fishery. In. *Proceedings of Summer School on Ecology, Fisheries and Fish Stock Assessment in Indian Rivers.* CIOFRI (ICAR) Publication.

Ganesan, V., Srinivasulu, K. and Pandey, A.K. (1991). Trace Metal Concentration in Water and Sediments of the River Khan and Kshipra (Ujjain). *Int. J. Eco. Env. Sci,* Vol. 17 No. 3. 225-236pp.

Ghosh, K.K., Sinha, M. and Srivastava, N.K. (1973). On the Escarpment of carp hatchlings from Shooting nets. *Indian J. Fish.,* Vol. 20 Issue 2. 395-410pp.

Ghosh, B.B., Bagchi, M.M. and De, D.K. (1983). Some Observation on the Status of Pollution in the Hooghly estuary with Reference to Heavy Metals deposited through Industrial Wastes. *J. Inland Fish. Soc.* India, Vol. 15 No. 1. 44-53pp.

Ghosh I, Mitra A, Trivedi S, Bag M, and Chowdhury A. (1996) Trace Metal Accumulation by the Gastropod *Neritina smithi wood* from Nayachar Island, Hooghly Estuary. *Proc. Acad. Environ. Biol.* 5(2); pp. 135-137.

Ghosh, A. (2008). Fishes of Hooghly Estuary. *CIFRI (ICAR) Publication,* Bulletin No. 155. i-iv pp.

Giesy, J.P., Versteeg, D.J. and Graney, R.I. (1988). A Review of Selected Clinical Indicators of Stress-Induced Changes in Aquatic Organisms. In. *Toxic Contaminants and Ecosystem Health* (M.S. Evans Ed.) Vol. 21. John Wiley and Sons Publication, New York. 169-200pp.

Gopal, V. and Maheswari Devi, K. (1991). Biomonitoring of Heavy Metal and Pesticide Pollution. *Indian Journal of Environmental Health,* Vol. 33, No. 4. 488-491 pp.

Gopalakrishnan, V., Ray, P. and Ghosh, B.B. (1970). Problem of Estuarine Pollution with Special Reference to the Hooghly Estuary. *Proc. Seminar Pollution and Human Environ. BARC, Trombay* (August 26-27). 313-324 pp.

Guhathakurta, H. and Kavaraj, A. (2000). Heavy Metal Concentration in Water, Sediment, Shrimp and Mullet in some brackishwater Ponds of Sundarban, *India. Mar. Poll. Bull.*, Vol. 40 Issue. 1. 914-920pp.

Haider, G. (1964). Studies on the Heavy Metal Poisoning of Fishes-Lead Poisoning of Rainbow trout *Salmo gairdnerii* (Richardson). *Z. Anqew. Zool.*, Vol. 51. 347-366pp.

Hellawell, J.M. (1986). Biological Indicators of Freshwater Pollution and Environmental Management. Elsevier Applied Science Publication, London.

International Union of Pure and Applied Chemistry (1993). *Glossary for Chemists of Terms used in Toxicology: Pure and Applied Chemistry*, Vol. 65, No. 9, 2003-2122 pp.

Israili, A.W. (1991). Occurrence of Heavy Metals in Ganga River Water and Sediments of Western Uttar Pradesh. *Poll. Res.*, Vol. 10 No. 2. 103-109pp.

Jhingran, A.G. and Joshi, H.C. (1987). Heavy Metals in Water, Sediments and Fish in the River Yamuna. *J. Inland Fish. Soc. India*, Vol. 19 No. 1. 13-23pp.

Kaushik, S., Sahu, B.K., Lawania, R.K. and Tiwari, R.K. (1999). Occurrence of Heavy Metals in Lentic Water of Gwalior Region. *Poll Res.*, Vol. 18 No. 2. 137-140pp.

Krishnamurti, S.R. and Bharat, S.G. (1994). Studies on the Metal Pollution of the River Kali Around Dandeli, Karnataka, India. *Poll. Res.*, Vol. 13 No. 3. 249-251 pp.

Jhingran, V.G. (1997). Fish and Fisheries of India. Hindusthan Publishing Company, New Delhi. 110-122pp.

Joseph, K.O. (1992). Heavy Metal Concentration in the Fishes of River Tungabhadra. *J. Inland Fish. Soc. India*, Vol. 24, No. 1. 73-76pp.

Joseph, K.O. and Shrivastava, J.P. (1992). Heavy Metal Load in Shrimp *Penaeus indicus* Inhabiting Ennore Estuary in Madras. *J. Inland Fish. Soc. India*, Vol. 24, No. 1. 30-33pp.

Joshi, H.C. (1991). Monitoring of Toxic and Hazardous Substances in the River Ganga. In. *R. Gupta Ed. Proc. Work. Trg. Biomon.* 62-68pp.

Kamble, S.K. and Patil, M.R. (2000). Heavy Metal Pollution from A Thermal Power Station in India. In. *B.B. Jana et al. Ed. Water Recycling and Resource Management in the Developing World. University of Kalyani,* West Bengal Publication. 411-413pp.

Katze, P., Preez, H.H.D. and Van Vuren, J.H.J. (1999). Bioaccumulation of Copper and Zinc in *Oreochromis mossambicus* and *Clarias gariepinus* from the Olifants River, South Africa. *Bull. Water Research Commission*, Vol. 25, No. 1. 99-110pp.

Kaunan, K., Sinha, R.K., Tanabe, S. and Tatsukawa, R. (1993). Heavy Metals and Organochlorine Residues in Ganga River dolphins from India. *Mar. Pollution. Bull.*, Vol. 26 No. 3. 159-162pp.

Kaviraj, A. (1989). Heavy Metal Concentration in Shrimp and Mullet from the Hooghly estuary. *Science and Culture*, Vol. 55. 695-699pp.

Kaviraj, A. and Guhathakurta, H. (2004). Heavy Metal Deposition in some Brackishwater Ponds of Sundarban during off Season of Shrimp Culture. *Asian Fisheries Science*, Vol. 17. 29-38pp.

Krishnamurthi, C.R. and Vishwanathan, P. (1991). Toxic Metals in the Indian Environment. Tata-McGraw Hill Publishing Company. Ltd. New Delhi.

Kumar, S. (1989). Heavy Metal Pollution in Gomti River Sediments Around Lucknow, Uttar Pradesh. *Curr Sci.*, Vol. 58 No. 10. 557-559.

Lokesh, S. and Somasekhar, R.K. (1989). Training of some Fungi to Heavy Metals – A Feasible Way of Monitoring Metal Pollution in Aquatic Environment. In *R.D. Khulbe Ed. Perspectives in Aquatic Biology,* Papyrus Publishing House, New Delhi. 31-40pp.

Madamba, L.S.B. and Pamulaklakin, M.A. (1994). Heavy Metal in Selected Fish Species Collected from Laguna De Bay. *Philipp. J. Sci.*, Vol. 123, No. 2. 135-146 pp.

Madhyastha, M.N., Rao, I.J. and Hosetti, B.B. (1996). Studies on some Heavy Metals in Nethravathi River. *Indian Journal of Environmental Health*, Vol. 38, No. 3. 181-187pp.

Mandal, P. (2008). Studies on Heavy Metal Pollution in Pond Environment of Sukhinda Valley, Orissa. MF.Sc. Dissertation submitted to Master of Fishery Science Unit, Utkal University, Bhubaneswar.

Maruthanayagam, C., Sharmila, G. and Kumar, A. (2002). Toxicity of Copper on the Morphological and Behavioural Aspects in *Labeo rohita*. In *Arvind Kumar Ed. Ecology and Ethology of Aquatic Biota*. Daya Publishing House, New Delhi. 119-127pp.

McLeay, D. (1986). Aquatic Toxicity of Pulp and Paper Mill Effluent. In. *Environment: Canada, Fisheries and Oceans, Canadian Pulp and Paper Association, Ontario, Ministry of Environment*. 1-234 pp.

Menon, A.G., Rama Rao, K.V. and Sen, T.K. (1972). The Hooghly and its Fisheries in the Past, the Present and the Future with Special Reference to the farakka barrage on the Ganga. *Sci and Cul.*, Vol. 38 No. 8. 338-343pp.

Mitra, A. and Chowdhury, A. (1993a). Metal Content in the Gastropod *Nerita articulata*. *Indian Journal of Environmental Health*, Vol. 35, No. 1. 31-35pp.

Mitra, A. and Chowdhury, A. (1993b). Heavy Metal Concentration in oyster *Crassostrea cucullata* in Sagar Island, India. *Indian Journal of Environmental Health*, Vol. 35, No. 2. 139-141 pp.

Mitra, A., Trivedi, S., Gupta, A. and Chowdhuri, A. (1996). Distribution of Trace Metals in the Sediments from Hooghly estuary, India. *Poll. Res.*, Vol. 15 No. 2. 137-141 pp.

Mohammad, A., Rozi, U. and Ullah, K.H. (1987). Monitoring of Heavy Metals in the Water and Sediment of Ganga River, India. *Water Sci. Tech.*, Vol. 19 No. 9. 107-117pp.

Moore, J.W. and Ramamurthy, S. (1984). 'Copper' Heavy Metals in Natural Waters – Applied Monitoring and Impact Assessment. In. *R.S. Desanta Ed. Springer-Verlag* New York, Berlin.

Mukhopadhyay, M.K. (2002). Status and Methods of Assessment of Heavy Metals in Aquatic Ecosystem in India in Relation to Fish Health. *In. Proceedings of Summer School on Methods of Assessment of Aquatic Ecosystem for Fish Health Care.* CIFRI (ICAR) Publication.

Panigrahi, A. and Chakraborti, A. (2002). Studies on Pollutional Impact of Tannery Effluent on Fish and Livestock. *In. Arvind Kumar Ed. Ecology and Ethology of Aquatic Biota.* Daya Publishing House, New Delhi. 85-88pp.

Patil, B.H. and Shrivastava, V.S. (2003). Heavy Metals in Cultivated Soils and River Sediments and their Correlation Study. *In. Aquatic Environment and Toxicology.* Daya Publishing House, New Delhi. 340-344 pp.

Pinta, M.D. (1975). Detection and Determination of Trace Elements. ANA Arbor Science Publication.

Post, G. (1987). Text-book of Fish Health. *TFH Publications*. 250-256pp.

Prasad, K.K. (2004). Analysis of Heavy Metals in Groundwater from Coal Mining Area in Jamtara District, Jharkhand. In. *Water Pollution – Abatement and Management*. Daya Publishing House, New Delhi. 283-288pp.

Prasad, S., Mathur, A. and Rupainwar, D.D. (1989). Heavy Metal Distribution in the Sediment and Sewer-river Confluence Points of River Ganga in Varanasi-Mirzapur Region. *Asian Env.*, Vol. 11 No. 2. 73-82pp.

Radhakrishnaiah, K., Venkataramana, P., Suresh, A. and Shivaramakrishna, B. (1982). Effect of Lethal and Sublethal Concentrations of Copper on glycolysis and Liver and Muscle of the Freshwater Teleost *Labeo rohita* (Hamilton). *J. Environ. Biol.*, Vol. 13. 63-68pp.

Ramesh, R., Ramanathan, A.L., James, R., Subramanian, V., Jacobsen, S.B. and Holland, H.D. (1999). Rare Earth Elements and Heavy Metal Distribution in Estuarine Sediments in East Coast of India. *Hydrobiologia*, Vol. 397. 89-99pp.

Rana, B.C. (1995). Pollution and Biomonitoring. Tata-McGraw-Hill Publishing Company, New Delhi. 1-416pp.

Reddy, G.N. and. Prasad, M. N. V. (1991). Heavy Metal Binding Proteins-peptides; Occurrence, Structure, Synthesis and Function – A review. *Envir. Exp. Bot.*, Vol. 30. 251-264pp.

Roy, D.N. and Dubey, N.K. (2002). Toxic Effects of Chromium sulphate on the Indian catfish *Heteropneustes fossilis* in Short-term and Long-term Exposure. *In Arvind Kumar Ed. Ecology and Ethology of Aquatic Biota.* Daya Publishing House, New Delhi. 107-114pp.

Sahgal, R. and Saxena, A.B. (1987). Determination of Acute Toxicity Levels of Cadmium and Lead to the Fish *Lebistes reticulate* (Peters). *Indian. J. Environ. Studies*, Vol. 29. 157-162pp.

Saikia, D.K., Mathur, R.P. and Srivastava, S.K. (1988). Heavy Metals in Water and Sediments of upper Ganga. *Indian J. Environment.*, Vol. 1. 11-17pp.

Samanta, S., Mitra, K., Chandra, K., Bandopadhyay, S. and Ghosh, A. (2005). Heavy Metal in Water of the Rivers Hooghly and Haldi at Haldia and their Impact on Fish. *J. Environ. Biol.*, Vol. 26 No. 3. 517-523pp.

Sarkar, R., Chaudhuri, P.R. and Gajghati, D.G. (1994). Toxicity Testing through Fish Bioassay and Its Application in India.

Sastry, K.V. and Gupta, P.K. (1978). Chronic Mercuric Chloride Intoxication in Digestive System of Channa Punctatus. *J. Toxicol. Environ. Health*, Vol. 4 No. 5-6. 777-784pp.

Seth, G.K. and Bhaskaran, T.R. (1950). Effect of Industrial Waste Disposal on the Sanitary Condition of the Hooghly River in and Around Calcutta. *Indian J. Med. Res.* Vol. 38 No. 4. 341-356.

Singh, H.P. and Mahaveer, L.P. (1997). A Note on Metal Concentration in Water and Soil Sediment in the Lower Stretch of River Ganga from Sultanpur to Farakka. *J. Inland Fish. Soc. India*, Vol. 29, No. 1. 78-80pp.

Singh, H.P. and Mahaveer, L.P. (1998). Concentration of Metal in Soil Sediments and Water in River Ghagara, Uttar Pradesh. *J. Inland Fish. Soc. India*, Vol. 30, No. 2. 87-89pp.

Singh, H.P., Ravish Chandra and Singh, B. (1993). Status of Heavy Metals in Water, Sediment and Fish Flesh in the Middle Stretch of River Ganga. *J. Inland Fish. Soc. India*, Vol. 25, No. 1. 62-65pp.

Singh, K.P. (1992). Measurement of Ganga River Quality with Particular Reference to Heavy Metal and Pesticides. *Project Report, NRCD Funded Project conducted by ITRC,* Lucknow.

Smith, J.A., Witkowski, P.J., and Fusillo, T.V. (1988). Manmade Organic Compounds in the Surface Waters of the United States – A Review of Current Understanding. *U.S. Geological Survey Circular* 1007, 92 p.

Solanki, J., Balogh, V.K. and Berta, E. (1982). Heavy Metals in Animals of Lake Belaton. *Water Res.*, Vol. 16. 1147-1152pp.

Srivastava, D.K. (1982). Comparative Effects of Copper, Cadmium and Mercury on tissue glycogen of catfish *Heteropneustes fossilis. Toxicol. Letters*, Vol. 11.135-140pp.

Srivastava, A.K. (1987). Changes Induced by Lead in Fish Testis. *J. Environ. Biol.*, Vol 8. 329-332pp.

Standard Methods for the Examination of Water and Wastewater 20th Edition (1998). In. *Clesceri, L.S., Greenberg, A.E. and Eaton, A.D. Ed. Published by American Public Health Association*, Washington D.C.

Subramanian, V., Dack. V.T. and Van Grieken, R. (1985). Chemical Composition of River Sediments from the Indian Subcontinent. *Chemical Geology*, Vol. 81. 241-253pp.

Suryawanshi, G.D. (2008). Seasonal Variations of Heavy Metals in Clam *Meretrix meretrix* from Ratnagiri Coast. *Proc. Zool. Soc. India*, Vol. 7, No. 1. 25-342pp.

Trivedi, S., Mitra, A., Bag, M., Ghosh, I. and Choudhury A. (1995). Heavy Metal Concentration in Mud Skipper *Boleophthalmus boddaerti* of Nayachar Island, India. *Indian Journal of Environmental Health, NEERI*, Vol. 37, No. 1, 42-45.

US Environment Protection Agency (1975). Methods for Acute Toxicity Tests with Fish, Macro-invertebrates and Amphibians. 600/3/75, Washington D.C.

Vass, K.K., Mukhopadhyay, M.K., Mitra, K., Bagchi, M.M. and Bandyopadhyay, S. (1998) Fish as Biomonitoring Tool for Environmental Impact Assessment in Ganga River System. In. *Changing Perspectives in Inland Fisheries (K.K. Vass and M. Sinha Ed.) CIFRI (ICAR) Publication*. 15-23pp.

Villareal, C.M., Morales, M.E.O. and Navarro, J.F.V. (1986). Bioaccumulation of Lead, Copper, Iron and Zinc by Fish in a Transect of the Santa Catarina river in Nuevo Leon, Mexico. *Bull. Environ. Contam. Toxicol.*, Vol. 37. 395-401pp.

Vinodhini, R. and Narayanan, M. (2008). Bioaccumulation of Heavy Meatals in Organs of Freshwater Fish *Cyprinus carpio* (common carp). *Int. J. Environ. Sci. Tech.*, Vol. 5, No. 2. 179-182pp.

Waldichuk, M. (1974). Some Biological Concern in Heavy Metal Pollution. In. *Vernberg, F.G. Ed. Pollution and Physiology of Marine Organisms.* Academic Press, New York. 1-57pp.

West Bengal Pollution Control Board Annual Report (2004). Assessment of Water Quality of River Ganga after idol Immersion Activities. *WBPCB*, Government of West Bengal Publication.

Whitton, B.A. and Say, P.J. (1975). Heavy Metals. In. *Whitton B. A. Ed. River Ecology. Blackwell Scientific Publications, Oxford*. 286-311pp.

Yazdandoost, M.Y. and Katdare, M.S. (1999). Study of the Heavy Metal Accumulation in the Tissues of Fish from Pune Rivers, India. *Asian Journal of Microbiology, Biotechnology and Environmental Science*, Vol. 1, No. 1-2. 115-118pp.

Pages 57-73

HEAVY METALS AND METALLOIDS IN BIOSPHERE: *IMPACTS AND ASSESSMENT*
***Edited by*: Dr. Avnish Chauhan; Dr. Sandeep Gupta & Dr. Pawan Kumar Bharti**
***Edition* : 2017**
ISBN : 978-93-5056-860-6
***Published by* : Discovery Publishing House Pvt. Ltd., New Delhi (India)**

Computational Study of Complexes of Delphinidin with Al^{3+} and Ni^{2+}

Prior to Reduce the Metal Toxicity

Vijisha. K. Rajan
K. Muraleedharan*

ABSTRACT

A computational study of interaction of Delphinidin with Al^{3+} and Ni^{2+} ions to reduce the toxic effects of free metal ions has been performed. All the computational works are carried out through Gaussian 09 software package. The level of theory adopted is B3LYP and the basis set employed is 6-31G (d, p) for C, H, O atoms and LANL2DZ for the metal ions. The solvent used is methanol. Both Al^{3+} and Ni^{2+} forms chelated complexes with Delphinidin. The metal co-ordination leads to increased conductivity and the absorption moves to lower energy region. The thermodynamic parameters show that the complexes are highly stable and thus metal is strongly co-ordinated. The complex formation is feasible at room temperature and atmospheric pressure and the resulting complex is so stable that the metal ions bind with the Delphinidin rather than existing freely in environment. The work is successful in removing the toxic metal ions from the ecosystem and thereby reducing the toxicity.

INTRODUCTION

Phenolic compounds act as antioxidants with mechanisms involving both free radical scavenging and metal chelation. They have ideal structural chemistry for free radical scavenging activities and have been shown to be more effective antioxidants in vitro than vitamin E and C on a molar basis. A large proportion of the flavonoids found in fruits and vegetables have sugar residues bound to their structures. Initially it was thought that only flavonoid aglycones (without bound sugars) were able to pass through the gut wall and that enzyme capable of cleaving the b-glycosidic bonds were not secreted

Department of Chemistry, University of Calicut, Malappuram 673 635, India.

into the gut or the intestinal wall. However, numerous studies have clearly shown that flavonoid glycosides can indeed enter into the circulation intact (Day *et al.* 1998; Noteborn, Jansen, Benito, and Mengelers, 1997; Shimoi *et al.* 1998), including anthocyanins (Miyazawa and Nakagawa, 1999; Tsuda, Horio, and Osawa, 1999).

Flavonoids represent the most common and widely distributed group of plant phenolics. Structural variation within the rings subdivides it into several families: flavonols, flavones, flavanols, isoflavanols, anthocyanidins and others. The basic flavonoid structure is the flavan nucleus, which consists of 15 carbon atoms arranged in three rings (C6-C3-C6), which are labeled A, B, and C (Figure 3.1). The various classes of flavonoids differ in the level of oxidation and pattern of substitution of the C ring, while individual compounds within a class differ in the pattern of substitution of the A and B rings (Pietta, 2000).

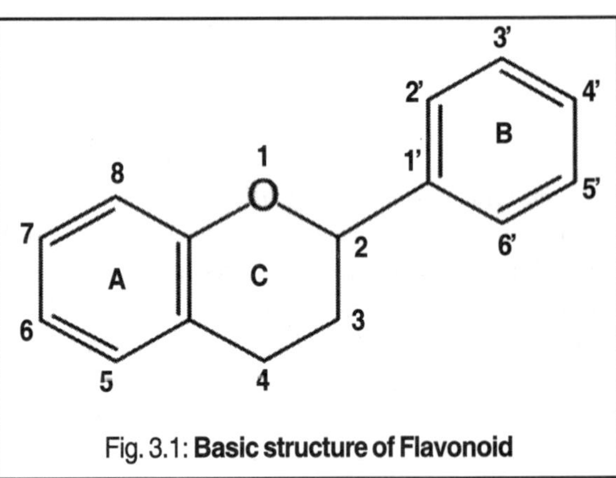

Fig. 3.1: **Basic structure of Flavonoid**

The anthocyanidins represents the most rottenly utilized vegetable colorants in the field of food chemistry. Anthocyanidins are the most important color pigments seen in vascular plants. Carrots, tomatoes, pepper, fruits like: blue berries, some flowers, etc., are the major source of these color pigments. They can be extracted from fruits. Their non-toxicity and high solubility in aqueous media enables them to use in food chemistry. Their main advantage is that their radical scavenging property which makes them to use as antioxidant in medicinal chemistry (Castañeda-ovando, Pacheco-hernández, Páez-hernández, Rodríguez, and Galán-vidal, 2009). Anthocyanidins are natural polyphenolic compounds, which are considered to be health promoting phytochemicals as they possess excellent antioxidant activity and exhibit beneficial antibacterial, antiglycemic, antiviral, anticarcinogenic, anti-inflammatory properties (Lu, Qiang, Li, Zhang, and Zhang, 2014). Researchers are found to give a noticeable attention to the study of flavanoids because of their fascinating phytochemical properties (Cody, Middleton, and Harborne, 1986). They play multiple roles in the ecology of plants. Since they serves as the colouring pigment in plants, helps to attract pollinating insects. They act as catalysts in the light phase of photosynthesis. They are actively involved in the UV protection of plants and fight against the microbes (DimitriæMarkoviæ, Markoviæ, Baranac, and Dašiæ, 2007). In this scenario the study of anthocyanidins are relevant.

Delphinidin (also delphinidine) is a common anthocyanidin, a primary plant pigment, and also an antioxidant. Delphinidin gives blue hues to flowers in the genera *Viola* and *Delphinium*. It also gives the blue-red color of the grape that produces Cabernet Sauvignon, and can be found in cranberries and Concord grapes as well as pomegranates. Delphinidin, like nearly all other anthocyanidins, is pH-sensitive, and changes from red in acidic solution to blue in basic solution (Afaq *et al.* 2007).

The presence of electronegative Oxygen in the Delphinidin, enables it to undergo metal chelation. This enables the accumulation of metals in the peripheral tissues of plants. These metal accumulations in plant tissues prevent the migration of these toxic metal ions to ecosystem resulting in the suppression of metal toxicity. This is useful to both ecosystem as well as the plant, since the deposited toxic metal ions prevent the attack of pathogens and plant eaters. This is the principle that is used in colorimetric titrations in the detection of metal traces (Dimitriæ Markoviæ *et al.* 2007).

Aluminium is the most aboundant metal in the earth crust. Plants are highly sensitive to even micromolar concentrations of Aluminum concentration in soil. This facilitates the chances of Aluminium toxicity in plants. The inhibition of root growth, a major symptom of Aluminium toxicity and this has become a widely accepted measure of Aluminium stress in plants. A micromolar concentrations of A1 is high enough to inhibit root growth within 60 min (Delhaize and Ryan, 1992). Aluminium, principally Al^{3+}, is released from soil clay minerals. These are active at a pH $\leq$ 5.5 and causes growth inhibition to plants. Aluminium toxicity is one of the major exixting environmental problems in the field of agriculture. Chemists are eagerly waiting for finding a solution to this environmental hazard. The Al-toxicity leads to low yield in crop production. Acidity in the soil enhances the inhibitory action of Al^{3+} ion. Al-toxicity alters the physiological and biochemical processes in plants, consequently their productivity decreases. The main symptoms of Al-toxicity is the decrease in the growth of roots (Kobayashi *et al.* 2013).

Nickel is another metal causing toxic effect to plants. It is present in soil only in trace amounts and is non toxic. But the concentration of Ni^{2+} in soil increases due to human activities. Even though Ni^{2+} is considered as an essential nutrient, an excess concentration of it leads to adverse effects in plants. It alters various physiological processes in plants resulting in detrimental effects and cause diverse toxicity symptoms. Chlorosis and necrosis are two examples of the toxicity of Ni^{2+} (Kopittke, Asher, and Menzies, 2007; Llamas, Ullrich, and Sanz, 2008).

In this scenario study of removal of toxic metal ions are highly significant. The present work computationally evaluates the interactions of Delphinidin with Aluminium (III) and Nickel (II) ions. Delphinidin is the most effective in producing the blueness which is associated with its availing as oxygen donating ligand in metal chelation reaction. Delphinidin forms metal chelated complexes with Al^{3+} and Ni^{2+} ion gas phase as well as in methanolic solution. The HOMO-LUMO energies, thermodynamic parameters, global descriptors are evaluated in the work. All the computational works are carried out in Gaussian 09 software package under DFT/B3LYP level of theory.

Materials and Method

Materials

The present work has used a computational approach to the study of interaction of delphinidin with metal ion. The input structures are drawn by using the Gaussview-5.0 graphical user interface. All the computational works have been carried out through Gaussian 09 software package (Frisch *et al.* 2009). Some of the structures are taken from the pubchem database (Bolton E., Wang Y., Thiessen P.A., Bryant S.H., 2008) and these are in SDF file format. To convert these SDF files to GJF (Gaussian Job File) input files an application called OpenBabel (O'Boyle, Banck, James, Morley, and Tim Vandermeersch Geoffrey R Hutchison, 2011) have employed. The present work uses DFT-B3LYP as level of theory with 6-31G (d, p) for Delphinidin and LANL2DZ for metal ions as the basis sets.

Computational Methodology

Mathematical description of chemistrty is called theoretical chemistry. It is of two types; computational theoretical chemistry and non-computational theoretical chemistry. Computational chemistry is a set of techniques for investigating chemical problems on a computer. These are developed by the implementation of suitable computer softwares. There are several tools to perform the computational works. Density Functional Theory (DFT) is one of the major and most oftenly used computational tool to solve the chemical problems. Density Functional Theory (DFT) in the Kohn – Sham version is an extended HF theory, where the many-body effect of electron correlation is modeled by a function of the electron density. DFT is, analogously to HF, an independent-particle model, and is comparable to HF computationally, but provides significantly better results. The main disadvantage of DFT is that there is no systematic approach to improving the results towards the exact solution.

The Density Functional Theory (DFT) is very convenient for computational analysis because of its large accuracy and high predicting power of physical and chemical properties (Cramer, 2004; Lewars, 2004). Most of the pKa value calculation studies are carried out by using DFT method. The level of theory adopted was B3LYP, which consists of Becke's exchange functional (Becke, 1993) in conjunction with Lee-Yang – Parr correlational functional (Lee, C.; Yang, W.; Parr, 1988) and the basis set used is 6-31+G (d, p). We can do the computations both in gas phase as well as in solution phase. The solution phase reactions are usually carried by using the continuum models. In the Polarization Continuum Models (PCM) the solvent is described by a dielectric medium and a cavity is defined inside this dielectric medium (Clementi and André, 2012). The evaluation of environment of the chemical reactions, *i.e.*, the salvation effects, is one of the major applications of computational chemistry. The solvent molecules can be characterized individually or by a continuum model in which solvent is considered as a continuous medium. In the present work the continuum model has been adopted. Here the solvent is considered as a uniform polarizable medium with a dielectric constant ε and the solute is placed inside the solvent cage/cavity (Fig. 3.2).

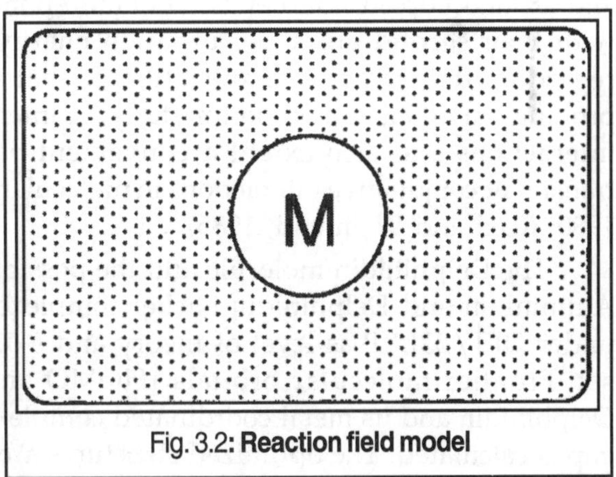

Fig. 3.2: Reaction field model

This cavity is formulated to insert the molecule in the solvent phase. These models are basically parameterized to calculate the free energy of solvation as given by Eq. (1):

$$\Delta G_{solv} = \Delta G_{es} + \Delta G_{vdw} + \Delta G_{cav} \quad (1)$$

where ΔG_{es} is the electrostatic, ΔG_{vdw} is the Van der Waals and ΔG_{cav} is the activation energy contributions to free energy of salvation which are obtained from the output of the Gaussian file. There are different PCM models available which are designed to improve the computational performance of the method. One example is the IEF-PCM model which have been used in this work, is an Integral Equation Formalism for solving relevant Self-Consistent Reaction Field (SCRF) equations which facilitates computation of gradients and molecular response properties an extension to permit application to infinite periodic systems in one and two dimensions, and an extension to liquid/liquid and liquid/vapor interfaces (Cramer, 2004; F., 2007).

NBO analysis is a computational method for optimally transforming a given wave function into localized form. The input atomic orbital basis set is transformed via natural atomic orbitals (NAOs) and natural hybrid orbitals (NHOs) into natural bond orbitals (NBOs). NBO is a useful tool enabling chemists to see intuitive picture of both electron orbitals and population analysis. NBO analysis is based on an approach of transforming multi electron wave functions of molecules into localized form that corresponds to single-center (lone pair (LP)) and two centered (natural bond and antibonding orbitals (BD and BD* respectively)) elements. It gives a deep insight into the intra and intermolecular orbital interaction in the molecules between filled donor and empty acceptor NBOs, which enables us to give a quantitative evaluation and thereby results a qualitative conclusion of donor-acceptor properties of substituents (Weinhold and Landis, 2001). By analyzing the interactions between occupied Lewis NBO (bond pair or lone pair) as donor and an unoccupied non-Lewis NBO (anti-bonding or Rydberg) as acceptor with their second order perturbation energy will give clear information regarding the origin of stabilization of that molecule. The NBO analysis provides an efficient method for studying inter and intra molecular bonding interactions and also extent a convenient basis for investigating charge transfer or conjugative interactions in molecular system (Foster and Weinhold, 1980; Reed and Weinhold, 1985).

The Delphinidin molecule and the possible conformers of Delphinidin-Aluminium and Delphinidin-Nickel complexes are optimized in Methanol under DFT/B3LYP as level of theory and 6-31G (d, p)/LANL2DZ as basis set. Frontier molecular orbitals (HOMO and LUMO) of the optimized Delphinidin and its metal coordinated complexes are analyzed and the band gap is calculated. The optimized structures are used for the TDDFT analysis for UV-Visible spectrum. The thermodynamic parameters of molecules are obtained from the thermochemistry part of output file. The present work employs Natural Bond Orbital (NBO) analysis for the determination of occupancy and bond orders of molecule.

Result and Discussion

Optimization of Stable Structure

Structure of Delphinidin

Stable conformer of Delphinidin is obtained by potential energy scanning and the 14 possible conformers along with the potential energy scanning graph are given in Figure 3.3a-3.3c. Among these the lowest energy conformer (12) has been selected for further studies.

Structure of Delphinidin-metal Complexes (D-Al-1, D-Al-2 and D-Ni)

The interaction of Delphinidin with Al^{3+}/ Ni^{2+} ion has been evaluated by placing Al^{3+}/ Ni^{2+} at different positions of Delphinidin. The Al^{3+}/ Ni^{2+} ions in the ecosystem get attracted by the Delphinidin molecule and coordinated to form stable complexes. Two possible conformers are obtained for Al and one for Ni. The Oxygen atom of the hydroxyl group of Delphinidin show affinity towards metal ions and forms a 5-membered chelated metal complex. When methanol is added as solvent, it has been observed that the oxygen atom of methanol binds with the Al^{3+}/ Ni^{2+} ion. The two conformers, designated as D-Al-1 and D-Al-2, are similar in structure but differ in energy by an amount of 188cal/mol.

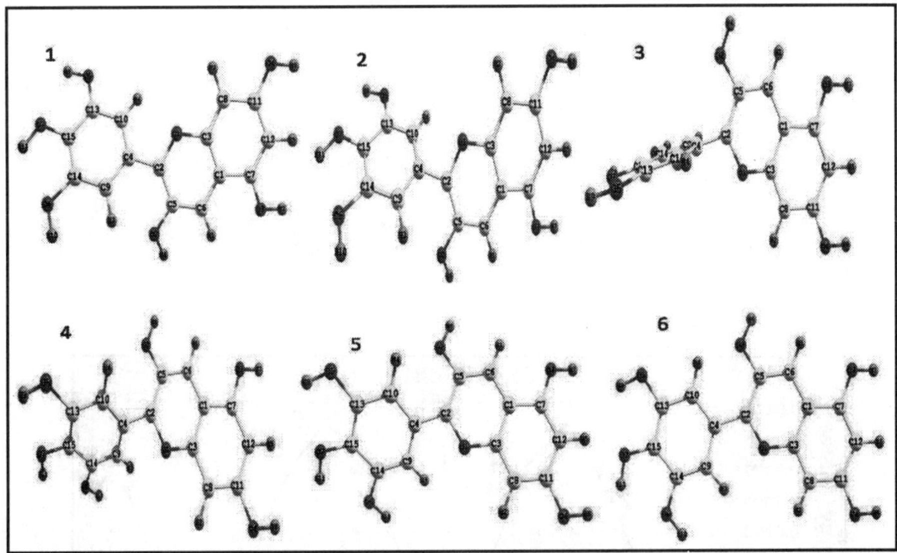

Fig. 3.3a: **Conformers 1-6 of Delphinidin**

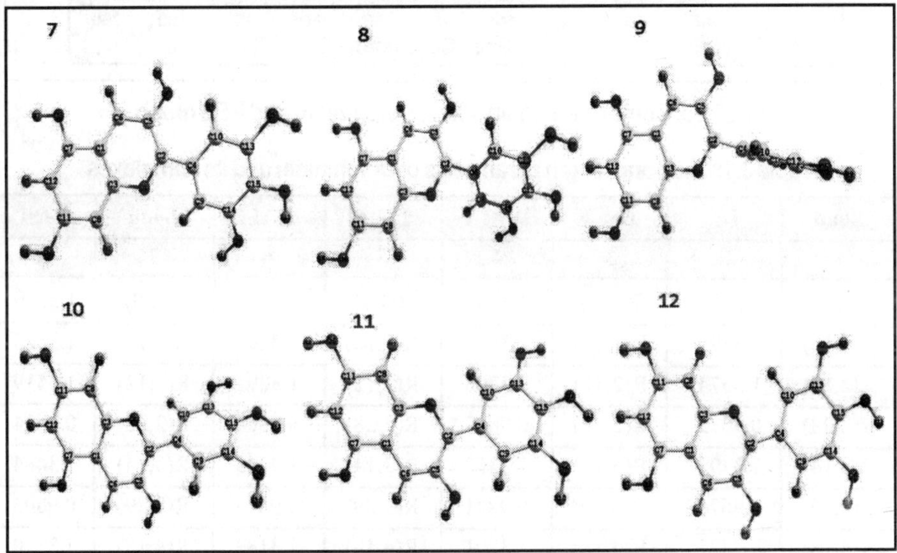

Fig. 3.3b: **Conformers 7-12 of Delphinidin**

The structures of Delphinidin and its metal complexes are shown in Figure 3.4. Although methanol is not a characteristic solvent to natural environment, complexation in methanol is investigated because it is well known as a good complexing medium, so that the results can be compared. The bond length parameters of Delphinidin (D), its complexes D-Al-1, D-Al-2 and D-Ni are given in Table 3.1.

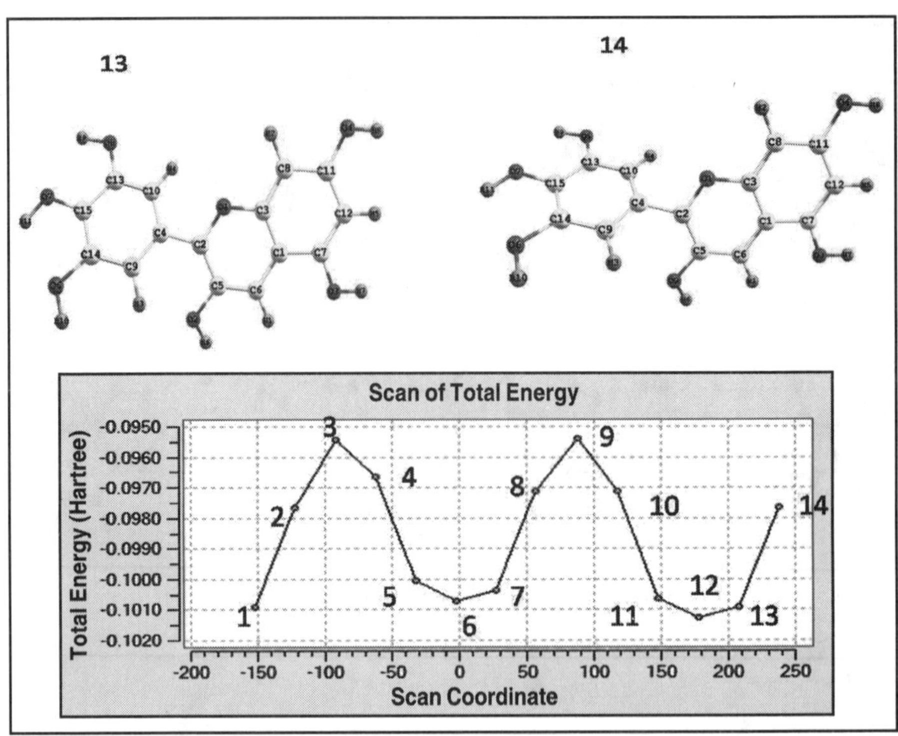

Fig. 3.3c: **Conformers 11 and 12 of Delphinidin and PES graph**

Table 3.1: The bond length parameters of Delphinidin and its complexes

Bond	D	Bond	D-Al-1	Bond	D-Al-2	Bond	D-Ni
1	2	3	4	5	6	7	8
R(1,9)	1.3492	R(1,9)	1.3799	R(1,9)	1.3762	R(1,9)	1.3839
R(1,10)	1.3599	R(1,10)	1.3910	R(1,10)	1.3893	R(1,10)	1.3825
R(2,12)	1.3574	R(2,12)	1.3305	R(2,12)	1.3291	R(2,12)	1.3519
R(2,28)	0.9675	R(2,28)	0.9867	R(2,28)	0.9864	R(2,28)	0.9814
R(3,14)	1.3492	R(3,14)	1.3353	R(3,14)	1.3345	R(3,14)	1.3484
R(3,29)	0.9676	R(3,29)	0.9841	R(3,29)	0.9844	R(3,29)	0.9803
R(4,18)	1.3425	R(4,18)	1.3201	R(4,18)	1.3183	R(4,18)	1.3340
R(4,30)	0.9677	R(4,30)	0.9868	R(4,30)	0.9873	R(4,30)	0.9823
R(5,20)	1.3500	R(5,20)	1.3684	R(5,20)	1.3374	R(5,20)	1.3199
R(5,31)	0.9699	R(5,32)	1.8085	R(5,31)	0.9835	R(5,32)	1.8578
R(6,21)	1.3647	R(6,21)	1.3348	R(6,21)	1.3705	R(6,21)	1.3469
R(6,32)	0.9661	R(6,31)	0.9834	R(6,32)	1.8011	R(6,31)	0.9805

Contd...

1	2	3	4	5	6	7	8
R(7,22)	1.3453	R(7,22)	1.3020	R(7,22)	1.3165	R(7,22)	1.2801
R(7,33)	0.9718	R(7,32)	1.9022	R(7,32)	1.9065	R(7,32)	1.8543
R(8,10)	1.4139	R(8,10)	1.4424	R(8,10)	1.4404	R(8,10)	1.4432
R(8,13)	1.4048	R(8,13)	1.3741	R(8,13)	1.3753	R(8,13)	1.3753
R(8,14)	1.4269	R(8,14)	1.4792	R(8,14)	1.4813	R(8,14)	1.4591
R(9,11)	1.4398	R(9,11)	1.4291	R(9,11)	1.4289	R(9,11)	1.4466
R(9,12)	1.4227	R(9,12)	1.4386	R(9,12)	1.4407	R(9,12)	1.4104
R(10,15)	1.3837	R(10,15)	1.3620	R(10,15)	1.3625	R(10,15)	1.3668
R(11,16)	1.4218	R(11,16)	1.4347	R(11,16)	1.4633	R(11,16)	1.4572
R(11,17)	1.4181	R(11,17)	1.4628	R(11,17)	1.4289	R(11,17)	1.4168
R(12,13)	1.3848	R(12,13)	1.4292	R(12,13)	1.4300	R(12,13)	1.4267
R(13,23)	1.0865	R(13,23)	1.0872	R(13,23)	1.0871	R(13,23)	1.0864
R(14,19)	1.3829	R(14,19)	1.3787	R(14,19)	1.3792	R(14,19)	1.3770
R(15,18)	1.3984	R(15,18)	1.4491	R(15,18)	1.4524	R(15,18)	1.4237
R(15,24)	1.0821	R(15,24)	1.0827	R(15,24)	1.0835	R(15,24)	1.0811
R(16,21)	1.3827	R(16,21)	1.3841	R(16,21)	1.3676	R(16,21)	1.3725
R(16,25)	1.0797	R(16,25)	1.0792	R(16,25)	1.0787	R(16,25)	1.0800
R(17,20)	1.3842	R(17,20)	1.3649	R(17,20)	1.3837	R(17,20)	1.3866
R(17,26)	1.0808	R(17,26)	1.0804	R(17,26)	1.0804	R(17,26)	1.0792
R(18,19)	1.4157	R(18,19)	1.4198	R(18,19)	1.4193	R(18,19)	1.4248
R(19,27)	1.0870	R(19,27)	1.0854	R(19,27)	1.0854	R(19,27)	1.0850
R(20,22)	1.4087	R(20,22)	1.4591	R(20,22)	1.4518	R(20,22)	1.4818
R(21,22)	1.4062	R(21,22)	1.4577	R(21,22)	1.4500	R(21,22)	1.4513
		R(32,41)	1.8310	R(32,33)	1.8361	R(32,41)	1.8446
		R(32,43)	1.8367	R(32,35)	1.8352	R(32,43)	1.8812
		R(33,34)	1.0887	R(33,34)	0.9817	R(33,34)	1.0900
		R(33,35)	1.0883	R(33,41)	1.5648	R(33,35)	1.0858
		R(33,36)	1.0889	R(35,36)	0.9824	R(33,36)	1.0900
		R(33,43)	1.5625	R(35,37)	1.5609	R(33,41)	1.5010
		R(37,38)	1.0878	R(37,38)	1.0878	R(37,38)	1.0882
		R(37,39)	1.0889	R(37,39)	1.0889	R(37,39)	1.0897
		R(37,40)	1.0886	R(37,40)	1.0888	R(37,40)	1.0898
		R(37,41)	1.5629	R(41,42)	1.0883	R(37,43)	1.5094
		R(41,42)	0.9817	R(41,43)	1.0888	R(41,42)	0.9761
		R(43,44)	0.9827	R(41,44)	1.0887	R(43,44)	0.9778

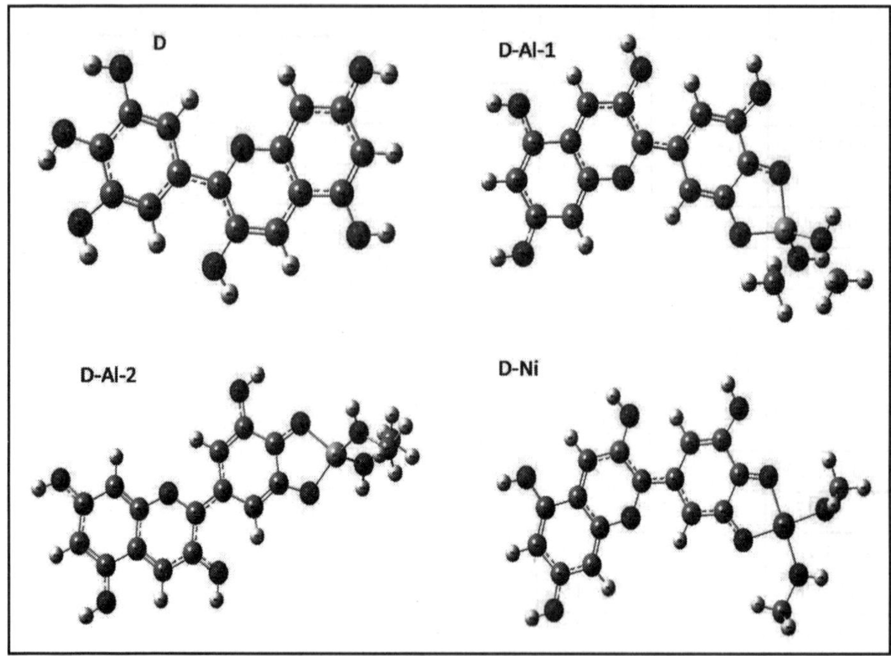

Fig. 3.4: **Structures of Delphinidin and its complexes**

Frontier Molecular orbital Analysis

The chemical reactivity of a molecule can be best understood by the Frontier Molecular Orbital (FMO) analysis, *i.e.*, HOMO-LUMO orbital analysis. The HOMO and LUMO energy value gives the information about the electron accepting and donating capacity of the molecule respectively. The difference between the HOMO-LUMO energy levels gives the energy gap and higher the energy gap lower is the reactivity and vice versa. By suitable substitution the energy gap can be altered and the reactivity can be tailored as per our necessities. Metals, being electron donating decrease the energy gap and thereby increasing the conductivity. The energy gap values of Delphinidin and D-Al-1, D-Al-2 and D-Ni complexes are given in Table 3.2. The HOMO-LUMO levels of Delphinidin and its complexes are given in Figure 3.5 and 3.6.

Table 3.2: Energy and energy gap values of Delphinidin and its complexes

Molecule	Energy (HF)	Energy Gap (eV)
D	-1104.5712	2.6
D-Al-1	-1575.6567	1.2
D-Al-2	-1575.6564	1.1
D-Ni	-2841.8498	1.3

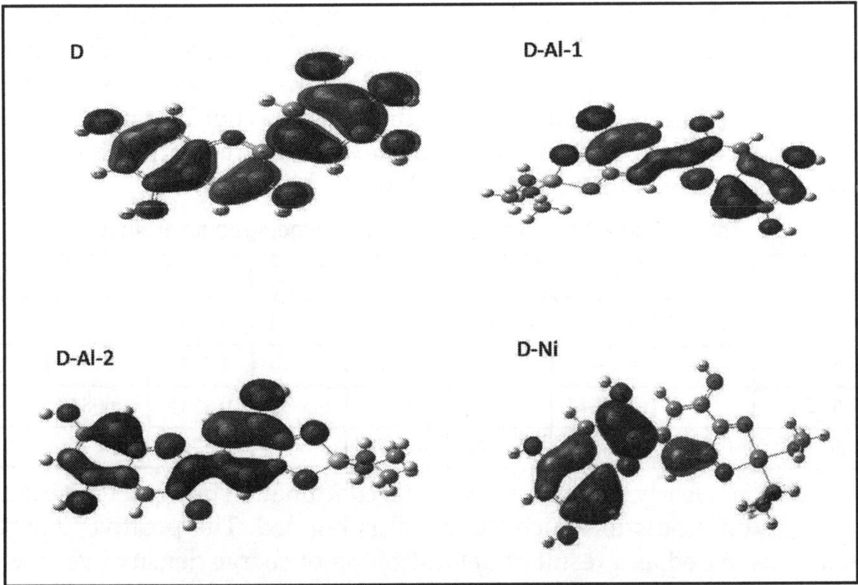

Fig. 3.5: HOMO of Delphinidin and its metal complexes

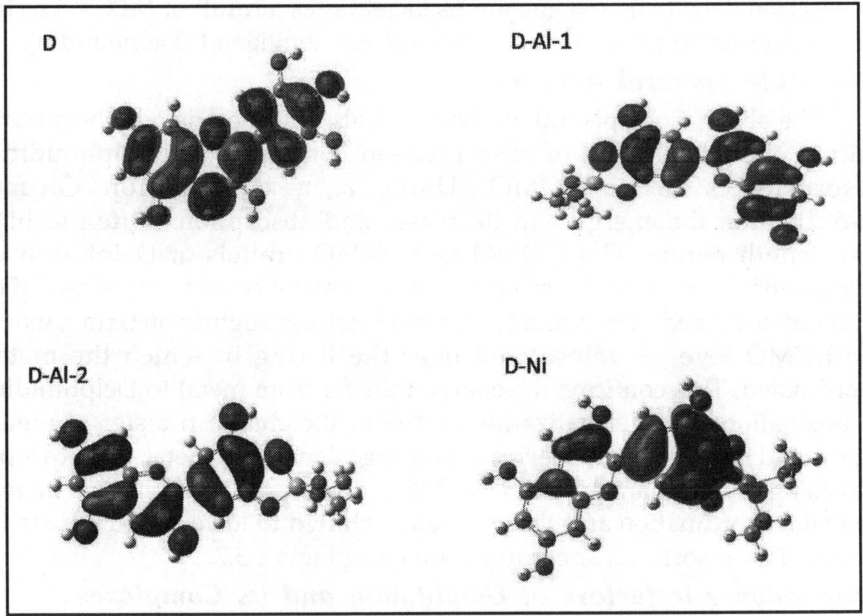

Fig. 3.6: LUMO of Delphinidin and its metal complexes

Since the energy gap decreases on metal co-ordination, it is easier for the electron in HOMO energy level to move to LUMO energy level resulting in the increased ionic mobility and conductivity of the resulting complex. The D-Al-2 complex, having lowest energy gap value, shows higher conductivity than the others. The D-Al-1 complex, more stable than D-Al-2 because of its lower energy and have higher energy gap than the latter. So D-Al-2 has higher conductivity than D-Al-1. The mulliken charge analysis shows that the charge density on metal decreases on coordination. The charge distribution of Delphinidin and complexes are given in Table 3.3. The conductivity follows the order D < D-Ni < D-Al-1 < D-Al-2.

Table 3.3: Mulliken charges on atoms undergoing complexation

Molecule	O5	O6	O7	C20	C21	C22	Al	Ni
D	-0.5455	-0.5815	-0.5501	0.3371	0.3121	0.3051	-	-
D-Al-1	-0.7503	-	-0.6005	0.3773	-	0.3947	1.6136	-
D-Al-2	-	-0.7515	-0.6495	-	0.3792	0.3546	1.6088	-
D-Ni	-0.5907	-	-0.5968	0.3678	-	0.3795	-	0.9626

Table 3.3 clearly shows that the metal coordination brings a redistribution of charges on atoms to which the metal is bonded. The positive charge on metal is decreased as a result of delocalization of charge density over the ring B. this is confirmed by the increased positive charge density on the carbon atom undergoing bond formation with metal. The negative charge density or the electron density on oxygen atoms increases as a result of MLCT. Electrons are transferred from metal to oxygen atom of the ligand (Delphinidin).

UV-Visible Spectral Analysis

The absorption spectral analysis reveals that there is a bathochromatic shift in the wavelength of absorption in complexes. In Delphinidin the absorption is due to HOMO-LUMO *i.e.,* π–π^* transition. On metal co-ordination the energy gap decreases and absorption shifted to higher wavelength region. The HOMO and LUMO orbitals of Delphinidin are delocalized over the entire molecule. But on metal co-ordination the HOMO level is delocalized over A and C ring and localized slightly on B ring, whereas the LUMO level is delocalized over the B ring in which the metal is coordinated. This confirms the charge transfer from metal to Delphinidin on co-ordination. The delocalization is due to the charge transfer of metal to ligand and resulting in the decrease of charge density on metal. The absorption wavelength values are given in Table 3.4. The dipole moment also increases on metal coordination and the absorption shifted to lower oscillator strength values. The absorption spectrum is given in Figure 3.7.

Thermodynamic factors of Delphinidin and its Complexes

The complex formation is conducted at 298K and 1 atm pressure. The thermodynamic parameters such as energy, enthalpy, Gibbs free energy and entropy of delphinidin and the metal coordinated complexes are given in Table 3.5. From these values the changes in thermodynamic parameters, stabilization energy, etc., are calculated. The S value is given in cal/mol and all others are given in HF units.

Table 3.4: Absorption wavelength and related parameters of Delphinidin and its complexes

Molecule	Energy Gap (eV)	Wavelength of Absorption (nm)	Oscillator Strength	Dipole Moment (Debye)
D	2.6	511.72	0.0308	6,78
D-Al-1	1.2	1466.57	0.0077	4.43
D-Al-2	1.3	2053.23	0.0018	7.43
D-Ni	1.1	1321.44	0.0062	5.21

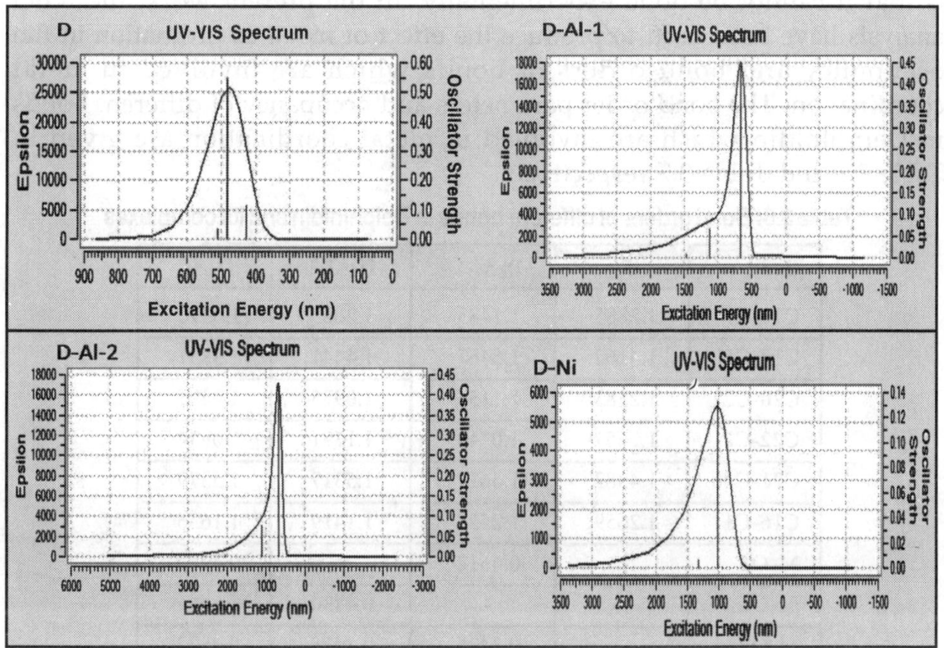

Fig. 3.7: **Absorption spectra of Delphinidin and its complexes**

Table 3.5: Thermodynamic parameters of Delphinidin and its complexes

Molecule	E	H	G	S	ΔH	ΔG	ΔS	E_{sta}
D	-1104.5712	-1104.30948	-1104.37595	139.901	-	-	-	-
D-Al-1	-1575.6567	-1575.29947	-1575.38458	179.144	-471.00863	-470.98999	39.243	471.08547
D-Al-2	-1575.6564	-1575.29975	-1575.38525	179.957	-471.0093	-470.99027	40.056	471.08373
D-Ni	-2841.8498	-2841.49218	-2841.57765	179.892	-1737.2017	-1737.1827	39.991	1737.2787

Table 3.5 clearly shows that the Gibbs free energy and enthalpy become more and more negative so that the complex formation reaction is feasible under normal conditions. The entropy value increase which is also a criterion for feasibility confirms that the complex formation is highly favorable. The

D-Ni complex is highly favored because of its more negative ΔG value. The stabilization of complex is indicated by the E_{sta} values called the stabilization energy, which is the negative of the energy of complex formation. More the E_{sta} value, more stable the complex. So the D-Ni complex is the most stable complex than the others.

NBO Analysis

The Natural Bond Orbital analysis gives an idea about the occupancy and bond orders of atoms in the molecule. The uniqueness of NBO analysis is that it cannot be done experimentally. In the present work, the NBO analysis have been used to produce the effect of metal co-ordination in the occupancy and bond orders of bonds which are involved in metal coordination. The bond order parameters and occupancy of different bonds in Delphinidin which are involved in metal coordination are given in Table 3.6 and Table 3.7 respectively.

Table 3.6: Bond orders of different bonds in Delphinidin and its complexes

Bond	D	D-Al-1	D-Al-2	D-Ni
C11-C17	1.2885	1.1483	1.2683	1.3370
C17-C20	1.4162	1.5467	1.4441	1.3857
C20-C22	1.2583	1.1157	1.0975	1.0285
C22-C21	1.2657	1.0748	1.1391	1.0834
C21-C16	1.4382	1.4617	1.5317	1.5379
C16-C11	1.2659	1.2528	1.1419	1.1636
M-O5	-	0.4612	-	0.4972
M-O6	-	-	0.4730	-
M-O7	-	0.3426	0.3435	0.4577

The bond orders of M-O are higher in D-Ni complex resulting in its high stability. This is supported by the energy values of complexes.

Table 3.7: Occupancy of different bonds in Delphinidin and its complexes

Bond	D	D-Al-1	D-Al-2	D-Ni
C11-C17	1.96924	1.97044	1.97200	1.96959
C17-C20	1.97335	1.97811	1.97451	1.97800
C20-C22	1.97466	1.98277	1.97864	1.98265
C22-C21	1.97344	1.97567	1.98197	1.97464
C21-C16	1.97763	1.98082	1.97843	1.98079
C16-C11	1.96598	1.97048	1.97056	1.97141

Table 3.7 clearly shows that the occupancies of bonds increased on co-ordination with the metal. This is because of the electron transfer from metal to Delphinidin.

Conclusion

In summary it is concluded that Delphinidin has strong affinity towards Al^{3+} and Ni^{2+} metal ions and it forms chelated metal complex. The complex formation is feasible at room temperature and atmospheric pressure. The complex formation satisfies all the thermodynamic criteria for feasible reaction. The metal coordination is results from the strong interaction of more electronegative oxygen atom and the metal ion. There is a metal to ligand charge transfer which results in the increased negative charge density on oxygen atoms to which the metal ion is bonded. The charge on metal is decreased as a result of delocalization over the ring B in Delphinidin molecule. This is further supported by NBO analysis. Metal coordination increases the conductivity due to the increased ionic mobility between HOMO and LUMO. There is a bathochromic shift in the wavelength of absorption due to the decreased energy gap by metal coordination. The affinity of Delphinidin towards the metal ion prevents the presence of these metal ions in the ecosystem. As the metal ions can strongly binds to the Delphinidin at room temperature itself and do not broken back easily, there is no adverse effect for the plants also. Thus the work successfully presents a way to reduce the metal toxicity in the ecosystem and give a solution to the environmental problem.

REFERENCES

Afaq, F., Syed, D.N., Malik, A., Hadi, N., Sarfaraz, S., Kweon, M.-H., and Mukhtar, H. (2007). Delphinidin, an Anthocyanidin in Pigmented Fruits and Vegetables, Protects Human HaCaT Keratinocytes and Mouse Skin Against UVB-Mediated Oxidative Stress and Apoptosis. *Journal of Investigative Dermatology*, 127(1), 222-232. http://doi.org/10.1038/sj.jid.5700510.

Becke, A.D. (1993). Density-functional Thermochemistry. III. The Role of Exact Exchange. *J. Chem. Phys.*, (98), 5648-5652.

Bolton E, Wang Y, Thiessen PA, Bryant SH., 2008, P. (2008). PubChem: Integrated Platform of Small Molecules and Biological Activities. Wheeler RA and Spellmeyer DC, Eds. Annual Reports in Computational Chemistry, VOxford, UK: Elsevier, 4, 217-241. http://doi.org/10.1016/S1574-1400(08)00012-1.

Castañeda-ovando, A., Pacheco-hernández, M.D.L., Páez-hernández, M. E., Rodríguez, J.A., and Galán-vidal, C. A. (2009). Chemical studies of anthocyanins/ : A review. Food Chemistry, 113(4), 859-871. http://doi.org/10.1016/j.foodchem.2008.09.001.

Clementi, E., and André, J. (2012). Theory and Applications in Computational Chemistry: The First Decade of the Second Millennium.

Cody, V., Middleton, E., and Harborne, J. (1986). Plant flavonoids in Biology and Medicine: Biochemical, Pharmacological, and Structure-activity Relationships. Alan R. Liss Inc., New York.

Cramer, C.J. (2004). Essentials of Computational Chemistry Theories and Models (2nd ed.). John Wiley and Sons Ltd.

Day, A.J., Dupont, M.S., Ridley, S., Rhodes, M., Rhodes, M.J., Morgan, M.R., and Williamson, G. (1998). Deglycosylation of flavonoid and isoflavonoid glycosides by Human Small Intestine and Liver β-glucosidase Activity. FEBS Letters, 436(1), 71-75. http://doi.org/10.1016/S0014-5793(98)01101-6.

Delhaize, E., and Ryan, P.R. (1992). Aluminum Toxicity and Tolerance in Plants. Plant Physiol, 107 (1 995), 315-321.

Dimitriæ Markoviæ, J. M., Markoviæ, Z. S., Baranac, J. M., and Dašiæ, M. L. (2007). Delphinidin-Aluminum(III) Complexes in Aqueous and Non-Aqueous Media: Spectroscopic Characterization and Theoretical Study. Monatshefte Für Chemie – Chemical Monthly, 138(12), 1225-1232. http://doi.org/10.1007/s00706-007-0741-z.

Foster, J.P., and Weinhold, F. (1980). Natural Bond Orbitals. *J. Am. Chem. Soc.*, 102, 7211-7218.

Frisch, M.J., Trucks, G.W., Schlegel, H.B., Scuseria, G.E., Robb, M.A., Cheeseman, J.R., and J., D. Fox. (2009). Gaussian 09 (Revision A.2) Gaussian, Inc., Wallingford, CT.

Jensen, F. (2007). Introduction to Computational Chemistry. Chichester: John Wiley and Sons.

Kobayashi, Y., Kobayashi, Y., Watanabe, T., Shaff, J.E., Ohta, H., Kochian, L. V, and Koyama, H. (2013). Molecular and Physiological Analysis of Al^{3+} and H^{+} rhizotoxicities at moderately Acidic Conditions. *Plant Physiology*, 163(1), 180-92. http://doi.org/10.1104/pp.113.222893.

Kopittke, P.M., Asher, C.J., and Menzies, N.W. (2007). Toxic Effects of Ni^{2+} on Growth of Cowpea (Vigna unguiculata). Plant and Soil, 292(1-2), 283-289. http://doi.org/10.1007/s11104-007-9226-4.

Lee, C., Yang, W. and Parr, R.G. (1988). Development of the Colle-Salvetti Correlation-Energy Formula into a Functional of the Electron Density. *Phys. Rev. B.*, 37, 785-789.

Lewars, E. (2004). Computational Chemistry Introduction to the Theory and Applications of Molecular and Quantum Mechanics. Kluwer Academic Publishers.

Llamas, A., Ullrich, C. I., and Sanz, A. (2008). Ni^{2+} Toxicity in Rice: Effect on Membrane Functionality and Plant Water Content. *Plant Physiology and Biochemistry*, 46(10), 905-910. http://doi.org/10.1016/j.plaphy.2008.05.006.

Lu, L., Qiang, M., Li, F., Zhang, H., and Zhang, S. (2014). Theoretical Investigation on the Antioxidative Activity of Anthocyanidins: A DFT/B3LYP Study. Dyes and Pigments, 103, 175-182. http://doi.org/10.1016/j.dyepig.2013.12.015.

Miyazawa, T., and Nakagawa, K. (1999). Direct Intestinal Absorption of Red Fruit Anthocyanins, Cyanidin-3-glucoside and Cyanidin-3 , 5-diglucoside, into Rats and Humans. *Journal of Agricultural and Food Chemistry*, 47(3), 1083-1091. Retrieved from http://pubs.acs.org/doi/abs/10.1021/jf9809582.

Noteborn, H.P.J.M., Jansen, E., Benito, S., and Mengelers, M.J.B. (1997). Cancer Oral Absorption and Metabolism of Quercetin and Sugar-conjugated, 114, 0-2.

O'Boyle, N.M., Banck, M., James, C.A., Morley, C., and Tim Vandermeersch Geoffrey R. Hutchison. (2011). Open Babel: An Open Chemical Toolbox. http://doi.org/doi:10.1186/1758-2946-3-33.

Pietta, P.G. (2000). Flavonoids as Antioxidants. *Journal of Natural Products*, 63(7), 1035-1042. http://doi.org/10.1021/np9904509.

Reed, A., and Weinhold, F. (1985). Natural Localized Molecular Orbitals. *J. Chem. Phys.*, 83, 1736-1740.

Shimoi, K., Okada, H., Furugori, M., Goda, T., Takase, S., Suzuki, M. and Kinae, N. (1998). Intestinal Absorption of luteolin and luteolin 7- O -β-glucoside in Rats and Humans. FEBS Letters, 438(3), 220-224. http://doi.org/10.1016/S0014-5793(98)01304-0.

Tsuda, T., Horio, F., and Osawa, T. (1999). Absorption and Metabolism of cyanidin 3-O-beta-D-glucoside in rats. FEBS Letters, 449, 179-182. http://doi.org/S0014-5793(99)00407-X [pii].

Weinhold, F., and Landis, C.R. (2001). Natural Bond Orbitals and Extensions of Localized Bonding Concepts. Chemistry Education Research and Practice in Europe, 2(2), 91-104. http://doi.org/10.1039/b1rp90011k

Pages 74-92

HEAVY METALS AND METALLOIDS IN BIOSPHERE: *IMPACTS AND ASSESSMENT*
***Edited by*: Dr. Avnish Chauhan; Dr. Sandeep Gupta & Dr. Pawan Kumar Bharti**
***Edition* : 2017**
ISBN : 978-93-5056-860-6
***Published by*: Discovery Publishing House Pvt. Ltd., New Delhi (India)**

Heavy Metals Contamination to Day-to-Day Life

Need of Sustainable Approach for Cure with Special Reference to Sorghum and Mycorrhiza

Prasann Kumar

ABSTRACT

Deprivation of accepted resources is perhaps one of the lethal lapses mankind has ever prepared in its voyage of progress and civilization. All the natural resources are contaminated with lethal lapses. Among them the land and water resources are worst affected and under continuous stress with both biotic and abiotic, due to anthropogenic interventions. If we talk about the soul of infinite life i.e., SOIL then it seems to appear the primary recipient by design or accident of a myriad of waste products and chemicals used in modern society. Soil contamination can be defined as the, addition of any substance to soil that may exert adverse effects on its functioning and capacity to yield a crop. Contamination of heavy metal is of special worry due to well-known reports emanating both from India and abroad. Various diseases and disorders observed both in human and livestock due to metal toxicity. Scientist reported that, the greatest problems most likely to involve mercury, cadmium, lead, chromium, arsenic, nickel etc. To a greater or lower degree all of these elements are toxic to humans and any others animals. Cadmium is extremely toxic causing heart and kidney disease, bone embrittleness; Cr, Ni, and Pb are moderately so which are responsible for mutagenic, lung cancer, convulsion and brain damage like some deadlier diseases. We have test several plant species for their capacity of scavenging heavy metals from soil and sludge and finally we reached on the conclusion that among the tested plants, Sorghum vulgare L is more adapted to grow on contaminated sites with respect to other plant and able to mitigate the heavy metal toxicity from hazardous waste site or cultivated site.

***Keywords*:** cadmium, density, effluents, grade.

Department of Plant Physiology, Institute of Agricultural Sciences, Banaras Hindu University, Varanasi, 221 005, India.

INTRODUCTION

Metals are defined as any element that has a silvery luster and is a good conductor of heat and electricity. There are many terms used to describe and categorise metals, including: traces metals, transition metals, micronutrients, toxic metals, heavy metals. Bjerrum's (1966) definition of 'heavy metals' is based upon the density of the elemental form of the metal, and he classifies 'heavy metals' as those metals with elemental densities above 7 g cm^{-3}. In 1964, the editor of Van Nostrand's International Encyclopedia of Chemical Science and in 1987, the editors of Grant and Hackh's Chemical Dictionary included metals with a density greater than 4 g cm^{-3}. The fate of various metals, including: chromium, nickel, copper, manganese, mercury, cadmium, and lead, and metalloids, including arsenic, antimony, and selenium, in the natural environment is of great concern (Adriano, 1986), particularly near former mine sites, dumps, tailing piles, and impoundments, but also in urban and industrial centers.

Cadmium

Cadmium is a soft, ductile metal which is usually obtained as a by-product from the smelting of lead and zinc ores. The principal use of cadmium is as constituents in alloys and in the electroplating industry. Other uses of cadmium include paints and pottery pigments, corrosion resistant coating of nails, screws, etc., in process engraving, in cadmium-nickel batteries, and as fungicides (Stoeppler, 1991). Cadmium is also naturally present in soils and mineral fertilizers. Origin of cadmium in soil is described as agricultural wastes (20%), sludge (38%), fertilizers (2%) and atmospheric fallouts (40%) (Juste, 1992). Cadmium is one of the most toxic elements with reported carcinogenic effects in humans (Goering *et al*. 1994). Cadmium and cadmium compounds are, compared to other heavy metals, relatively water soluble and mobile compound in most soils, generally more bio-available and tends to bio-accumulate. It induces cell injury and death by interfering with calcium (Ca) regulation in biological system. Cadmium is not essential for plant or animal life (IPCS monographs/WHO 1995a; WHO 1995b). It is more mobile than zinc but less mobile than nickel. Cadmium is readily accumulated by many organisms, particularly by microorganism and mollusks where the bio-concentration factors are in the order of thousands. Its mobility essentially depends on the pH; the metal's adsorption to the soil's solid phase can be multiplied threefold for every unitary increase in pH in a range from 4 to 8. Terrestrial plants may accumulate cadmium in the roots and cadmium is found bound to the cell walls (AMAP 2002). The pH level is one of the most important factors controlling cadmium absorption. Compared with other micropolluants such as: Cu or Pb, transfer of Cd to the above ground parts of the plant may be considered as significant. Concentration in roots represents only 2 to 5 times that in the above ground parts but cadmium is transferred only with difficulty to reproductive or storage organs of the plant (Mench, 1997). No deficiency level for cadmium is known.

Sorghum: As Contrivence of Cure to Cadmium

Sorghum is one of the main staple foods for the world's poorest and most food-unsecured people across the semi-arid tropics. Heavy metal contamination threats the critical limit of alarm in most of the cultivated and periurban area around us. That's why it is considered as the major concern in India and abroad. The remediation of these heavy metal contaminated soils can be attempted through conventional treatment such as: land filling and leaching, excavation and burial or soil washing. However, these approaches are cost intensive and thus not economically viable, besides being intrusive in nature and deteriorating soil structure. The use of specially selected and engineered metal accumulating plants for environmental cleanup is an emerging frontline technology called 'Green Cure'; which describes a system wherein plants in association with soil organism can remove or transform contaminants into harmless and often valuable and adsorb pollutant, mainly metals, from cultivated area, waste area, water bodies and aqueous waste streams. We have tested several plant species for their capacity of scavenging heavy metals from soil and sludge and finally we reach on the conclusion that among the tested plants, *Sorghum vulgare* L is more adapted to grow on contaminated sites with respect to other plant and able to mitigate the heavy metal toxicity from hazardous waste site or cultivated site. It has tremendous capacity to tolerate and mitigate the wider range of heavy metal contamination. Root system of *Sorghum vulgare* is fibrous in nature which leads to accumulation of metals more in the root. But interestingly, grains of the plant remain free from contamination because transfer and transportation ratios remain low for the metals within the plants under field condition. So, amelioration of metals from contaminated site can be possible through cultivation of *Sorghum vulgare* L. without disturbing the soil natural properties along with sustainable harvest for longer period (Figure 4.1 and 4.2).

Fig. 4.1

Fig. 4.2

Source of Fig. 4.1 and Fig. 4.2: Photographs taken by Prasann Kumar, Unpublished, 2015.

Where, Fig. 4.1 = Sorghum plants treated with mycorrhiza in contaminated soil with heavy metal cadmium nitrate at the higher concentration.

Fig. 4.2 = Sorghum plants treated without/absent mycorrhiza in contaminated soil with the heavy metal cadmium nitrate at the higher concentration.

On the contrary, cadmium is well known as a highly phyotoxic element. Besides retarding growth, phytotoxicity also occurs above 5.0-30.0 mg/kg dry weight, though chlorosis, which can be followed in the case of acute cadmium poisoning by necrosis (Browen, 1979). Other compounds including Fe, Se, Mn and particularly Zn are antagonistic to Cd. A draft commission regulation process to set maximum level for some heavy metals in foodstuff as 0.05 mg kg^{-1} in fish, vegetables and fruits, excluding leafy vegetables, root vegetables and potatoes; 0.1 mg kg^{-1} cereals, except wheat grain and rice; 0.2 mg kg^{-1} in wheat grain and rice, leafy vegetables and mushrooms.

Toxic Metal Cadmium Removal from Soil through am Fungi Inoculated *Sorghum*

Cadmium is one of the components of the earth's crust and found everywhere in the environment. The natural occurrence of cadmium in the environment results mainly from gradual phenomenon such as: rock erosion and abrasion that estimate for 15,000 mt per annum (WHO, 1992). Naturally existing concentration of Cd in atmosphere is 0.1-0.5 ng/m^3, in earth crust 100-500 mg/gm but much higher level may be accumulated in sedimentary rocks and marine phosphates. The wide spade use of Cd is based on its unique physical and chemical properties. It is highly resistant to chemicals, high temperature and ultraviolet light (Morrow and Keatings, 1997). Cd is widely used in special alloys, pigments coatings stabilizers above all (almost 70% of its use) in Ni-Cd batteries (Morrow, 1996). It can enter air from the burning of coal, household waste, and metal mining as well as refining process which may increase the level of Cd in the soil varying from 100-600 mg/kg dry weight (Ernest and Neilson, 2000; Lombi *et al.* 2000) or more (Meaghler *et al.* 2000). The general trends of metal enhancement appears to urban > rural > remote locations (depends on authors personal idea). I have test the sample of Glomus inoculated sorghum with FTIR and found interesting picks at different wave lengths (Figure 4.3).

Some countries have set tolerance limits on heavy metal addition to soil because their long-term effects are unknown. These limits are usually set for plough layer of soil where most of the root activity occurs. The value of potentially toxic elements (PTE) proposed by council of European Economic Committee (Smith, 1996) for Cd concentration in soil is 1.0-3.0 mg/kg of dry soil and maximum annual addition of total cadmium to soils is 150gm per hectare (Palanaippan, 2002). Phytoremediation of metal contaminated sites offers a low cost method for soil remediation and some extracted metals

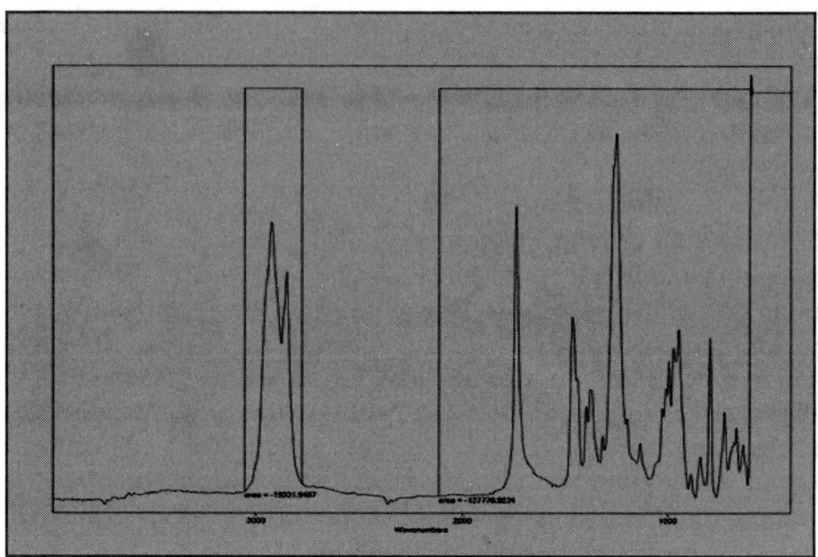

Fig. 4.3: FTIR data of sorghum inoculated with Glomus mycorrhiza in contaminated soil with heavy metal cadmium

Source: Drawn on the basis of author research work, unpublished, 2016.

may be recycled for value. Cost of growing a crop is minimal compared to those of soil removal and replacement, so the use of plants to remediate the hazardous soils seems to have great promise. Other recent reviews on many aspects of soil phytoremediation are available. Phytoremediation is the use of plants to make soil contaminants non-toxic and is also often referred to as bioremediation, botanical-bioremediation, or green remediation. The idea of using rare plants which hyper-accumulate metals to selectively remove and recycled excessive soil metals was introduced in 1983 (Cheny, 1997), gained public exposure in 1990 (Anonymous 1990), and has increasingly been examined as a potential practice and more cost effective technology than soil replacement, solidifications, or washing strategies recently used (Salt *et al.* 1995; Cunningham *et al.* 1996). In the experiment conducted by Arora and Sharma, 2009, it was found that health hazard posed by the accumulation of toxic metals in the environment accompanied by high cost of removal and replacement of metal polluted soil have prompted effort to develop bioremediation strategies. In their experiment, plants of sorghum were grown in AM and non AM inoculated substrate and subjected to five soil-[Cd] concentrations (0.1%, 1.0%, 2.0% and 5.0%). The inoculation of AM fungi resulted in significantly better absorption, and accumulation of Cd accumulation was 47.1 per cent, 45.2 per cent, 35.7 per cent, 33.9 per cent and 23.5 per cent for 0.1 per cent, 0.2 per cent, 1.0 per cent, 2.0 per cent and 5.0 per cent, respectively after 80 days of treatments. Table a, deals with the value of soil pH at different concentrations of Cd. The pH of soil having 0.1

per cent concentration of Cd was more or less near to the pH of control for both AMF and non-AMF treatments. For non-AMF treatments, there was a decrease in pH as the concentration of Cd was increased. At 0.2 per cent and 1 per cent of Cd, pH was slightly acidic but at 5 per cent concentration soil was found to be acidic. The AMF treatments didn't show much variation in pH *i.e.,* no significant changes in pH was observed. For AMF treatments, pH seemed to be independent of the concentrations of the metal Cd (Pawloska *et al.* 1996).

Table 4.1: Effects of Cadmium at different concentrations on soil pH

Days	Control	Concentration of Cd (%)									
		0.1		0.2		1		2		5	
		AMF	NAMF	AMF	NAMF	AMF	NAMF	AMF	NAMF	AMF	NAMF
0	7.3	7.08	6.8	7.02	6.36	6.97	6.16	6.95	6.69	6.94	5.2
20	7.36	7.1	6.75	7.06	6.21	7.01	6.11	7	5.79	6.98	5.16
40	7.26	7.09	6.65	7.04	6.18	6.99	6.07	6.96	5.75	6.95	5.15
60	7.2	7.07	6.6	7.03	6.08	6.94	6.02	6.91	5.69	6.93	5.1
80	7.18	7.05	6.45	7	6	6.9	5.98	6.9	5.6	6.89	5.06

Source: Arora and Sharma, 2009.

From the experiment of Arora and Sharma 2009, it is clear that the accumulation of cadmium in plants was at low concentration because as the concentration of the metal increases it becomes toxic to the plant and thus retards its growth (Table 4.1). With the inoculation of the AM fungi, the potential of sorghum to accumulate Cd from the soil increases significantly. The efficiency of phytoremediation of heavy metal contaminated site increases with the presence of higher proportion of metal resistant microbial population in the soil, which may likely; confer a better nutritional assimilation and protective effect on plant (Doelman, 1985). There have been reports of significant inhibition of mycorrhizal colonization by the heavy metals like Cd (Griffioen *et al.* 1994; Leyval *et al.* 1995). The increase in AM root colonization is likely the results of numerous factors including increase in soil-metal (Cd) concentration and the subsequent decrease in soil pH (Rufyikiri *et al.* 2003), who assessed root-and hypha-induced substrate. pH groups of soluble proteins and non-proteins thiol operating as tolerating mechanism in root cells (Chaui *et al.* 1997). So, finally Arora and Sharma, 2009 suggested that, in addition to the metal immobilization in the mycorrhizosphere, mycorrhizal fungi may also act as effective barrier controlling excessive metal uptake into the root cells. It is also suggested that inoculation with AM fungi can facilitate plant growth and thus increase phytoremediation sufficiency. Plant – mycorrhizal relationship in relation to toxic metal removal from soil can be an effective tool to enhance plant efficiency. I have compared the FTIR spectra with standard curve of different hydrocarbon compounds for getting the unknown hydrocarbons produced. In the Figure 4.4, the red line shows the known standard line and the black line shows the unknown lines.

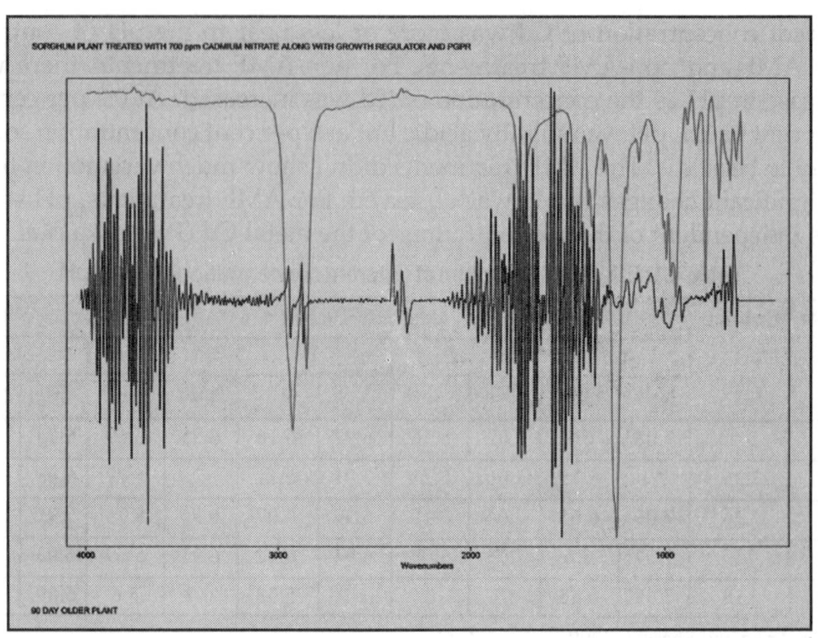

Fig. 4.4: **Comparison of unknown picks with the known standard picks**

Source: Drawn on the basis of author's research work, unpublished, 2015.

Effects of Cadmium on the Growth and Physiological Characteristics of Sorghum Plants

With the rapid industrial development, soil environmental pollution in India has become increasingly serious. Cadmium (Cd) is a highly toxic heavy metal in the environment (Davis, 1984; Guo, 1994). Cd is a non-essential nutrient for plants, and excessive Cd has not only significant adverse effects (Shamsi *et al.* 2008), but also endangers human health via food chain (Naidu and Harter, 1998). The alleviation or inhibition of Cd damage in plants has, therefore, caused extensive attention of the whole society (Uraguchi *et al.* 2009; Wang *et al.* 2008). Heavy metals have an adverse impact on growth and development of the plants, showing some physiological and biochemical characteristic of damages. To a certain extent, plant growth and physiological characteristic can reflect the adverse impact of heavy metal externally or internally (Zhang and Shu, 2006). The research of the poisoning effect of the heavy metal Cd on plant mainly focuses on food crops such as: rice, wheat and maize, but less on *Sorghum* plants, which is known often as animal feed sources. Sorghum scientist reported some important changes in growth and physiological characteristic of sorghum plant under cadmium stress. In their experiment, the major physiological parameters for observation were like this *(a)* effects of cadmium on height of different species of sorghum; *(b)* effects of cadmium on chlorophyll contents of different species of sorghum plants; *(c)* effects of cadmium on root activities in leaves of different species of sorghum plants; *(d)* effects of cadmium on MDA contents in leaves of different species of sorghum plants. They found several interesting observations and these can be summarized such as: a kind of oxidative stress, heavy metal stress affects the growth of plants. Jalil *et al.* (1994) reported that low concentration of cadmium can promote the growth of hard wheat, while under a relatively high concentration, the growth of wheat and tillering were both inhibited and the degree varied among different varieties. Liu's (2004) research also showed that corn seedling's height under cadmium treatment reduced significantly as the concentration of cadmium increased with prolonged growth period. These studies showed that lower concentration of cadmium stimulates the increase of sorghum height, which may be related to the certain resistance of sorghum plants to Cd, while higher levels of cadmium inhibited height growth of sorghum genus plant. Thus, lower concentration of cadmium stress stimulates the growth of sorghum plants to a certain extent, and higher concentrations inhibited their growth.

Reason for the inhibitory effect of heavy metals to plant growth was probably due to:

(a) A series of physical and chemical reactions between excess heavy metal and soil components changes soil properties, thus affecting soil fertility levels (Cieslinski *et al.* 1996; Chang and Wu, 2005). For example, heavy metal pollution can enhance the fixation of soil phosphorous, which affected the plants absorbing phosphorous, thus influenced the growth of plants (Li *et al.* 2004; Zhang *et al.* 2004).

(b) Heavy metal poisonous effects caused a reduction in plant photosynthesis, thereby reducing the plant water and nutrient adsorption, which affected the normal growth and development of plants (Qin *et al.* 2000).

In the plant body, photosynthesis is the most fundamental and important physiological and biochemical process, and its initial link is chlorophyll synthesis and function realization. The results from experiments conducted by Liu *et al.* (2004) showed that chlorophyll synthesis was affected by cadmium stress and with the increase of cadmium stress levels; the inhibitory effect was increasingly severe. The reason for change in chlorophyll contents in the leaves of sorghum plants might be that chlorophyll synthesis was formed under the action of a series of enzymes in proplastid and chloroplast (Stobart and Griffith, 1985; Wang, 2000). Cd stress inhibited relevant enzymes activities in the leaves of sorghum plants in the process of chlorophyll synthesis, affecting chlorophyll synthesis process and leaf chlorosis, thus leading to the change in chlorophyll contents. There have been many reports about heavy metal pollution linked to root activities of *Graminae*. For example, through the hydroponic way, Yang *et al.* (2005) researched the effect of sewage irrigation accelerated the decline of wheat seedlings and root, reducing the root number and the root activities significantly. Jiang *et al.* (2004) research also showed that infected soil made the roots of rice seedling yellow and red, enlarged the rhizome and the root colour was brown and yellow. Under Cd stress, root activities of three kinds of sorghum plants decreased significantly in different growth stages. Underground part and aerial part of plants existed with interdependence and mutual restriction relevance. Roots and leaves of plants not only existed in sink-source relationships in assimilation products, but also in supply-demand relationships between water and inorganic nutrition. Cd stress could directly reduce root activities, impending water and mineral nutrient absorption and influencing the aerial part of growth by showing a drop in height, leaf area and tillering number. It might also influence the root growth by reducing the allocation of photosynthesis products to root, thus influencing the photosynthesis products to root, thus influencing the photosynthetic capacity in leaf (Foy *et al.* 1978; Kastori *et al.* 1992). Under senescence and stress, plant organs undergo lipid membrane peroxidation because of free radical toxicity, and the product, malondialdehyde, damage cell membrane system severely. In normal circumstances, because of the active oxygen scavenging system in plant body, active oxygen in cells exists at very low levels, so it cannot cause damage. When adversity exceeds a certain degree, the active oxygen scavenging system in plant is destroyed, and active oxygen become accumulated (Richter and Schweizer, 1997; Shah *et al.* 2001), deflating or reducing the structure, activities and contents of active oxygen scavengers such as: SOD, POD, CAT etc., which lead to further accumulation of active oxygen, thus destroying the oxygen balance. Meanwhile, the increase of reactive oxygen not only cause or aggravates membrane lipid peroxidation (Filek *et al.* 2009), but also dehydrogenated protein and produces proteins free radicals, causing damage to chain polymerization and membrane system, with the accumulation of MDA acting as an indicator of the degree of damage of membrane system cells (Phindsa *et al.* 1981).

Lead

Lead is largely used in the industry for plastics, fishing tools, lead crystal glass inclusive cathode ray tubes, ceramics, solders, pieces of lead flashing, pipes, battery, and ammunition production and most common for its anti-knocking property. Industrial effluents may also contain lead. Their contribution to the sludge is of about 20 per cent. Origin of lead in soil is described as agricultural wastes (12%) sludge (19%) fertilizers (1%) and atmospheric fallouts (68%) (Juste, 1992). Lead is not essential for plant or animal life. It does not bio-accumulate in most organisms, but accumulate in biota feeding primarily on particles, *e.g.*, mussels and worms. Bioavailability of lead in soil is low. Plant absorption is therefore also low. Moreover, eventual lead readily transferred to the upper parts of plant. It has been reported that lead concentration in plants grown on soil containing several hundreds of mg/kg of total Pb rarely exceeded 30 to 50 mg kg^{-1} DMBOWEN (1979). Translocation of the ion in plants is limited and most bound lead stays at root or leaf surfaces. Thus, lead is only likely to affects at sites with very high environmental concentrations. It seems that only 5 to 10 per cent of lead ingested via drinking water or foodstuffs is assimilated and, up to 90 per cent of which are stored in the skeleton (Danish EPA, 1997). It transfers then slowly into the blood. A draft Commission regulation proposes to set maximum levels for some heavy metals in foodstuff, Cow's milk 0.02 mgl^{-1}, Cereals, leguminous and pulses, excluding bran and germ, fish 0.2 mg kg^{-1}, fruits (as consumed) 0.1 mg kg^{-1}.

Lead and it's Salt

It is reported that, the elemental lead is odorless, silver in color and chemically most of the form is insoluble in water, whereas, physically it is soft, highly malleable, ductile and a relatively bad conductor of electricity. It generally occurs in two oxidation state, Pb^{+2} and Pb^{+4}. Stereochemistry of Pb^{+2} is more rather than Pb^{+4}. In general, if we see the abundance for the same, than it is found that, Pb^{+2} will be 80 per cent more than Pb^{+4} (Figure 4.5).

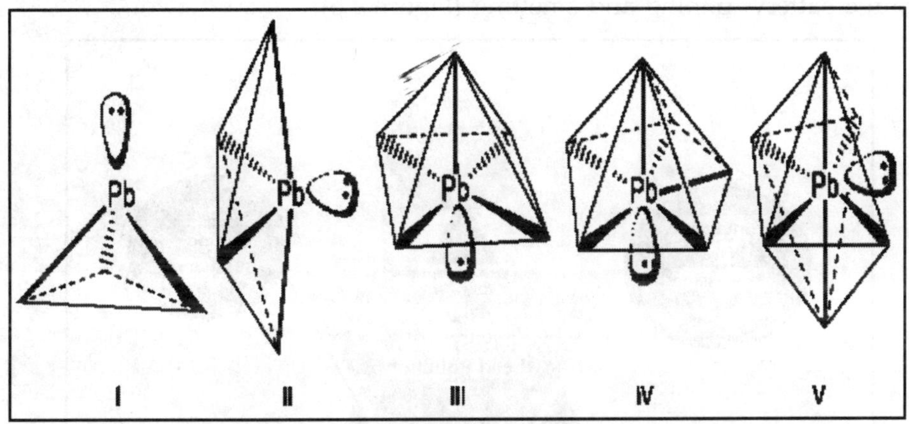

Fig. 4.5: **Co-ordinate polyhedral in Pb(II) complexes with O-donor ligands**

Source: Davidovich *et al.* 2009.

The cationic metals occur naturally in soils as oxides and hydroxides to a lesser extent they can occurs as carbonates, phosphates and sulfates and in reducing soils as sulfides, which are highly insoluble. The soil parameters important in affecting sorption and precipitation reactions and the extent of their influence-and thus contaminants bioavailability-depend on the intrinsic properties of the contaminants. In general, within the soil environment, the metals can remain in the form of cation, anion and neutral ions. These forms of ions significantly affect their sorption, solubility, and mobility. Physical and chemical properties of lead and lead compounds are listed in Table 4.2.

Table 4.2: Properties of lead and lead compounds

Substance	Specific Gravity	Melting Point (°C)	Boiling Point (°C)
Lead	11.34	327	1,740
Lead acetate	3.25	280	DEC
Lead chloride	5.85	501	950
Lead nitrate	4.53	470	DEC
Lead subacetate	NR	75	DEC
Tetraethyl lead	1.659	-136.8	200
Tetramethyl lead	1.995	-30.2	110

Source: Report on Carcinogen, Twelfth Edition, 2011, CAS No.7439-92-1(Lead), 2011).
where, NR = Not responding, DEC = decomposes.

Sources of Lead Contamination Worldwide

Lead contamination is a major concern in both aquatic and terrestrial ecosystems. Both anthropogenic and geological activity is responsible for contamination of lead in natural environment. Geological activity includes weathering, whereas anthropogenic activity includes automobiles exhaust, storage battery, mining and smelting (Figure 4.6).

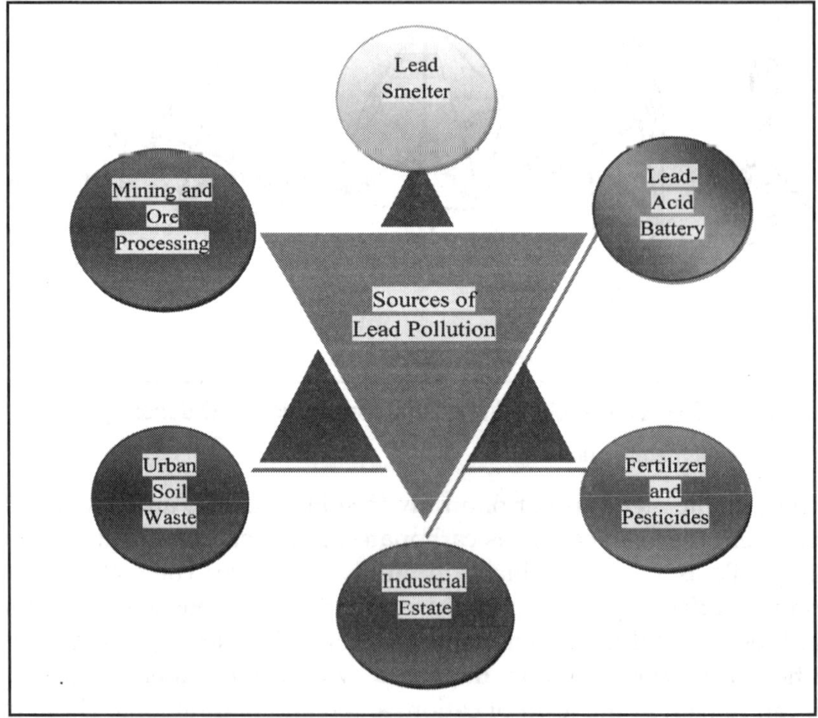

Fig. 4.6: **Different sources of lead pollution**

Source: Drawn by author

1. *Lead Pollution from used Lead-acid Battery Recycling:* Lead-acid batteries are rechargeable batteries that are broadly available throughout the world and are commonly used in motor vehicles. These batteries are made up of lead plates and sulfuric acid that are contained within a plastic cover. The lead plates are perfect for use in batteries because of their ability to be recharged multiple times. After sustained use, the lead plates eventually weaken and are no longer able to store energy. Used lead-acid batteries (ULABs) are either discarded or recycled. Because of the toxic materials within these used batteries, the Basel Convention has included ULABs on its list of materials classified as 'hazardous waste' (Figure 4.7).

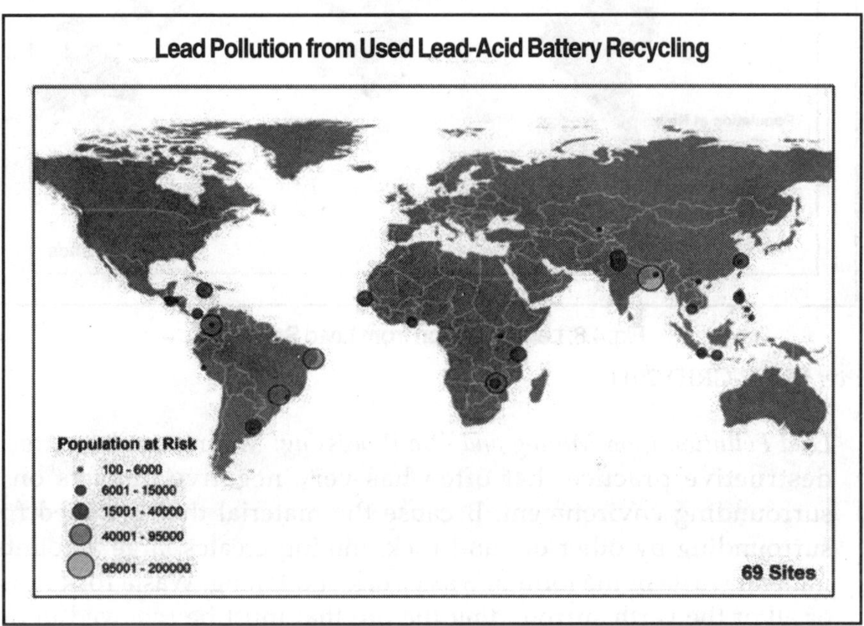

Fig. 4.7: **Lead pollution from used lead-acid battery recycling**

Source: UNEP GRID 2011.

2. *Lead Pollution from Lead Smelters:* Lead processing and smelting plants work with both primary and secondary lead. Primary lead is mined, separated from ore, and refined into various products, whereas secondary lead is recovered from used objects – such as: used lead-acid batteries – for reuse in other products. Smelting is a key process in lead product production, and involves heating lead ore or recovered lead with chemical reducing agents. Both secondary and primary smelting processes can be responsible for releasing large amounts of lead contamination into the surrounding environment (Figure 4.8).

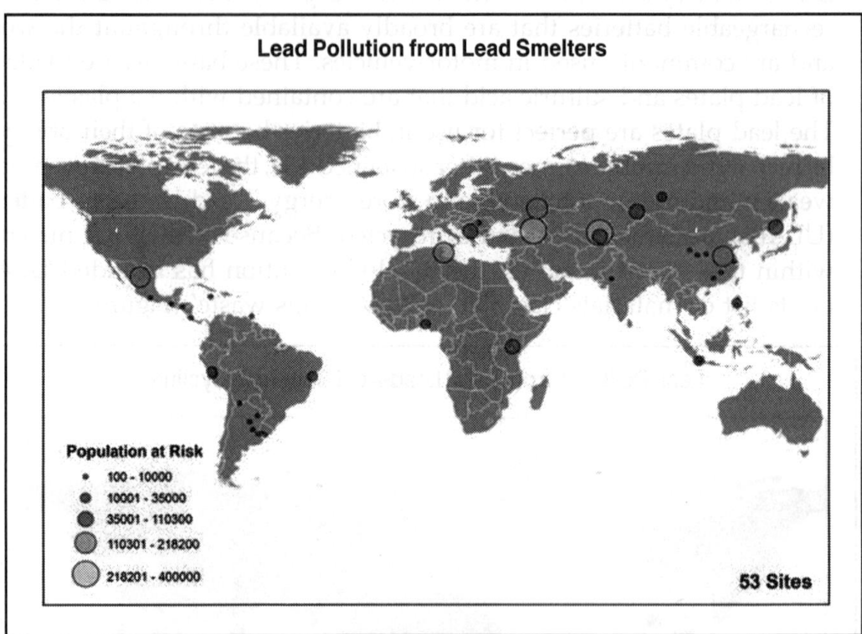

Fig. 4.8: **Lead Pollution from Lead Smelters**

Source: UNEP-GRID 2011.

3. *Lead Pollution from Mining and Ore Processing:* Mining can be extremely destructive practice that often has very negative impacts on the surrounding environment. Because the material that is mined fro is surrounding by other ore and rock, mining creates large amounts of mineral waste in the form of waste rock and tailing. Waste rock consists of all of the earth surrounding the ore that must be removed in order to access the desired minerals, metals and gems. Tailing are the waste material from the ore processing phase, and often contain toxins left over from the ore separating process along with small amounts of heavy metals that were not fully removed. Lead is almost always contained in sulfide ores as galena, or lead sulfide. Waste rock material from mines that contain metal sulfides can lead to sulfuric acid drainage when left out in the open air. Tailings also contain minerals and materials that can lead to dangerous runoff and water contamination when stored improperly. Some mine waste and tailing dump sites are structurally unsound and often overflow and break, allowing contaminants to spill out over the surrounding environment. In some cases, mines will have long pipes or waste canals that carry tailings to waterways for dumping (Figure 4.9).

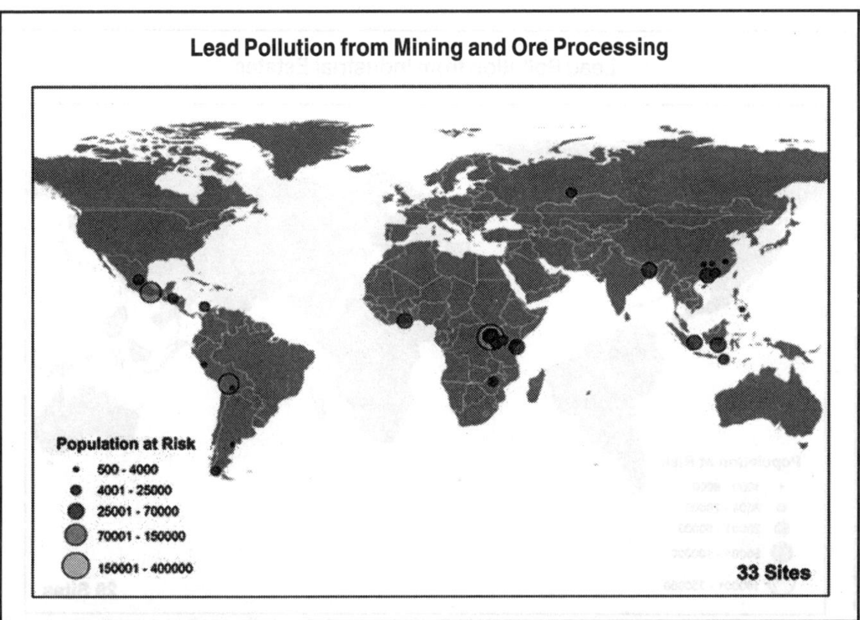

Fig.4.9: **Lead Pollution from Mining and Ore Processing**

Source: UNEP-GRID 2011.

4. *Lead Pollution from Industrial Estate:* Industrial Estates are planned, zoned areas that are set aside for a variety of industries, offices and production. These areas, also known as industrial parks, are frequently built outside of major population areas or residential neighborhoods and are easily accessible *viz;* roads, rail and boat. Industrial estates are often governed by regulatory regimes that are set up to advance and encourage industry. Industrial parks contain a large variety of businesses ranging from food production to heavy metals smelting. The multilateral investment guarantee agency of the World Bank recommended that industrial estates have effluent treatment centers, proper infrastructure for containing and disposing of toxic waste, emissions standards, proper monitoring and reporting systems, and clear emergency preparedness plans. If proper precautions are taken, industrial estates can reduce community and environmental impacts by isolating potentially hazardous process in areas far away from residential neighborhoods and by ensuring safety and environmental standards for all of the industries in the zone. Unfortunately, in many low-and middle-income countries, industrial estates have little to no waste treatment and disposal in infrastructure, and they are often located near populated areas. In the case of an industrial estate that has no pollution control mechanisms, lead, this is often a main contaminant caused by industrial estates, can be released into surrounding air, soil, water and food (Figure 4.10).

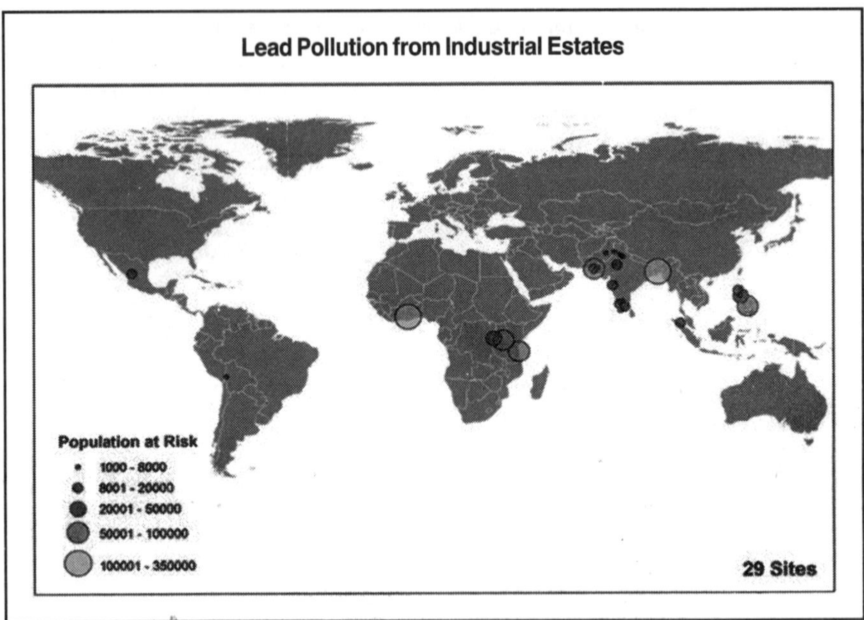

Fig. 4.10: **Lead pollution from Industrial estates**

Source: UNDP GRID 2011.

Chromium

Large amounts of chromium are found in terrestrial crust. The most important part of the extracted chromium is used in alloys, for instance to produce stainless steel. It is also used for its heat resistance and wood protection properties, and, in chemical industry, as tanning agent, and pigment. Whatever its form, the metal concentrates essentially in the roots and is very little transfers to the upper parts of the plant (<10 % of the total). Hexavalent chromium, contrary to the trivalent form, easily crosses membranes and binds to cellular proteins. The tolerable daily intake of chromium has been set at 5.0 $\mu g\ kg^{-1}$ body weights (RIVM Report 711701025, 2001).

Nickel

Nickel is used for the production of stainless steel and in alloys for coins and different instruments production. It is also used for metal surface treatment and battery production. Nickel in sludge originates from households effluents (cosmetic production and pigments) but also from industrial effluents from the activities mentioned above (Merian, 1984). The high mobility and bioavailabity of nickel of exogenous origin (sludge, salts) in comparisons with other metals has frequently been observed. The majority of plants only absorb with difficulty. In the case of cereals crops, and particularly barley and oats, Ni may be transferred to the grain at the moment of senescence.

Nickel's phyto toxic effects are well known. Nickel however is also important for plants and is involved in the metabolism of nitrogen. The production of biomass is rapidly affected. In non accumulative plants it can be suspected that phyto-toxicity would occur at nickel levels in plant in excess of 10 to 100 mg/ kg of dry matter (Bowen 1979). Palacios *et al.* (1999) studies the specific impact of sewage sludge application on tomato fruit yield and quality. It was reported that sewage sludge addition to the calcareous soil of the experiment significantly increased fruit yield but did not adversely affect the quality and the nutritional status of the tomato fruit. Only the highest addition rate of Ni to the sludge amended calcareous soil (240 mg kg^{-1}) had negative effects on fruit yield and quality and caused a Ni accumulation in fruit which could be considered as a hazard for human health.

Conclusion

Heavy metal is considered as one of the most significant inorganic pollutant at worldwide level. Several extensive studies on its behaviour indicate that it will show the biomagnifications in the successive tropics. All of us read in the earlier part of the review that lead can form the stable compounds with the components of the soil. The function and behaviour will depend on its form. These forms will be affected by soil physio-chemical properties such as: pH, EC, Cation Exchange Capacity, redox condition, aeration, soil microbial level etc. In the endodermic of the roots, Casparian strips are present. It is he suberized part of the endodermal cells and important thing is that this acts as one of the natural barrier in the plant which prevents the entry of the lead at its own level. Cadmium has been proved to the toxic to the plants and it will affect the growth and development of the plants at cellular and molecular levels. The efficiency of detoxification mechanisms determines the final tolerance or sensitivity of the plants to metal-induced stress. Plants that have efficient detoxification methods are generally distinguished as being the Hyperaccumulators in the plant groups. Such plants are useful in soil clean up for many hazardous metals. Better knowledge of these mechanisms may lead to:

1. Identification of novel genes and the subsequent development of transgenic plants with superior remediation capacities.
2. Better understanding of the ecological interactions involved (*e.g.*, plant-microbe interactions).
3. Appreciation of the effect of the remediation process on ecological interactions.
4. Knowledge of the entry and movement of the pollutant in the ecosystem.

REFERENCES

AMAP. AMAP Assessment. (2002). Heavy Metals in the Arctic - Pre-print Files. Arctic Monitoring and Assessment Programme; Oslo, Norway, pp. 870.

Adriano DC. (1986). Chromium. In "Trace Elements in the Terrestrial Environment" Springer, New York, pp. 58-76.

Arora K., Sharma S. (2009). Toxic Metal (Cd) Removal from Soil by AM Fungi Inoculated Sorghum. *Asian J Exp. Sci.*, 23(1): 341-438.

Bjerrum J. (1959). Metal Amine Formation in Aqueous Solution. In: Treatise on Analytical Chemistry. Vol. I. *J. Elving* (eds.). New York: The Interscience Encyclopedia.

Browen HJM. (1979). In "Environmental Chemistry of the Elements" 2nd Edition Academic Press, London, pp. 333-335.

Chaney R.L., Malik M., YM Li, Brown S.L., Brewer E.P., Angle J.S., Baker AJM. (1997). Phytoremediation of Soil Metals. *Curr. Opi. Biotechnol.*, 8: 279-284.

Chang ZM, Wu XH. (2005). Difference Comparison of three Alfalfa Varities Resistant to Cadmium Pollution. *Pratacult. Sci.*, 22(12): 20-23.

Cieslinski G., Neilser GH., Hogue EJ. (1996). Effect of Soil Cadmium Applicat ion and pH on Growth and Cadmium Accumulation in Roots, Leaves and Fruit of Strawberry Plants. *Plant Soil*, 180: 267-271.

Cunningham SD, Ow DW. (1996). Promises and Prospects of Phytoremediation. *Plant Physiol.*, 110 (3): 715-719.

Danish Environmental Protection Agency. (1997). Use of Waste Products in Agriculture, Environmental Project No. 366.

Davidovich R.L., Stavila V., Marinin D.V., Voit IE, Whitmire KH. (2009). Steriochemistry of Lead (II) Complexes with Oxygen Donor Ligands, Coordq. Chem. Revi., 253: 1316-1352.

Davis RD. (1984). Cadmium - A Complex Environmental Problem: Cadmium in Sludge used as Fertilizer. Experiment, 40(2): 117-126.

Ernest WHO, Nielson HJM. (2000). Life cycle phases of Zn and Cd resistant ecotypes of in Risk Assessment of Polymetallic Metallic Mine Soils. Environ. Pollut., 107: 329-338.

Filek M., Zenbalab M., Hartikainen H., Miszalski Z., Komas A., Wietecka-Posluszny R., Walas P. (2009). Changes in wheat Plastid Membrane Properties Induced by cadmium and Selenium in Presence/Absence of 2, 4-dichlorophenoxyacetic Acid. Plant Cell Tissue Organ Cult., 96: 19-28.

Foy C.D., Chaney R.L., White M.C. (1978). The Physiology of Metal Toxicity in Plants. *Ann. Rev. Plant Physiol.*, 29: 511-566.

Guo DF. (1994). Lead and Cadmium Source in Environment and the Harms on Human and Animal. *Environ. Sci. Prog.*, 12(3): 71-76.

Jalil A., Selles F., Clark J.M. (1994). Effects of Cadmium on Growth and the uptake of Cadmium and other Elements by Durum Wheat. Plant Nutr., 17: 1839-1895.

Jiang Y., Liang W.J., Zhang Y.G., Xu Y.F. (2004). Research on Effects of Sewage Irrigation on Soil Heavy Metal Environmental Capacity and Rice Growth. *China Ecol. Agric. J.*, 12(3): 124-127.

Kastori RK, Sawhney VP. (2002). Polyamines Research in Plants: A Changing Perspective. *Physiol. Planta*, 116: 281-291.

Kumar P., Mandal B., Dwivedi P. (2014). Phytoremediation for Defending Heavy Metal Stress in Weed Flora. *Intl. J. Agri, Environ and Biotechnol.*, 6(4): 587-595.

Li F, Li M.Y., Pan XH, Xu YF. (2004). Biochemical and Physiological Characteristic in Seedlings Roots of different Rice Cultivars under Low Phosphorous Stress. *Chinese J Rice Sci.*, 18(1): 48-52.

Liu JH, Kitashiba H, Wang J, Ban Y, Moriguchi T. (2007). Polyamines and their Ability to Provide Environmental Stress Tolerance to Plants. *Plant Biotechnol*, 24: 117-126.

Liu JX. (2004). Effects of Cadmium and zinc Interaction on Corn Seedlings Physiological and Biochemical Characteristics. *Yi Chun College J.*, 26(6): 55-57.

Lombi E., Zhao F.J., Dunham S.J., Mcgrath S.P. (2001). Phytoremediation of Heavy Metal-contaminated Soils: Natural hyperaccumulation *vs.* Chemically Enhanced Phytoextraction. *J Environ. Qual.*, 30: 1916-1926.

RIVM Report 711701012/2001. Bioaccessibility of Contaminants from Ingested Soil in Humans. pp. 1-61.

Stoeppler M. (1991). Cadmium. In: Merian E (ed.) Metals and their Compounds in the Environment: Occurrence, Analyses and Biological Relevance. VCH, New York, pp. 803-851.

Goering PL, Waalkes MP, Klaassen CD. (1994). Toxicity of Cadmium. In "Handbook of Experimental Pharmacology: Toxicity of Metals, Biochemical Effects" (Ed) By Goyer R.A.C., Herian M.G. Springer Verlag, New York. pp 189-213.

USEPA. (1996). SW846, third ed., Office of Solid Waste and Emergency Response, Washington, DC, 1996.

Juste M. (1992). Long-term Application of Sewage Sludge and its Effects on Metal Uptake by Crops. In: Biogeochemistry of Trace Metals.

Mench (1998). Cadmium Availability to Plants in Relation to Major Long-term Changes in Agronomic Systems', Agrosys. Ecosys. Environ.

Meagher R.B., Rugh C.L., Kandasamy M.K., Gragson G., Wang NJ. (2000). Engineered Phytoremediation of Mercury Pollution in Soil and Water Using Bacterial Genes. In: Terry N, Bañuelos G (eds) Phytoremediation of Contaminated Soil and Water. Lewis Publishers, Boca Raton, FL. pp. 201-219.

Morrow H., Keating J. (1997). "Overview Paper for OECD Workshop on the Effective Collection and Recycling of Nickel-Cadmium Batteries" OECD Workshop on the Effective Collection and Recycling of Nickel-Cadmium Batteries, Lyon, France, September 23-25. Proceedings to be published by OECD, Paris, France.

Morrow H. (1996). "Questioning the need to Develop Alternatives for Cd Coatings". Proceedings of Second Annual Cd Alternatives for Cd Conference, National Defense Centre or Environment Excellence, Johnstown, Pennsylvania, USA, May 13-15.

Naidu R, Harter RD. (1998). Effects of different Ligands on Cadmium Sorption by and Extract Ability from Soils. *Soil Sci. Am. J*, 62: 644-650.

Palanaippan M., Shannumugam K., Ponnusamy S. (2002). Soil Degradation due to Heavy Metal Accumulation under Long-term Fertilization. The 17th World Congress of Soil Science (WCSS), Bangkok (Thailand).

Pawlowska T.E., Blaszkowski J., Rushling A. (1996). The mycorrhizal Status of Plants Colonizing a Calamine Spoil Mound in Southern Poland. Mycorr., 6: 499-505.

Phindsa R.S., Dhindsaa P.P., Thorpa TA. (1981). Leaf Senescence: Correlated with Increased Levels of Membrane Permeability and Lipid Peroxidation and Decreased Levels of superoxide dismutase and catalase. *J Exp. Bot.*, 32: p. 93.

Qin T.C., Ruan J., Wang L.J. (2000). Effects of Cadmium on Plant Photosynthesis. *Environ. Sci. Technol.*, 13: 33-35.

Report on Carcinogen, Twelfth Edition, 2011, CAS No.7439-92-1(Lead), 2011)).

Richter C., Schweizer M. (1997). Oxidative Stress in Mitochondria. Cold Spring Harbor Laboratory Press, 34: 169-200.

Salt D.E., Blaylock M., Kumar NPBA, Dushenkov V., Ensley BD, Chet I, Raskin I. (1995). Phytoremediation: A Novel Strategy for the Removal of Toxic Metals from the Environment using Plants. Biotechnol., 13: 468-475.

Shah K., Kumar R.G., Verma S, Dubey RS. (2001). Effect of Cadmium on Lipid Peroxidation, Superoxide Anion Generation and Activities of Antioxidant Enzymes in Growing Rice Seedlings. *Plant Sci.,* 161(6): 1135-1144.

Shamsi I.H., Wei K., Zhang G.P., Jilani G.H., Hassan M.J. (2008). Interactive Effects of Cadmium and Aluminium on Growth and Antioxidative Enzymes in Soyabean. *Biol. Plant.,* 52: 165-169.

Smith C.J., Hopmans P., Cook FJ. (1996). Accumulation of Cr, Pb, Cu, Ni, Zn and Cd in Soil Following Irrigation with Untreated urban Effluents in Australia. *Environ. Poll.,* 94(3): 317-323.

Stobart AK, Griffiths WT. 1985. Effects of Cd^{2+} on the biosynthesis of chlorophyll in Leaves of Barley. *Physiol. Plant,* 63: 293-298.

UNEP GRID 2011.

Uraaguchi S, Mori S, Kuramata M, Kawasaki A, Arora T, Ishikawa S. (2009). Root-to Shoot Cd Translocation via the xylem is the Major Process Determining Shoot and Grain Cadmium Accumulation in Rice. *J Exp. Bot.,* 60: 2677-2688.

Wang L., Zhou Q.X., Ding L.L., Sun Y. (2008). Effect of Cadmium Toxicity on Nitrogen Metabolism in Leaves of *Solanum nigrum* L. as a Newly Found Cadmium hyperaccumulator. Hazard. Mat., 154(1-3): 818-825.

Wang Z. (2000). Plant Physiology. China Agriculture Press. Beijing.

WHO. (1992). Cadmium - Environmental Aspects. Geneva, World Health Organization, pp. 156.

Yang JF, Bu YS, Guo XY. (2005). Research on Effects of Soil Exogenous Cadmium and Lead Pollution on Rape Growth, *Shanxi Agri. Sci.,* 3: 26-28.

Zhang J, Shu WS. (2006). Mechanisms of Heavy Metal Cadmium Tolerance in Plants. *J Plant Physiol. Mol. Biol.,* 32(1): 1-8.

Pages 93-112

HEAVY METALS AND METALLOIDS IN BIOSPHERE: *IMPACTS AND ASSESSMENT*
***Edited by*: Dr. Avnish Chauhan; Dr. Sandeep Gupta & Dr. Pawan Kumar Bharti**
***Edition* : 2017**
ISBN : 978-93-5056-860-6
***Published by* : Discovery Publishing House Pvt. Ltd., New Delhi (India)**

Biochar Reduces the Bioavailability and Phytotoxicity of Heavy Metals

S. Ponmani*
P. Kannan

INTRODUCTION

Biochar

Biochar is the carbon-rich product obtained when biomass is heated in a closed container with little or no available air through a process called pyrolysis (Lehmann *et al.* 2006). Biochar is a pyrogenic black carbon that has attracted increased attention in both research and academic areas. The ability to attract such a global attention is due to biochar's potential to mitigate climate change (Feng *et al.* 2012) and provide food security as well as providing an alternative for organic waste management. Application of biochar to soils is currently gaining considerable interest globally due to its potential to improve soil nutrient retention capacity, water holding capacity and also to sustainably store carbon, thereby reducing greenhouse gas (GHG) emissions (Duku *et al.* 2011). Farmers will be motivated to apply biochar on their farms if these benefits can be demonstrated explicitly through various farming methods such as: mixing the biochar with fertilizer and seed, applying through no till systems, uniform soil mixing, deep banding with plow, top-dressed, hoeing into the ground, applying compost and char on raised beds. However, the type of application of biochar to soil depends on the farming system, available machinery and labour. Biochar has the potential to mitigate climate change because the inherent fixed carbon in raw biomass that would otherwise degrade to greenhouse gases is sequestered in soil for years. Assessments of the realistic potential for biochar in carbon abatement have

Dryland Agricultural Research Station, Tamil Nadu Agricultural University, Chettinad - 630 102, Tamil Nadu, India.

converged on a figure of about 1 Gt C yr^{-1} (Lehmann, 2007) presenting a potential wedge for climate change mitigation. It can act as a soil amendment tool because of its beneficial impact on cation exchange capacity (CEC; 40 to 80 meq per 100 g, high surface area (51 to 900 m^2g^{-1}), which leads to increased soil pH and water holding capacity and affinity for micro and macro plant nutrients. The use of biochar as a soil amendment has been investigated since the early 1800's. A number of studies have suggested that terrestrial application of biochar could effectively sequester carbon in soils and thus mitigate global warming (Sohi *et al.* 2010) reveals that applying biochar to agricultural soil is proposed for three reasons:

1. Only the soil seems to have a capacity sufficient to accommodate biochar at the scale relevant to the long-term mitigation of climate change.
2. There is a potential for biochar to enhance soil function for agricultural productivity and thus offset the opportunity cost associated with its residual energy value.
3. The possible suppression of methane and nitrous oxide release would increase the value of biochar as a means to offset agricultural GHG emissions. In their study on biochar and its function in soil, (Sohi *et al.* 2010) assert that a strategy to deploy biochar on a large scale would divert a portion of the existing global carbon flux that resides within managed ecosystems or to intercept enhanced net primary productivity production in the form of increased harvest or waste biomass. This reveals the great need and potential for technologies relevant for sustainable biochar production. Pyrolysis of the biomass feedstocks enables the biomass conversion to biochar whose subsequent application to soil is in a more stabilized form. When little or no oxygen is supplied, biochar is formed under the pyrolysis process and with a controlled amount of supplied air, it is formed under the gasification process. The later optimizes the gaseous phase of biomass conversion while the former optimizes char yield. Biochar is currently the accepted term for pyrolysis-derived charcoal when used as a soil amendment (Kannan *et al.* 2016). The quest for a good biochar suitable for soil application is largely attributed by a number of social, technological as well as the environmental factors.

Properties of Biochar

Characterization of biochar for proximate and ultimate analysis reveals the different biochar properties. Important physico-chemical properties include porosity, surface area and pH which all have an effect on its application to soil. Biochar is made up of elements such as: carbon, hydrogen, sulphur, oxygen, nitrogen as well as minerals in the ash fraction. The properties of biochar will thus vary depending upon the production conditions and the nature of the feedstock used. For example, during the thermal oxidation of biomass to produce biochar, the inherent carbon is lost in the forms of CO_2, CO, CH_4 and various hydrocarbons. Also, there is more cracking and devolatilization creating bigger pore holes inside the biochar if produced at higher temperatures. Results from Peterson and Jackson (2014) for biochar BET analysis revealed that samples with low surface area seem to have large, flat surfaces that have partial cracking, compared to the higher surface area samples, for which the cracking is further developed and there are more individually shaped spherical particles. Biochar surface area increases directly with treatment temperature due to increased volatilization of organic material, leaving a porous structure consisting of the mineral and carbon-based vascular tissue but if volatilization is allowed to continue beyond the optimum, the pores become wider and a drop in BET surface area may be observed (Ghani *et al.* 2013). Thus, a biochar with desirable properties can be deduced from both its proximate and ultimate analysis. The lower the O/C and H/C ratios, the higher are the loss of oxygen and hydrogen during the combustion process producing a product richer in higher elemental carbon. The International Biochar Initiative (IBI) recommends a maximum value of 0.7 for the molar H/C ratio (Wiedner *et al.* 2013) to distinguish biochar from biomass that has not been or only somewhat thermo-chemically altered. Thus suitable working conditions and technologies must be selected in order to produce a biochar of high quality.

Heavy Metal

Industrializations and technical advances have led to an increase in the use of heavy metals and heavy metal pollution. Contrary to organic substances, heavy metals are non-degradable and accumulate in the environment. While some soils can have a high background level of heavy metals due to volcanic activity or weathering of parent materials, in other soils anthropogenic activities, including; smelting, mining, use of pesticides, fertilizers and sludges are responsible for these high levels of heavy metals.

Soil heavy metal pollution has a pernicious effect on soil microbial properties (Yang *et al.* 2012) and on the taxonomic and functional diversity of soils (Vacca *et al.* 2012). Soil heavy metal pollution poses a risk to the environment and to human health (Roy and McDonald, 2014) due to biomagnifications (increases in metal concentration as the element passes from lower to higher trophic levels). Some of these elements can be essential for living organisms while some others are non-essential. Even concentrations of essential elements beyond a certain threshold will have pernicious health effects, as they interfere with the normal metabolism of living systems. Kabata-Pendias and Pendias (2001) provide a list of toxic effects of heavy metals on plants and the mechanism involved, while a summary of adverse effects of heavy metals on human health was provided by Ali *et al.* (2013). We would like to remind the reader that studies on heavy metal pollution are focused on As, Cd, Cr, Hg and Pb as they are toxic, non-essential heavy metals, and on Cu, Ni and Zn which, although essential, can cause health problems in humans or can result in phytotoxicity at high concentrations.

Biochar for Remediation of Soils Contaminated with Heavy Metals

Heavy metals are not biodegradable, and persist for a long time in contaminated soils. It is expensive and time consuming to remove heavy metals from contaminated soils (Cui and Zhang 2004). Stabilization of heavy metals *in-situ* by adding soil amendments such as: lime and compost is commonly employed to reduce the bioavailability of metals and minimize plant uptake (Komárek *et al.* 2013). Biochar can stabilize heavy metals in the contaminated soils, improve the quality of the contaminated soil (Ippolito *et al.* 2012) and has a significant reduction in crop uptake of heavy metals. Therefore, application of biochar can potentially provide a new insight for remediation of the soils contaminated by heavy metals.

Stabilization of heavy metals in soils with application of biochar could involve a number of possible mechanisms, as illustrated in Fig. 5.1 (Lu *et al.* 2012). Taking Pb^{2+} as an example, the various mechanisms for Pb^{2+} sorption by sludge-derived biochar that could include: *(i)* heavy metal exchange with Ca^{2+}, Mg^{2+}, and other cations associated with biochar, attributing to co-precipitation and innersphere complexation with complexed humic matter and mineral oxides of biochar; *(ii)* the surface complexation of heavy metals with different functional groups, and innersphere complexation with the free hydroxyl of mineral oxides and other surface precipitation; and *(iii)* the physical adsorption and surface precipitation that contribute to the stabilization of Pb $^{2+}$ (Lu *et al.* 2012).

In case of acidic contaminated soils, depending on the type of biochars and exchangeable cations (Na, Mg, K and Ca) present in it could hold the key for the release of some of the these cations during sorption process with the heavy metal, and thus may enrich the stabilization process. Lu *et al.* (2012) further demonstrated that the heavy metal exchange with Ca^{2+}, Mg^{2+}, and other cations (Na^+ and K^+) associated with sludge-derived biochar was the main mechanism responsible in their study; however, contribution of monovalent (Na^+ and K^+) cations for heavy metal exchange was found to be negligible. Therefore, it is conceivable that under realistic field situation, sorption mechanisms for metal contaminated soils by biochar could be dependent on the type of soils and the cations present in both soils and biochar, and thus implications for metal remediation in contaminated soils could vary.

The mineral components such as: phosphates and carbonates in biochar play an important role in stabilization of heavy metals in soils because these salts can precipitate with heavy metals and reduce their bioavailability (Cao *et al.* 2009). Cao and Harris (2010) propose that the main mechanism for dairy manure biochar to be effective to retain Pb was the precipitation of insoluble Pb phosphates. Generally, during the manufacture of biochar, water-soluble P, Ca and Mg increased when heated to 200°C but decreased at higher temperatures probably due to increased crystallization of Ca–Mg–P, as evidenced by the formation of whitlockite $(Ca, Mg)_3(PO_4)^2$ when pyrolysis temperature increased to 500°C, thereby facilitating the precipitation of Pb

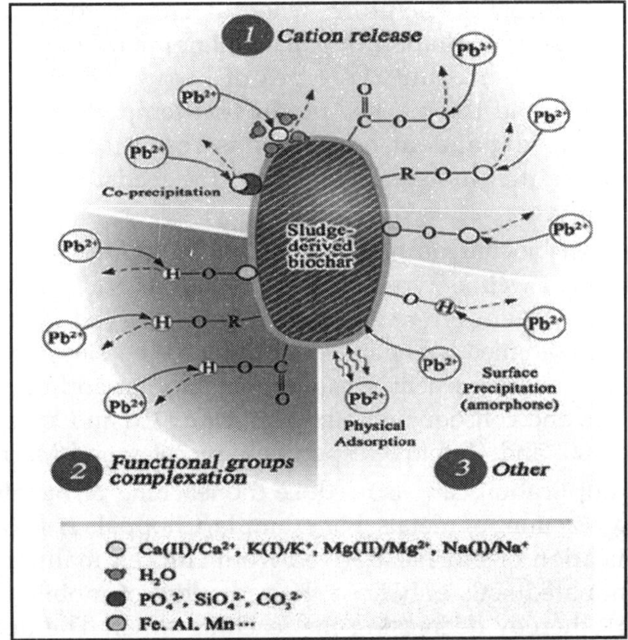

Fig. 5.1: Conceptual illustration of the possible mechanisms of Pb adsorption on biochar (from Lu *et al.* 2012)

(Cao and Harris 2010). Alkalinity of biochar can also promote heavy metal precipitation in soils. Chan and Xu (2009) reviewed biochar pH values from a range of feedstocks in the literature and obtained a mean value of pH 8.1. With the same feedstock material, biochar pH value increases with pyrolysis temperature because of increased ash content in biochar (Wu *et al.* 2012). Therefore, most biochars are alkaline material and have a liming effect, which contributes to the reduction of the mobility of the heavy metals in contaminated soils (Sheng *et al.* 2005). However, the adsorption ability of the same type of biochar varies with different types of heavy metals.

Effect of Biochar on Heavy Metal Mobility

Biochar application can reduce the mobility of heavy metals in contaminated soils (Table 5.1), which renders a reduced risk of taking up by plants. Studies have shown that biochar derived from bamboo can adsorb Cu, Hg, Ni, and Cr from both soils and water, and Cd in polluted soils (Cheng *et al.* 2006). Cao *et al.* (2009) reported that dairy manure-derived biochar pyrolyzed at 200°C was more effective in sorbing Pb than biochar produced at 350°C because the 200°C biochar had the higher concentration of soluble phosphate. Given that biochar characteristics are a function of feedstock and pyrolytic conditions, not one type of biochar could be universally used to remediate soils contaminated with various types of heavy metals. Additionally, not one type of mechanism, or a particular feedstock, or pyrolytic condition could hold true for heavy metal remediation of soil using biochar as an adsorbent. Therefore, when biochar is to be utilized as an amendment for the remediation of soils contaminated with heavy metals, one should take into account the types of heavy metals present in the contaminated soil, and the biochar production temperature as the biochar characteristics are dependent on pyrolysis conditions such as: highest treatment temperature, moisture content of the feedstock, residence time, and the type of feedstock used.

The effect of biochar on metal bioavailability varies with the types of biochar products as well as types of heavy metals. A soil contaminated with Cd and Zn was amended with a hardwood-derived biochar and the concentration of both metals in pore water reduced (Beesley *et al.* 2010). Using the same soil in a column leaching experiment, biochar addition immobilized both Cd and Zn, and consequently, the pore water Cd and Zn concentrations were reduced 300- and 45-folds, respectively (Beesley and Marmiroli 2011).

Biochar application can also reduce the leaching of metals through its effect of redox reactions of metals. For example, Choppala *et al.* (2012) showed that the application of biochar derived from chicken manure to chromate (CrVI)-contaminated soils enhanced the reduction of mobile Cr(VI) to less mobile Cr(III), thereby decreasing the leaching of Cr. The decrease in the leaching of Cr(III) is attributed to the adsorption of Cr(III) onto cation exchange sites and also to the precipitation as $Cr(OH)_3$ resulting from the release of OH, ions during the Cr(VI) reduction process (Fig. 5.2).

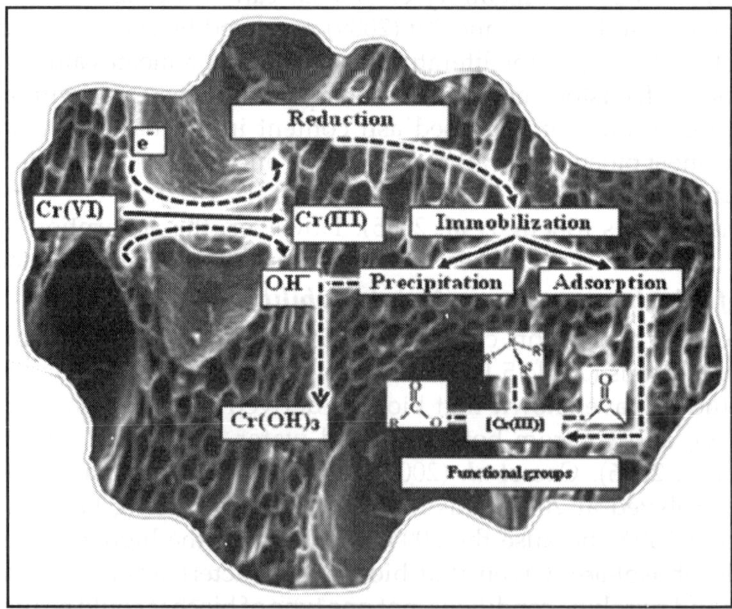

Fig. 5.2: **Concomitant reduction and immobilization of chromium in biochar carbon-amended soils (from Bolan *et al.* 2013)**

Table 5.1: Effect of biochar application on the mobility of heavy metals in soils

Feedstock	Production Temperature	Contaminant	Effect	Reference
Hardwood	450ºC	As, Cd, Cu, Zn	Reduction in Cd in soil pore water by 10-folds; Zn concentrations reduced 300- and 45-folds, respectively, in column leaching tests	Beesley *et al.* (2010); Beesley and Marmiroli (2011)
Hardwood	450ºC	As, Cd, Cu, Pb, Zn	Biochar surface mulch enhanced as and Cu mobility in the soil profile; little effect on Cd and Pb	Beesley and Dickinson (2011)
Wood	200ºC and 400ºC	Cd, Zn	Reduction in Zn and Cd leaching loss by >90%	Debela *et al.* (2012)

Effect of Biochar on the Bioavailability of Heavy Metals

The bioavailability of heavy metals determines the toxicity in the soil and potential risk in entering human food chain. The bioavailability of pollutants governs their eco-toxicology and degradation in contaminated soils. Environmental microbiologist defines bioavailability as the contaminant fraction which represents the accessibility of a chemical to a living organism for assimilation, degradation and eco-toxicology expression (Naidu *et al.* 2008). A number of studies have shown that biochar application is effective in heavy metal immobilization, thereby reducing the bio-availability and phyto-toxicity of heavy metals (Table 5.2). Fellet *et al.* (2011) evaluated the potential of application of biochar to ameliorate the heavy metal toxicity in the mine tailings. They applied biochar derived from orchard prune residues at four rates (0 %, 1 %, 5 % and 10 % biochar in the mine tailings). The pH, cation exchange capacity and the water-holding capacity increased as the biochar rates increase and the bioavailability of Cd, Pb and Zn of the mine tailings decreased, with Cd having the greatest reduction. Zhou *et al.* (2008) used cotton stalk derived biochar to amend Cd-contaminated soil and studied the uptake of Cd by the cabbage. They found that the cotton stalk-derived biochar can reduce the bioavailability of soil Cd through adsorption or co-precipitation. Méndez *et al.* (2012) evaluated the effects of biochar derived from sewage sludge on heavy metals solubility and bioavailability in a Mediterranean agricultural soil and compared with those of sewage sludge, which was not charred. The biochar treatments reduced plant availability of Ni, Zn, Cd and Pb when compared to sewage sludge treatments.

Table 5.2 summarizes the effect of different biochar types on the bioavailability and uptake of range of contaminants. Park *et al.* (2011) reported that both chicken manure and green waste-derived biochars significantly reduced Cd, Cu and Pb uptake by Indian mustard. The study also found that the reduction of the plant metal concentrations increased with biochar application rates except for Cu concentration. Elsewhere, a study conducted by Jiang *et al.* (2012) demonstrated that the rice straw biochar was more efficient in the immobilization of Cu and Pb than Cd. Therefore, when the purpose of utilization of biochar is to immobilize heavy metals, particular attention should be paid to the selection of feedstock, as biochar properties are dependent on the feedstock's inherent properties as well as the pyrolysis conditions under which the biochar is prepared.

In a pot experiment, Namgay *et al.* (2010) applied an activated wood biochar to a soil spiked with heavy metals in order to investigate the impact of biochar on the availability of As, Cd, Cu, Pb and Zn to maize. Biochar treatment decreased the concentration of As, Cd and Cu in maize shoots. However, the effects of adding biochar were inconsistent on Pb and Zn concentrations in the shoots. Soil pH is closely related to the bioavailability of heavy metals in soils. Uchimiya *et al.* (2010) suggested that biochar application can increase the soil pH and cation exchange capacity, and subsequently enhance the immobilization of heavy metals in soil. Ahmad *et al.* (2012) used mussel shell, cow bone and biochar to reduce Pb toxicity in the highly contaminated military shooting range soil. Bioavailability of Pb in the soils was found to decrease by 75.8 per cent with biochar treatment. Increases in soil pH and the adsorption capacity were considered as the mechanisms of remediation effect of the biochar. For example, the bioavailability of Pb in the soils was decreased by up to 92.5 per cent with mussel shell, a liming material (Ahmad *et al.* 2012).

Mechanism of Adsorption of Heavy Metal by Biochar

For evaluating the removal efficiency of the contaminants by biochars, the identification of the underlying mechanisms of the adsorption process is needed. The adsorption behaviour of biochar is different and well correlated with the properties of contaminants. In addition, the adsorption mechanism may also depend on biochar's various properties including surface functional groups, specific surface area, porous structure and mineral components.

As for heavy metals, the possible adsorption mechanisms usually involved integrative effects of several kinds of interactions including: electrostatic attraction, ion-exchange, physical adsorption, surface complexation and/or precipitation. The various mechanisms proposed for the interaction of biochar with heavy metals are summarized in Figure 5.3. The specific mechanisms of different heavy metals are different and the appropriate properties of biochars make a great contribution to the adsorption of heavy metals.

Table 5.2: Effect of biochar application on the bioavailability of heavy metals in soils

Feedstock	Production Temperature	Contaminant	Effect	Reference
Cotton stalks	450ºC	Cd	Reduction of the bioavailability of Cd in soil by adsorption or co-precipitation	Zhou *et al.* (2008)
Hardwood derived biochar	400ºC	As	Significant reduction of As in the foliage of *Miscanthus*	Hartley *et al.* (2009)
Eucalyptus	550ºC	As, Cd, Cu,Pb, Zn	Decrease in As, Cd, Cu, and Pb in maize shoots	Namgay *et al.* (2010)
Orchard prune residue	500ºC	Cd, Cr, Cu,Ni, Pb, Zn	Significant reduction of the bioavailable Cd, Pb, and Zn, with Cd showing the greatest reduction; an increase in the pH, CEC, and water-holding capacity	Fellet *et al.* (2011)
Chicken manure and green waste	550ºC	Cd, Cu, Pb	Significant reduction of Cd, Cu, and Pb accumulation by Indian mustard	Park *et al.* (2011)
Chicken manure	550ºC	Cr	Enhanced soil Cr(VI) reduction to Cr(III)	Choppala *et al.* (2012)
Sewage sludge	500ºC	Cu, Ni, Zn,Cd, Pb	Significant reduction in plant availability of the metals studied	Méndez *et al.* (2012)
Rice straw		Cu, Pb, Cd	Significant reduction in concentrations of free Cu, Pb, and Cd in contaminated soils; identification of functional groups on biochar with high adsorption affinity to Cu	Jiang *et al.* (2012)
Quail litter	500ºC	Cd	Reduction of the concentration of Cd in physic nut; greater reduction with the higher application rates	Suppadit *et al.* (2012)
Oak wood	400ºC	Pb	Bioavailability reduction by 75.8%; bioaccessibility reduction by 12.5%	Ahmad *et al.* (2012)

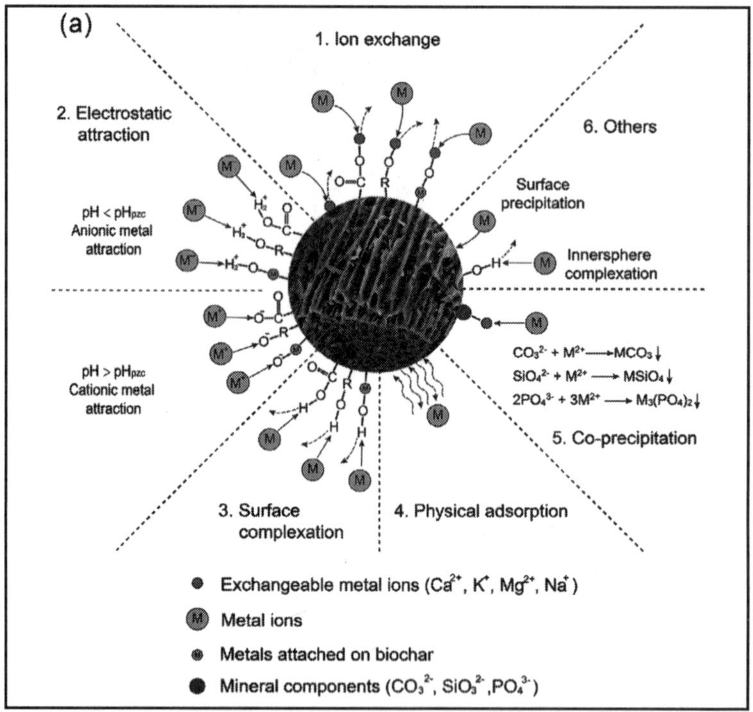

Fig. 5.3: **Mechanisms of heavy metal adsorption on biochar (Xiaofei Tan *et al.* 2015)**

Abundant surface functional groups (mainly oxygen-containing groups, *e.g.*, carboxylate, ACOOH and hydroxyl, AOH) are existed on biochar's surface, which can have strong interactions with heavy metals such as: electrostatic attraction, ion-exchange and surface complexation. These effects can be evidenced by the changes in functional groups of biochar before and after the metal adsorption. Dong *et al.* (2011) hypothesized that sugar beet tailing biochar effectively removed Cr(VI) via electrostatic attraction of Cr(VI) coupled with Cr(VI) reduction to Cr(III) and Cr(III) complexation. They summarized the adsorption process into three parts: *First*, the negatively charged Cr(VI) species were migrated to the positively charged surfaces of biochar (at low pH) with the help of electrostatic driving forces; *Second*, Cr(VI) was reduced to Cr(III) by the participation of hydrogen ions and the electron donors from biochar; And finally, part of the Cr(III) reduced from Cr(VI) was released to the aqueous solution, and the other part of Cr(III) was complexed with the function groups on biochar. Lu *et al.* (2012) also proposed that the functional groups played an important role in Pb adsorption on a sludge derived biochar, which including metal exchange with K^+ and Na^+ due to the electrostatic outer-sphere complexation, surface complexation with free carboxyl functional groups and free hydroxyl functional groups, and inner-sphere complexation with free hydroxyl groups. Similar mechanisms can also be seen in the adsorption of Hg(II) onto soybean stalk-based biochar (Kong *et al.* 2011) and the adsorption of Cd(II) on corn straw biochar (Sun *et al.* 2014).

In addition, the mineral components in biochar played a crucial role in the adsorption process. Xu *et al.* (2013) compared the simultaneously removal effect of Pb, Cu, Zn, and Cd from aqueous solutions by rice husk biochar and dairy manure biochar. The results indicated that the removal ability varied with different biochar feedstock sources and the mineral components such as: CO_3^{2-} PO_4^{3-} originated from the feedstock play an important role in the adsorption ability of biochar. In another study of Cu, Zn, and Cd removal by the dairy manure-derived biochar, the researchers found that the biochar produced from dairy manure were rich in PO_4^{3-} and CO_3^{2-}. These mineral components served as additional adsorption sites, contributing to the biochar's high adsorption capacity for heavy metals. Similar result was found in the adsorption of Pb by dairy-manure derived biochar. They hypothesized that high Pb removal efficiency by biochar may be attributed to the formation of Pb-phosphate precipitate $Pb^9(PO_4)^6$ and the Pb-carbonate precipitation $Pb^3(CO_3)_2(OH)_2$ (Cao *et al.* 2009). Qian and Chen (2013) stated that the complexation of Al with organic groups (hydroxyl and carboxyl), the surface adsorption, and co-precipitation of Al with silicate particles (as $KAlSi_3O_8$) all contributed to Al adsorption onto biochar.

Furthermore, the surface area and porous structure of biochar can also have effects on the adsorption of heavy metals. Biochars have various magnitudes of surface areas and pores within the particles, which enable them easily accessible to metals. However, the surface area and porous structure of biochar seem to have less effect on heavy metal adsorption than oxygen-containing functional groups. Ding *et al.* (2014) reported that the oxygen functional groups were probably responsible for the high Pb sorption onto low temperature biochars (250 and 400°C) whereas intraparticle diffusion was mainly responsible for low Pb sorption onto high temperature biochars (500 and 600°C). Samsuri *et al.* (2014) used oil palm biochar and rice husk biochar to adsorb different heavy metals, the results showed that the former with lower surface area exhibited a higher adsorption capacity for the heavy metals than the latter, suggesting that surface area was less important than oxygen-containing functional groups.

Studies on the Effect of Biochar on Soil Heavy Metals

Table 5.3 shows a brief summary of the latest works about the effect of biochar on soil heavy metals. Uchimiya *et al.* (2012) analysed the effects on soil heavy meals concentrations of 10 biochars prepared from 5 feedstocks at 2 different temperatures. They observed that manures with a high or low proportion of ash or P were less effective to immobilize heavy metals. In contrast, biochars prepared at 700°C were more effective, which could be attributed to transformations in the material, including the removal of nitrogen containing heteroaromatic and leachable aliphatic functional groups. They found Cu and Pb relatively easy to stabilize in soil, while Cd and Ni response depended strongly on the type of biochar added to the soil.

Beesley and Marmiroli (2011) detected retention of As, Cd and Zn on biochar surfaces. These authors proved that sorption of the metal were produced at the biochar surface and that this process was not immediately reversible. Leachate concentrations of Cd and Zn were reduced 300-and 45-fold, respectively. However, leachate concentrations of As did not diminish.

Namgay *et al.* (2010) reported that the concentrations of Cd, As and Pb in maize shoots decreased after biochar application. Beesley *et al.* (2013) reported interesting results, finding that As can increase in soil pore water after biochar addition, but transfer to the plant be reduced. This would imply that at least some biochars could pose no risk of increasing heavy metals in plants and hence are safe in terms of food chain transfer, but leaching of As to nearby waters must be considered. Karami *et al.* (2011) added biochar to a mine soil polluted with Pb and Cu. They found that biochar addition reduced pore water Pb concentrations to half their values in the mine soil. When biochar was combined with greenwaste compost the levels of Pb concentrations in the pore water were 20 times lower than in the control. Jiang *et al.* (2012) found that the acid-soluble fractions of Pb^{2+} and Cu^{2+} diminished by 18.8-77.0 per cent and 19.7-100.0 per cent, respectively, depending on biochar concentration. However, only 5.6-14.1 per cent of acid-soluble Cd^{2+} was immobilized. Park *et al.* (2013) compared the sorption capacity of two biochars, made from chicken manure and from green waste. They found chicken manure biochar more effective to immobilize Cd and Pb compared to green waste biochar. Both biochars presented a higher sorption capacity for Pb, possibly as a consequence of precipitation and complexation of Pb with carbonate, sulphate and phosphate present in the biochar.

Hydrochars are produced after pyrolysis of organic-matter rich materials in the presence of subcritical liquid water. This technique can be applied to obtain pyrolysed products from wet feedstocks. In principle, the adsorption capacity of hydrochars seems to be reduced compared to biochars or other adsorbents due to the fewer functional groups containing oxygen present on hydrochar surfaces. However, Xue *et al.* (2012) have demonstrated experiments that the use of activated hydrochars could overcome these problems. They performed a series of batch and columns experiments to show how this type of hydrochar could reduce Pb on water. The potential applicability of hydrochar to address soil heavy metal pollution remains untested. However, hydrochars tend to be acidic and could possess phytotoxic or genotoxic risks (Busch *et al.* 2013), which would deem them unsuitable in restoration projects.

There is a lack of studies concerning how pyrolysis conditions affect biochar properties as heavy metal sorbent. To fill this gap, Uchimiya *et al.* (2011a) performed an experiment using wood and grass biochars prepared at five different temperatures and another one (Uchimiya *et al.* 2011b) used poultry litter prepared at four different temperatures to study lead retention. From the first experiment they suggested using biochars prepared at high temperature (650°C to 800°C) for remediation purposes. In addition they recommended performing acid or other oxidant post-treatment in order to increase oxygen-containing surface functional groups (carboxyl, carbonyl and hydroxyl) which have a great importance in relation to heavy metal sorption into biochar.

In the case of the chicken litter biochar, they found that lower production temperatures were more suitable than higher ones due to the stabilising effect. Higher rates of amendment were necessary in their experiments for chicken manure biochar to get the same remediation effect as plant-derived biochars. It is expected that as biochar is in contact with soil for a prolonged period of time, oxidation, both biotic and abiotic, would result in the alteration of biochar, a process known as aging. This process, which would result in the formation of carboxylic, phenolic, carbonyl, quinones and hydroxyl functional groups and which can be emulated under laboratory conditions was studied by Uchimiya *et al.* (2010). The immobilization of heavy metals by biochar was related to the metal lability, this means that heavy metal immobilization followed the order $Cu^{2+} > Cd^{2+} > Ni^{2+}$. Heavy metal immobilization was not affected by biochar aging, except for a small increase in Ni observed in soils with aged biochar.

Earthworms can be added to soil at some stages of ecological restoration due to their well-established positive effects on soil properties as organic matter content, soil formation, soil aeration and nutrient cycling. Sizmur *et al.* (2011) tested a polluted soil collected in the vicinity of a Cu mine using biochar in combination with compost and earthworms (*Lumbricus terrestris*). They found all treatments (biochar alone, biochar + compost, and biochar + compost + earthworms) to reduce the amount of heavy metals compared to the control soils. A limiting aspect when using earthworms with remediation purposes is that their addition to soil could lead to the mobilization of heavy metals and hence to an increase of plant heavy metal concentrations. Interestingly, Sizmur *et al.* (2011) found that the treatments containing biochar and earthworms did not result in higher heavy metal mobility or plant availability. As a consequence of heavy metal immobilization, biochars can reduce the phytotoxicity of polluted soils, resulting in increases in the percentage of germinated seeds and root length (Ahmad *et al.* 2012).

All of the above experiments have been conducted under laboratory conditions. We would urge scientists to design experiments to help to demonstrate the benefits of biochar against heavy metal pollution under field conditions, as done by Zheng *et al.* (2012) and Cui *et al.* (2011, 2012). Zheng *et al.* (2012) studied the effect of three biochars on different heavy metals (Table 5.2) using a multi-polluted soil planted with rice. They found Cd, Pb and Zn to be reduced on rice shoots, in particular when using straw-derived biochar. However, as in rice shoots was increased by biochar addition. More importantly, we believe that this is one of the first studies considering the effects of biochar particle size on plant heavy metals. The authors found that decreases in particle size resulted in less Cd, Zn and Pb accumulating in the rice plants. Similarly, Cui *et al.* (2011) and Cui *et al.* (2012) found reduced Cd uptake in paddy fields and in a soil cropped with wheat, respectively. Both studies consisted of two annual measurements, so the need to reapply biochar after more extended periods of time remains to be explored.

Table 5.3: Studies considering the effect of biochar application on soil heavy metals

Feedstock (Temperature)	Soil Type	Heavy Metals	Reference
1	2	3	4
Sewage sludge	Haplic Cambisol	Cu, Ni, Zn, Cd, Pb	Méndez *et al.* (2012)
Rice husk, rice straw and ricebran (400°C)	Technosol	As, Cd, Pb, Zn	Zheng *et al.* (2012)
Wastewater sludge (550°C)	Chromosol	As, Cd, Cr, Cu, Pb, Ni, Se, Zn, Sb, B, Ag, Ba, Be, Co, Sn, Sr	Hossain *et al.* (2010)
Broiler litter (350 and 700°C), pecan shells (450°C)	Abruptic Durixeralfs	Cu, Cd, Ni	Uchimiya *et al.* (2010)
Pecan shell (450°C), broilerlitter samples (700°C)	Typic Kandiudult and Abruptic Durixeralfs	Cu	Uchimiya *et al.* (2011a)
Chicken manure (550°C), green waste (550°C)		Cd, Cu, Pb	Park *et al.* (2011)
Forest green waste (600-800°C)	Peat	Cu	Buss *et al.* (2012)
Dairy manure (350 and 700°C), paved feedlot manure (350 and 700°C), poultry litter (350 and 700°C), turkey litter (350 and 700°C), separated swine solids (350 and 700°C)	Typic Kandiudult	Pb, Cu, Ni, Cd	Uchimiya *et al.* (2012)
Mix of hardwoods (400°C)		As, Cd, Zn	Beesley and Marmiroli (2011)
Mix of hardwoods (400°C)	Technosol	Pb, Cu	Karami *et al.* (2011)

Contd...

1	2	3	4
Orchard prune residue (500°C)	Technosol	Cd, Cr, Cu, Ni, Pb, Tl, Zn	Fellet *et al.* (2011)
Eucalyptus		As, Cd, Cu, Pb, Zn	Namgay *et al.* (2010)
Wheat straw (350-550°C)	Technosol	Cd	Cui *et al.* (2012)
Orchard prune residues (500°C)	Technosol	As	Beesley *et al.* (2013)
Miscanthus (600°C)		Cd, Zn, Pb	Houben *et al.* (2013)
Chicken manure (550°C), green waste (550°C)		Cd, Pb	Park *et al.* (2013)
De-inking paper sludge (300 and 500°C)	Vertisol	Ni	Méndez *et al.* (2014)

Problems, Sustainability and Potential Application of Biochar

Potential Negative Effects

It is noted that biochars have significant removal ability for heavy metals. However, further use of biochar in environmental management, potential negative effects associated with the use of biochar in aqueous must be considered before expanding use in practice. The potential toxic elements, specifically, heavy metals and metalloids inevitably form and associate with biochar. Some researchers have investigated the concentrations of extractable toxic elements contained within the biochar and made some recommendations regarding to minimizing the risk of potential toxic element. Based on the presently reported, most toxic element associated with biochar are likely to be minimal and can thus be acceptable (Agrafioti *et al.* 2013). Pyrolysis may also inhibit the potential release of heavy metals from the biochars (Zhang *et al.* 2013). The yield and composition of toxic element associated with the biochars are strongly dependent upon feedstock material and pyrolytic temperature. In this context, the application of biochar may not be easily brought into schedule. More and more specific and persuasive researches are needed in the future. Despite several studies presently reported that most toxic element associated with biochar are likely to be minimal and can thus be acceptable, it is unknown how variations in pyrolytic temperature and feedstock type affect concentration and composition of these toxic elements. And the stability of these toxic elements in a longer period is still equivocal. To close these knowledge gaps, the security of biochars produced with different feed stocks under varying production conditions should be continuously investigated at large time scale.

Sustainable use of Biochar

For a sustainable biochar development and its safe use as a soil amendment, the International Biochar Initiative (IBI) has established standards (Standardized Product Definition and Product Testing Guidelines for Biochar That Is Used in Soil) to identify certain qualities and characteristics of biochar materials and report common research requirements for researchers (Initiative, 2012). These standards are updated continually. The further application of biochar in water should imitate this way. Guidelines for biochar that is used in water are also needed.

Potential Application of Biochar

Very little information is now available regarding biochar application in the treatment of contaminated site. Considering biochar's excellent adsorption ability in heavy metals, it can be used as new potential *in-situ* amendments sorbent for contaminated site (Ghosh *et al.* 2011). Consequently, further research studies should focus on analyzing the feasibility of this assumption, which offers an exciting opportunity for both carbon sequestration and sediment remediation.

Conclusion

Biochar has the potential to be developed as a viable technology for remediation of contaminated soils. Obviously, biochar can conceivably reduce the bioavailability and efficacy of heavy metal pollutants in soil. Biochars produced from different biomass materials and with different pyrolysis conditions (*e.g.*, temperatures) showcase highly heterogeneous physicochemical properties, which can affect the efficacy in the remediation of contaminated soils. We should understand, firstly, how these properties are relevant for heavy metal adsorption and how they contribute to the different mechanism of heavy metal immobilization, and secondly how to optimize the choice of pyrolysis conditions and feedstocks in order to produce the desired biochar exclusively for different heavy metal abatement in the contaminated soil.

Future Research

For biochar most of the experiments (both in field and under laboratory conditions) have been conducted in the short-term, which poses an interrogation on the long-term fate of these heavy metals. In fact it could be expected that, due to aging processes, the ability of biochar to sequester heavy metals decreases with time. More research will be needed to understand the mechanism of aging process in biochar with respect to different heavy metals.

REFERENCES

Agrafioti, E. Kalderis, D and Diamadopoulos, E (2014). Arsenic and Chromium Removal from Water using Biochars Derived from Rice Husk, Organic Solid Wastes and Sewage Sludge. *J. Environ Manage,* 133: 309-314.

Ahmad, M. Lee, S.S. Yang, J.E. Ro, H.M. Lee, Y.H and Ok, Y.S (2012). Effects of Soil Dilution and Amendments (mussel shell, cow bone and biochar) on Pb Availability and Phytotoxicity in Military Shooting Range Soil. *Ecotox Environ Safe,* 79: 225-231.

Ali, H. Khan, E and Sajad, M.A. (2013). Phytoremediation of Heavy Metals – Concepts and Applications. *Chemosphere,* 91:869-881.

Beesley, L. Moreno-Jiménez, E and Gomez-Eyles, JL (2010). Effects of Biochar and Green Waste Compost Amendments on Mobility, Bioavailability and Toxicity of Inorganic and Organic Contaminants in Multi-element Polluted Soil. *Environ Pollut,* 158: 2282-2287.

Beesley, L. and Dickinson, N. (2011). Carbon and Trace Element Fluxes in the Pore Water of An Urban Soil following Greenwaste Compost, Woody and Biochar Amendments, Inoculated with the Earthworm *Lumbricus Terrestris. Soil Biol Biochem,* 43:188-196.

Beesley, L. and Marmiroli, M. (2011). The Immobilisation and Retention of Soluble Arsenic, Cadmium and Zinc by Biochar. *Environ Pollut,* 159:474-480.

Beesley, L. Marmiroli, M. Pagano, L. Pigoni, V. Fellet, G. Fresno, T. Vamerali, T. Bandiera, M and Marmiroli, N (2013). Biochar Addition to An Arsenic Contaminated Soil Increases Arsenic Concentrations in the Pore Water but Reduces Uptake to Tomato Plants (*Solanum lycopersicum* L.). *Sci Total Environ,* 454-455: 598-603.

Bolan, N.S. Choppala, G. Kunhikrishnan, A. Park, J and Naidu, R. (2013). Biotransformation of Trace Elements in Soils in Relation to Bioavailability and Remediation. *Rev Environ Contaminat Toxicol,* 225:1-56.

Busch, D. Stark, A. Kammann, C. I and Glaser, B. (2013). Genotoxic and phytotoxic Risk Assessment of Fresh and Treated Hydrochar from Hydrothermal Carbonization Compared to Biochar from Pyrolysis. *Ecotox Environ Safe,* 97: 59-66.

Buss, W. Kammann, C. and Koyro, H.W. (2012). Biochar Reduces Copper Toxicity in *Chenopodium quinoa* Willd. in a Sandy Soil. *J. Environ Qual,* 41: 1157-1165.

Cao, XD. Ma, LN. Gao, B and Harris, W (2009). Dairy-manure Derived Biochar Effectively Sorbs Lead and Atrazine. *Environ Sci Technol,* 43:3285-3291.

Cao, XD and Harris, W. (2010). Properties of Dairy-manure-Derived Biochar Pertinent to Its Potential use in Remediation. *Bioresource Technol,* 101:5222-5228.

Chan, KY and Xu, Z. (2009). Biochar: Nutrient Properties and their Enhancement In: Lehmann, J and Joseph, S (Eds), Biochar for Environmental Management: Science and Technology. Earthscan, London and Sterling, VA USA.

Cheng, CH. Lehmann, J. Thies, JE. Burton, SD and Engelhard, MH (2006). Oxidation of Black Carbon by Biotic and Abiotic Processes. *Organ Geochem,* 37:1477-1488.

Choppala, GK. Bolan, NS. Megharaj, M. Chen, Z and Naidu, R. (2012). The Influence of Biochar and Black Carbon on Reduction and Bioavailability of Chromate in Soils. *J. Environ Qual,* 41:1175-1184.

Cui, D.J. and Zhang, Y.L. (2004). Current Situation of Soil Contamination by Heavy Metals and Research Advances on the Remediation Techniques. *Chinese J. Soil Sci,* 35:366-370.

Cui, L. Li, L. Zhang, A. Pan, G. Bao, D. and Chang, A. (2011). Biochar Amendment Greatly Reduces Rice Cd uptake in a Contaminated Paddy Soil: A two-year Field Experiment. *Bioresources,* 6: 2605-2618.

Cui, L. Pan, G. Li, L. Yan, J. Zhang, A. Bian, R. and Chang, A. (2012). The Reduction of Wheat Cd uptake in Contaminated Soil via Biochar Amendment: A Two-year Field Experiment. *Bioresources,* 7: 5666-5676.

Debela. F. Thring, R.W. and Arocena, J.M. (2012). Immobilization of Heavy Metals by Co-pyrolysis of Contaminated Soil with Woody Biomass. *Water Air Soil Pollut,* 223:1161-1170.

Ding, W. Dong, X. Ime, I.M. Gao, B and Ma, L.Q (2014). Pyrolytic Temperatures Impact Lead Sorption Mechanisms by Bagasse Biochars. *Chemosphere,* 105: 68-74.

Dong, X. Ma, L.Q and Li, Y (2011). Characteristics and Mechanisms of Hexavalent Chromium Removal by Biochar from Sugar Beet Tailing. *J. Hazard Mater,* 190: 909-915.

Duku, M.H. Gu, S and Hagan, E.B (2011). Biochar Production Potential in Ghana – A Review. *Renewable and Sustainable Energy Reviews,* 15: 3539-3551.

Fellet, G. Marchiol, L. Delle Vedove, G and Peressotti, A (2011). Application of Biochar on Mine Tailings: Effects and Perspectives for Land Reclamation. *Chemosphere,* 83: 1262-1297.

Feng, Y. Xu, Y. Yu, Y. Xie, Z and Lin, X (2012). Mechanisms of Biochar Decreasing Methane Emission from Chinese Paddy Soils. *Soil Biology and Biochemistry,* 46: 80-88.

Ghani, W.A.W. A.K. Mohd, A. Da Silva, G. Bachmann, R.T. Taufiq-Yap, Y.H. Rashid, U and Al-Muhtaseb, A.H (2013). Biochar Production from Waste Rubber-Wood-Sawdust and Its Potential Use in C Sequestration: Chemical and Physical Characterization. *Industrial Crops and Products,* 44: 18-24.

Ghosh, U. Luthy, R.G. Cornelissen, G. Werner, D and Menzie, C.A (2011). In-situ sorbent Amendments: A New Direction in Contaminated Sediment Management. *Environ Sci Technol,* 45: 1163-1168.

Hartley, W. Dickinson, N.M. Riby, P and Lepp N.W. (2009). Arsenic Mobility in Brownfield Soils Amended with Green Waste Compost or Biochar and Planted with Miscanthus. *Environ Pollut,* 157: 2654-2662.

Hossain, M.K. Strezov, V. Chan, K.Y. and Nelson, P.F. (2010). Agronomic Properties of Wastewater Sludge Biochar and Bioavailability of Metals in Production of Cherry Tomato (*Lycopersicon esculentum*). *Chemosphere,* 78: 1167-1171.

Houben, D. Evrard, L and Sonnet, P. (2013). Mobility, Bioavailability and pH-dependent Leaching of Cadmium, zinc and Lead in a Contaminated Soil Amended with Biochar. *Chemosphere,* 92: 1450-1457.

Initiative, I.B (2012). Standardized Product Definition and Product Testing Guidelines for Biochar that is used in Soil. International Biochar Initiative.

Ippolito, J.A. Laird, D.A. and Busscher, W.J. (2012). Environmental Benefits of Biochar. *J. Environ Qual,* 41: 967-972.

Jiang, J. Xu, R. Jiang, T. and Li, Z. (2012). Immobilization of Cu (II), Pb (II) and Cd (II) by the Addition of Rice Straw Derived Biochar to a Simulated Polluted Ultisol. *J. Hazard Mater,* 229-230:145-150.

Kabata-Pendias, A and Pendias, H (2001). Trace Elements in Soil and Plants. 3rd Edn., CRC Press, 403-415.

Kannan, P. Ponmani, S. Prabukumar, G and Swaminathan, C (2016). Effect of Biochar Amendment on Soil Physical, Chemical and Biological Properties and Groundnut Yield in Rainfed Alfisol of Semi-Arid Tropics. *Archives of Agronomy and Soil Science,* http://dx.doi.org/10.1080/03650340.2016.1139086.

Karami, N. Clemente, R. Moreno-Jiménez, E. Lepp, N and Beesley, L (2011). Efficiency of Green Waste Compost and Biochar Soil Amendments for Reducing Lead and Copper Mobility and Uptake to Ryegrass (*Lolium perenne*). *J Hazar Mater,* 191: 41-48.

Komárek, M. Vanìk, A and Ettler, V (2013). Chemical Stabilization of Metals and Arsenic in Contaminated Soils using Oxides – A Review. *Environ Pollut,* 172: 9-22.

Kong, H. He, J. Gao, Y. Wu, H and Zhu, X (2011). Cosorption of phenanthrene and Mercury (II) from Aqueous Solution by Soybean Stalk-based Biochar. *J. Agric Food Chem,* 59: 12116-12123.

Lehmann, J. Gaunt, J and Rondon, M (2006). Bio-Char Sequestration in Terrestrial Ecosystems – A Review. *Mitigation and Adaptation Strategies for Global Change,* 11: 395-419.

Lehmann, J. (2007): Bio-Energy in the Black. *Frontiers in Ecology and the Environment,* 5: 381-387.

Lu, H. Zhang, Y.Y. Huang, X. Wang, S. and Qiu, R. (2012). Relative Distribution of Pb^{2+} sorption Mechanisms by Sludge-derived Biochar. *Water Res,* 46: 854-862.

Méndez, A, Gómez, A. Paz-Ferreiro, J. and Gascó, G. (2012). Effects of Sewage Sludge Biochar on Plant Metal Availability after Application to a Mediterranean Soil. *Chemosphere,* 89:1354-1359.

Méndez, A. Paz-Ferreiro, J. Araujo, F and Gasco, G. (2014). Biochar from Pyrolysis of de-inking Paper Sludge and its use in the Treatment of a Nickel Polluted Soil. *J. Anal Appl Pyrol,* doi:10.1016/j.jaap.2014.02.001.

Naidu, R. Semple, KT. Megharaj, M. Juhasz, AL. Bolan, NS. Gupta, S. Clothier, B. Schulin, R. and Chaney, R. (2008). Bioavailability, Definition, Assessment and Implications for Risk Assessment. In: Naidu, R (Ed.), Chemical Bioavailability in Terrestrial Environment. Elsevier, Amsterdam, pp. 39-52. ISBN: 978-0-444-52.

Namgay, T. Singh, B and Singh, B.P. (2010). Influence of Biochar Application to Soil on the Availability of As, Cd, Cu, Pb, and Zn to maize (*Zea mays* L.). *J. Aust Soil Res,* 48:638-647.

Park, J.H. Choppala, G.K. Bolan, N.S. Chung, J.W. and Chuasavathi, T. (2011). Biochar Reduces the Bioavailability and Phytotoxicity of Heavy Metals. *Plant Soil,* 348:439-451.

Park, J.H. Choppala, G.H. Lee, S.J. Bolan, N. Chung, J.W. and Edraki, M. (2013). Comparative Sorption of Pb and Cd by biochars and its Implication for Metal Immobilization in Soil. *Water Air Soil Poll,* 224: 1711, doi:10.1007/s11270-013-1711-1.

Peterson, S.C. and Jackson, M. (2014). Simplifying Pyrolysis: Using Gasification to Produce Corn Stover and Wheat Straw Biochar for Sorptive and Horticultural Media. *Industrial Crops and Products,* 53: 228-235.

Qian, L. and Chen, B. (2013). Dual Role of Biochars as Adsorbents for Aluminum: The Effects of Oxygen-containing Organic Components and the Scattering of Silicate Particles. *Environ Sci Technol,* 47: 8759-8768.

Roy, M. and McDonald, L.M. (2014). Metal Uptake in Plants and Health Risk Assessments in Metal-contaminated Smelter Soils. *Land Degrad Dev,* doi:10.1002/ldr.2237.

Samsuri, A. Sadegh-Zadeh, F and Seh-Bardan, B. (2014). Characterization of Biochars Produced from Oil Palm and Rice husks and their Adsorption Capacities for Heavy Metals. *Int J. Environ Sci Technol,* 11: 967-976.

Sheng, GY. Yang, YN. Huang, M.S. and Yang, K. (2005). Influence of pH on Pesticide Sorption by Soil Containing Wheat Residue-derived char. *Environ Pollut,* 134:457-463.

Sizmur, T. Wingate, J. Hutchings, T and Hodson, M.E (2011). *Lumbricus terrestris L.* does not Impact on the Remediation Efficiency of Compost and Biochar Amendments. *Pedobiologia,* 54: S211-S216.

Sohi, S. Krull, E. Lopez-Capel, E and Bol, R (2010). A Review of Biochar and Its Use and Function in Soil. *Advances in Agronomy,* 105: 47-82.

Sun, J. Lian, F. Liu, Z. Zhu, L. and Song, Z. (2014). Biochars Derived from Various Crop Straws: Characterization and Cd (II) Removal Potential. *Ecotoxicol Environ Safe,* 106: 226-231.

Suppadit, T. Kitikoon, V. Phubphol, A and Neumnoi, P. (2012). Effect of Quail Litter Biochar on Productivity of Four New Physic nut Varieties Planted in Cadmium-contaminated Soil. *Chilean J. Agric Res,* 72:125-132.

Uchimiya, M. Lima, I.M. Klasson, K.T. and Wartelle, L.H. (2010). Contaminant Immobilization and Nutrient Release by Biochar Soil Amendment: Roles of Natural Organic Matter. *Chemosphere,* 80: 935-940.

Uchimiya, M. Klasson, K.T. Wartelle, L.H and Lima, I.M. (2011a). Influence of Soil Properties on Heavy Metal Sequestration by Biochar Amendment: Copper Sorption Isotherms and the Release of Cations. *Chemosphere,* 82: 1431-1437.

Uchimiya, M. Wartelle, L.H. Klasson, K.T. Fortier, C.A and Lima, I.M .(2011b). Influence of Pyrolysis Temperature on Biochar Property and Function as a Heavy Metal Sorbent in Soil. *J. Agr Food Chem,* 59: 2501-2510.

Uchimiya, M. Cantrell, K.B. Hunt, P.G. Novak, J.M and Chang, S.C. (2012). Retention of Heavy Metals in a Typic Kandiudult amended with different manure-based Biochars. *J Environ Qual,* 41: 1138-1149.

Vacca, A. Bianco, M.R. Murolo, M and Violante, P. (2012). Heavy Metals in Contaminated Soils of the Rio Sitzerri floodplain (Sardinia, Italy): Characterization and Impact on Pedodiversity. *Land Degrad Dev,* 23: 250-364.

Wiedner, K. Rumpel, C. Steiner, C. Pozzi, A. Maas, R and Glaser, B (2013). Chemical Evaluation of Chars Produced by Thermochemical Conversion (Gasification, Pyrolysis and Hydrothermal Carbonization) of Agro-Industrial Biomass on a Commercial Scale. *Biomass and Bioenergy,* 59: 264-278.

Wu, W. Yang, M. Feng, Q. McGrouther, K. Wang, H. Lu, H and Chen, Y (2012). Chemical Characterization of Rice Straw-derived Biochar for Soil Amendment. *Biom Bioene,* 47:268-276.

Xiaofei Tan, Yunguo Liu, Guangming Zeng, Xin Wang, Xinjiang Hu, Yanling Gu and Zhongzhu Yang (2015). Application of Biochar for the Removal of Pollutants from Aqueous Solutions. *Chemosphere,* 125:70-85.

Xu, X. Cao, X and Zhao, L. (2013). Comparison of Rice Husk-and Dairy Manure-Derived Biochars for Simultaneously Removing Heavy Metals from Aqueous Solutions: Role of Mineral Components in Biochars. *Chemosphere,* 92: 955-961.

Xue, Y.W. Gao, B. Yao, Y. Inyang, M. Zhang, M. Zimmerman, A.R and Ro, K.S (2012). Hydrogen Peroxide Modification Enhances the Ability of Biochar (hydrochar) Produced from Hydrothermal Carbonization of Peanut Hull to Remove Aqueous Heavy Metals: Batch and column tests. *Chem Eng J.,* 200-202: 673-680.

Yang, D. Zeng, D. H. Li, L. J and Mao, R (2012). Chemical and Microbial Properties in Contaminated Soils Around a Magnesite Mine in Northeast China. *Land Degrad Dev,* 23: 256-262.

Zhang, W. Mao, S. Chen, H. Huang, L. and Qiu, R. (2013). Pb (II) and Cr (VI) Sorption by Biochars pyrolyzed from the Municipal Wastewater Sludge under different Heating Conditions. *Bioresour Technol,* 147: 545-552.

Zheng, R.L. Cai, C. Liang, J.H. Huang, Q. Chen, Z. Huang, Y.Z. Arp, H. P. H and Sun, G.X. (2012). The Effects of Biochars from Rice Residue on the Formation of Iron Plaque and the Accumulation of Cd, Zn, Pb, As in Rice (*Oryza sativa* L.) Seedlings. *Chemosphere,* 89: 856-863.

Zhou, J.B. Deng, C.J. Chen, J.L. and Zhang, QS (2008). Remediation Effects of Cotton Stalk Carbon on Cadmium (Cd) Contaminated Soil. *Ecol Environ,* 17:1857-1860.

Pages 113-125

HEAVY METALS AND METALLOIDS IN BIOSPHERE: *IMPACTS AND ASSESSMENT*
***Edited by*: Dr. Avnish Chauhan; Dr. Sandeep Gupta & Dr. Pawan Kumar Bharti**
***Edition* : 2017**
ISBN : 978-93-5056-860-6
***Published by*: Discovery Publishing House Pvt. Ltd., New Delhi (India)**

Inductive Coupled Plasma Mass Spectrometry

What Can it Do with Special Reference to Heavy Metal Toxicity in Sorghum

Prasann Kumar

ABSTRACT

Inductive Coupled Plasma Mass Spectrometry has been proved as the one of the best tool for the study of the heavy metals toxicity concerned with the food and other thing else. We are biased for the statement because this is our personal interest. We have conducted a lot of experiments related to the screening capacity of the plant(s). These plants are of different groups such as: ornamental, medicinal, cereals, weed, leafy and woody species etc. ICP-MS plays an important role for the test of minimum level of concentration for concerned heavy metals like: cadmium, lead, nickel and chromium in the plant samples. The concentration can be measured up to the lowest level which is further described in to the forthcoming text by us. Contamination of heavy metal is of special worry due to well-known reports emanating both from India and abroad. Various diseases and disorders observed both in human and livestock due to metal toxicity. Scientist reported that, the greatest problems most likely to involve mercury, cadmium, lead, chromium, arsenic, nickel etc. To a greater or lower degree all of these elements are toxic to humans and any others animals. Cadmium is extremely toxic causing heart and kidney disease, bone embrittleness; Cr, Ni, and Pb are moderately so which are responsible for mutagenic, lung cancer, convulsion and brain damage like: some deadlier diseases. Sorghum bicolor L. is an imperative crop due to its extensive use as food, feed and energy crop. India has a prosperous and mottled heritage of biodiversity surrounding a wide range of habitats. The present review is written for partial fulfillment of some of the promising used instrument like: Inductive Coupled Mass Spectrometry mediated by workers with

Department of Plant Physiology, Institute of Agricultural Sciences, Banaras Hindu University, Varanasi, 221 005, UP., India.

special reference to heavy metal toxicity in sorghum. I am interested in sorghum because in my experiment I have found that, it has the tremendous capacity to tolerate the high level of cadmium toxicity. The detection of cadmium in plant samples was performed with the help of ICP-MS in the year 2015 at Banaras Hindu University.

Keywords: absorption, cadmium, density, inductive, mass, spectrometry.

INTRODUCTION

ICP-MS is very popular for the elemental determinations in the plant or animal samples. In the year 1983, this technology was comes in to the notice (Aceto 2002). And after that it was frequently used in to the day-to-day life and recently it has been proved as the one of the best analytical technique for the elemental determination (Figure 6.1). With respect to other elemental analyzer, I have found that ICP-MS has more advancement rather than others, these are:

- Detection limits for most elements equal to or better than those obtained by Graphite Furnace Atomic Absorption Spectroscopy (GFAAS).
- Higher throughput than GFAAS.
- The ability to handle both simple and complex matrices with a minimum of matrix interferences due to the high temperature of the ICP source.
- Superior detection capability to ICP-AES with the same sample throughput.
- The ability to obtain isotopic information.

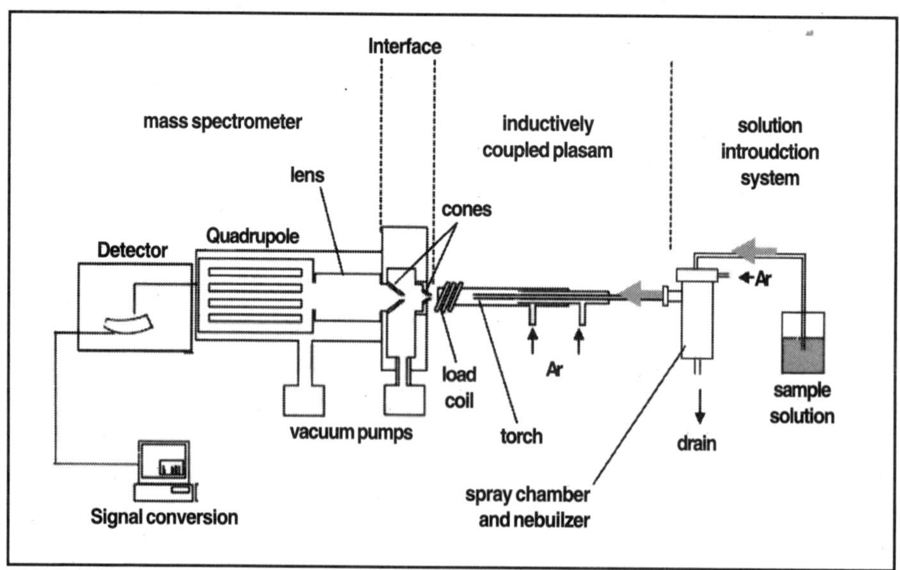

Fig. 6.1: **Schematic diagram of ICP-MS**

Source: Review Literature, 2016.

Besides above mention reasons for the popularity of ICP-MS, the growing popularity of ICP-MS can be summarized as:

1. Isotopic examination can be achieved readily.
2. The operation range of analysis is nine order of scale.
3. The output is unmatched by any other technique.
4. The instrument revealing limits are at or below the single part per trillion level for most of the element.

An ICP-MS combines a high temperature ICP (Inductively Coupled Plasma) source with a mass spectrometer. The ICP source converts the atoms of the elements in the sample to ions. These ions are then separated and detected by the mass spectrometer. Argon gas flows inside the concentric channels of the ICP torch. The RF load coil is connected to a radiofrequency (RF) generator. As power is supplied to the load coil from the generator, oscillating electric and magnetic fields are established at the end of the torch. When a spark is applied to the argon flowing through the ICP torch, electrons are stripped off of the argon atoms, forming argon ions. These ions are caught in the oscillating fields and collide with other argon atoms, forming an argon discharge or plasma. The most important things to remember about the argon ICP plasma are: *(i)* the argon discharge, with a temperature of around 6000-10000ºK, is an excellent ion source; *(ii)* the ions formed by the ICP discharge are typically positive ions, M^+ or M^{+2}, therefore, elements that prefer to form negative ions, such as: Cl, I, F, etc., are very difficult to determine via ICPMS; *(iii)* the detection capabilities of the technique can vary with the sample introduction technique used, as diverse techniques will allow differing amounts of sample to reach the ICP plasma; *(iv)* recognition capabilities will vary with the sample matrix, which may affect the degree of ionization that will occur in the plasma or allow the formation of species that may interfere with the analyze determination (Stefánsson *et al.* 2007; Mermet 2003) (Figure 6.2).

Sample Prepration of Soil/Sludge for the Detection of Heavy Metals by the Application of ICP-MS

Sludge samples were air dried grounded and sieved through 2 mm sieve. Then the samples were stored in refrigerator after packing in polyethylene bags. Plant samples were cleaned thoroughly with 0.01N HCl followed by distilled water. Finally these were dried at 60ºC and grinded.

1. *Total heavy metal content of sludge*: 0.5 gram of the processed samples was digested with di-acid mixture (HNO_3:$HClO_4$, 9:4) on a hot plate (APHA, 1992). The clear solutions were filtered through Whatman No. 42 filter paper and diluted to 50 ml for analysis by Atomic Absorption Spectrophotometer (GBS-902).
2. *Heavy metal content in plant samples*: 0.5 gram of dried sample was digested with di-acid mixture (HNO_3:$HClO_4$, 9:4) on a hot plate (APHA, 1992) until the discoloration of solution.

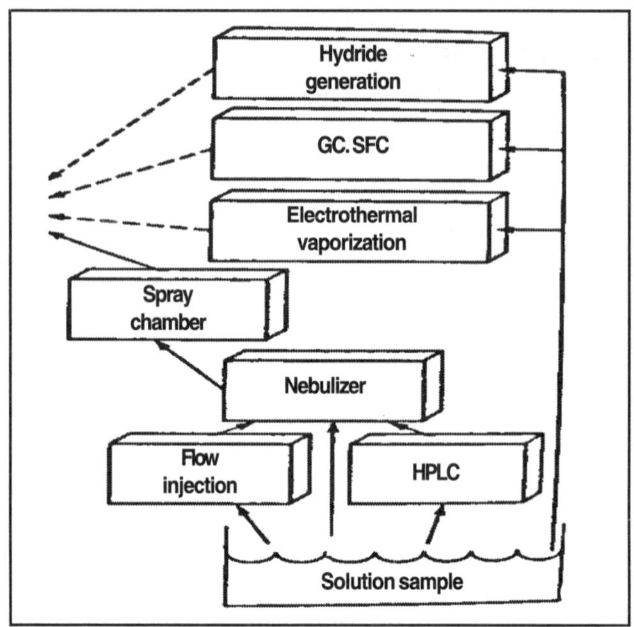

Fig. 6.2: **Sample entry pathway**

Source: Skoog, Hollar and Cronch, 2007.

We use the sample in liquid form for detection the heavy metal through ICP-MS. The liquid sample is pumped into the sample introducing system (Mermet 2005). This introducing chamber is made up of a spray chamber and nebulizer. The sample travels through the different heating zones of the plasma torch it is dried, vaporized, atomized and finally ionized (Hieftje 2006). When the sample finally arrives at the analytical zone of the plasma, it exists as excited atoms and ions and this will represent the elemental composition of the sample. The excitation of the outer electron of a ground-state atom, to produce wavelength-specific photons of light, is the fundamental basis of atomic emission (Figure 6.3). However, there is also enough energy in the plasma to remove an electron from its orbital to generate an ion (Haung 1989). It is the generation, transportation, and detection of significant numbers of these positively charged ions that give ICP-MS its characteristic ultra trace detection capabilities (Thomas R. 2001). It is also important to mention that, although ICP-MS is predominantly used for the detection of positive ions, negative ions (such as: halogens) are also produced in the plasma (Thomas R. 2001). However, because the extraction and transportation of negative ions is different from that of positive ions, most commercial instruments are not designed to measure them (Thomas R. 2001). The process of the generation of positively charged ions in the plasma is shown conceptually in greater detail in Figure 6.3 and 6.4.

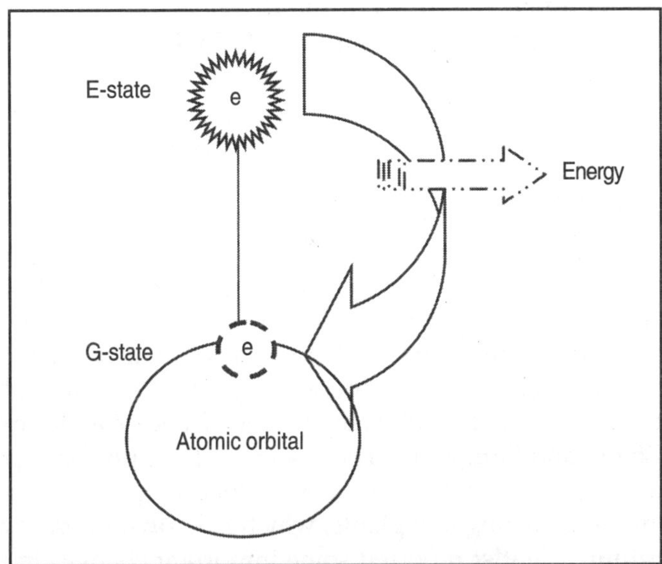

Fig. 6.3: **Schematic diagram of energy release and electron excitation from ground state to excited stated**

Source: Drawn by author, unpublished, 2016.

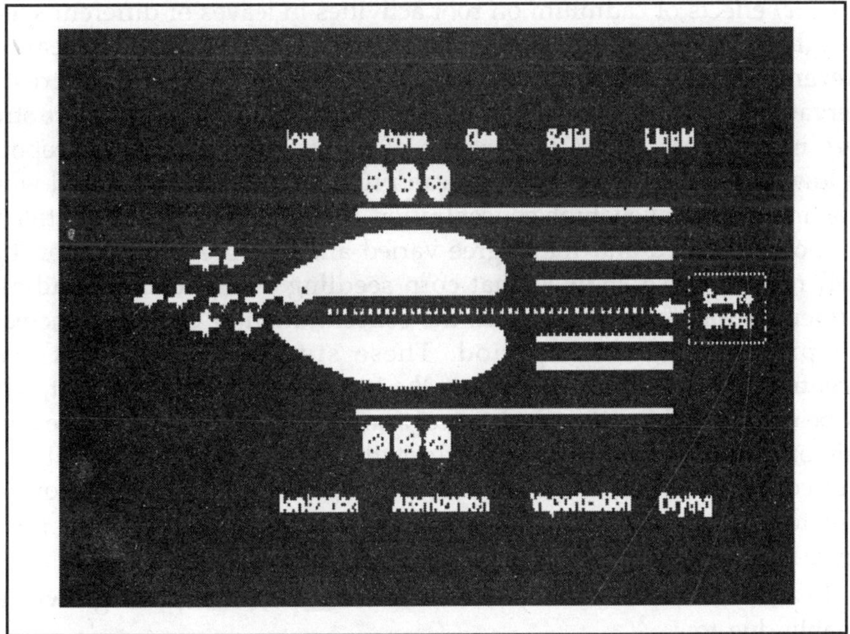

Fig. 6.4: **Schematic diagram generation of cation in the plasma**

Source: Thomas R., 2001.

Why I am Bother about the Study of the Heavy Metal Especially Concerned with Cadmium Toxicity in Sorghum

With the rapid industrial development, soil environmental pollution in India has become increasingly serious. Cadmium (Cd) is a highly toxic heavy metal in the environment (Davis, 1984; Guo, 1994). Cd is a non-essential nutrient for plants, and excessive Cd has not only significant adverse effects (Shamsi *et al.* 2008), but also endangers human health via food chain (Naidu and Harter, 1998). The alleviation or inhibition of Cd damage in plants has, therefore, caused extensive attention of the whole society (Uraguchi *et al.* 2009; Wang *et al.* 2008). Heavy metals have an adverse impact on growth and development of the plants, showing some physiological and biochemical characteristic of damages. To a certain extent, plant growth and physiological characteristic can reflect the adverse impact of heavy metal externally or internally (Zhang and Shu, 2006). The research of the poisoning effect of the heavy metal Cd on plant mainly focuses on food crops such as: rice, wheat and maize, but less on *Sorghum* plants, which is known often as animal feed sources. Sorghum scientist reported some important changes in growth and physiological characteristic of sorghum plant under cadmium stress. In their experiment, the major physiological parameters for observation were like this *(a)* effects of cadmium on height of different species of sorghum; *(b)* effects of cadmium on chlorophyll contents of different species of sorghum plants; *(c)* effects of cadmium on root activities in leaves of different species of sorghum plants; *(d)* effects of cadmium on MDA contents in leaves of different species of sorghum plants. They found several interesting observations and these can be summarized such as: a kind of oxidative stress, heavy metal stress affects the growth of plants. Jalil *et al.* (1994) reported that low concentration of cadmium can promote the growth of hard wheat, while under a relatively high concentration, the growth of wheat and tillering were both inhibited and the degree varied among different varieties. Liu's (2004) research also showed that corn seedling's height under cadmium treatment reduced significantly as the concentration of cadmium increased with prolonged growth period. These studies showed that lower concentration of cadmium stimulates the increase of sorghum height, which may be related to the certain resistance of sorghum plants to Cd, while higher levels of cadmium inhibited height growth of sorghum genus plant. Thus, lower concentration of cadmium stress stimulates the growth of sorghum plants to a certain extent, and higher concentrations inhibited their growth (Figure 6.5).

Reason for the inhibitory effect of heavy metals to plant growth was probably due to:

(a) A series of physical and chemical reactions between excess heavy metal and soil components changes soil properties, thus affecting soil fertility

levels (Cieslinski *et al.* 1996; Chang and Wu, 2005). For example, heavy metal pollution can enhance the fixation of soil phosphorous, which affected the plants absorbing phosphorous, thus influenced the growth of plants (Li *et al.* 2004; Zhang *et al.* 2004).

(b) Heavy metal poisonous effects caused a reduction in plant photosynthesis, thereby reducing the plant water and nutrient adsorption, which affected the normal growth and development of plants (Qin *et al.* 2000).

In the plant body, photosynthesis is the most fundamental and important physiological and biochemical process, and its initial link is chlorophyll synthesis and function realization. The results from experiments conducted by Liu *et al.* (2004) showed that chlorophyll synthesis was affected by cadmium stress and with the increase of cadmium stress levels; the inhibitory effect was increasingly severe. The reason for change in chlorophyll contents in the leaves of sorghum plants might be that chlorophyll synthesis was formed under the action of a series of enzymes in proplastid and chloroplast (Stobart and Griffith, 1985; Wang, 2000).

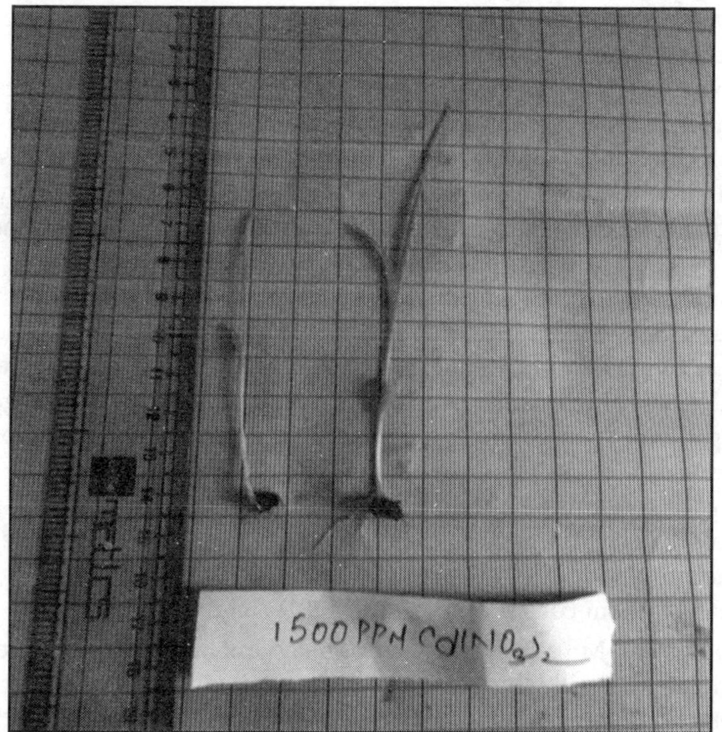

Fig. 6.5: **Two leaf stage of sorghum grown under 1500 ppm cadmium nitrate**

Source: Photograph taken by Prasann Kumar at BHU, unpublished, 2016.

Cd stress inhibited relevant enzymes activities in the leaves of sorghum plants in the process of chlorophyll synthesis, affecting chlorophyll synthesis process and leaf chlorosis, thus leading to the change in chlorophyll contents. There have been many reports about heavy metal pollution linked to root activities of *Graminae*. For example, through the hydroponic way, Yang *et al.* (2005) researched the effect of sewage irrigation accelerated the decline of wheat seedlings and root, reducing the root number and the root activities significantly. Jiang *et al.* (2004) research also showed that infected soil made the roots of rice seedling yellow and red, enlarged the rhizome and the root colour was brown and yellow. Under Cd stress, root activities of three kinds of sorghum plants decreased significantly in different growth stages. Underground part and aerial part of plants existed with interdependence and mutual restriction relevance. Roots and leaves of plants not only existed in sink-source relationships in assimilation products, but also in supply-demand relationships between water and inorganic nutrition. Cd stress could directly reduce root activities, impending water and mineral nutrient absorption and influencing the aerial part of growth by showing a drop in height, leaf area and tillering number. It might also influence the root growth by reducing the allocation of photosynthesis products to root, thus influencing the photosynthesis products to root, thus influencing the photosynthetic capacity in leaf (Foy *et al.* 1978; Kastori *et al.* 1992). Under senescence and stress, plant organs undergo lipid membrane peroxidation because of free radical toxicity, and the product, malondialdehyde, damage cell membrane system severely. In normal circumstances, because of the active oxygen scavenging system in plant body, active oxygen in cells exists at very low levels, so it cannot cause damage. When adversity exceeds a certain degree, the active oxygen scavenging system in plant is destroyed, and active oxygen become accumulated (Richter and Schweizer, 1997; Shah *et al.* 2001), deflating or reducing the structure, activities and contents of active oxygen scavengers such as: SOD, POD, CAT etc., which lead to further accumulation of active oxygen, thus destroying the oxygen balance. Meanwhile, the increase of reactive oxygen not only cause or aggravates membrane lipid peroxidation (Filek *et al.* 2009; Tames *et al.* 2009), but also dehydrogenated protein and produces proteins free radicals, causing damage to chain polymerization and membrane system, with the accumulation of MDA acting as an indicator of the degree of damage of membrane system cells (Phindsa *et al.* 1981) (Figure 6.6).

Through ICP-MS a large number of heavy metals can be detected in the plant samples and soil/sludge samples respectivelly. It is a powerfull tool for the detection of trace metal in environmental sample also. For the instance in the Figure 6.7, I am giving the name of the elements which can be measurable with the help of ICP-MS.

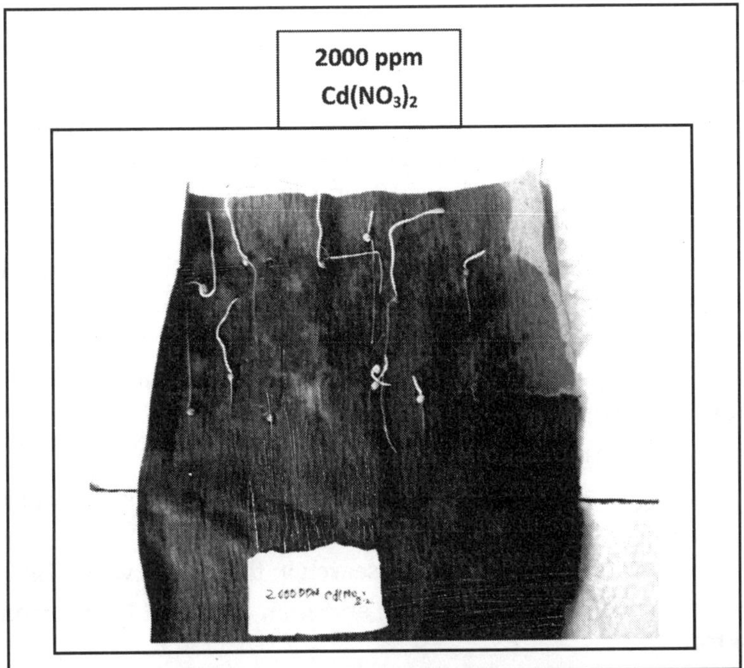

Fig. 6.6: **Effect of cadmium concentration (2000 ppm using germination paper) on germination of sorghum seeds CSU15 (along with primary roots)**

Source: Photograph taken by Prasann Kumar at BHU, 2015.

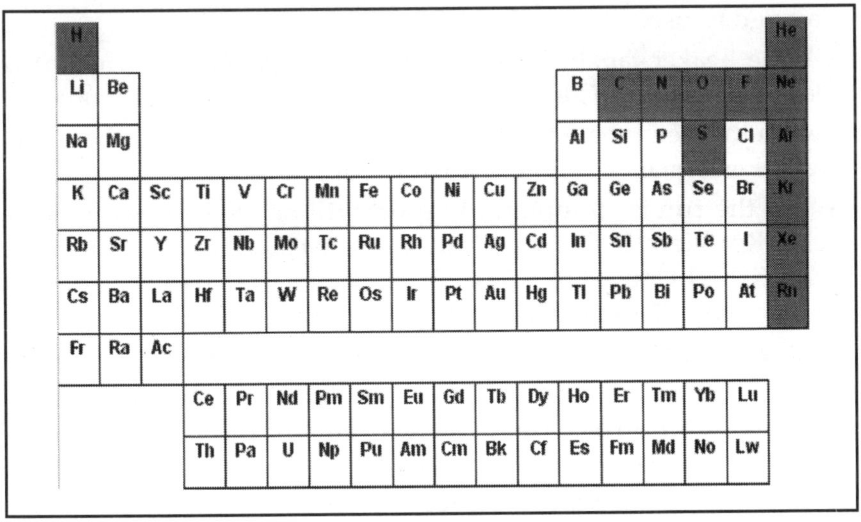

H																	He
Li	Be											B	C	N	O	F	Ne
Na	Mg											Al	Si	P	S	Cl	Ar
K	Ca	Sc	Ti	V	Cr	Mn	Fe	Co	Ni	Cu	Zn	Ga	Ge	As	Se	Br	Kr
Rb	Sr	Y	Zr	Nb	Mo	Tc	Ru	Rh	Pd	Ag	Cd	In	Sn	Sb	Te	I	Xe
Cs	Ba	La	Hf	Ta	W	Re	Os	Ir	Pt	Au	Hg	Tl	Pb	Bi	Po	At	Rn
Fr	Ra	Ac															
			Ce	Pr	Nd	Pm	Sm	Eu	Gd	Tb	Dy	Ho	Er	Tm	Yb	Lu	
			Th	Pa	U	Np	Pu	Am	Cm	Bk	Cf	Es	Fm	Md	No	Lw	

Fig. 6.7: **Elements meserable with ICP-MS**

Source: Skoog, Hollar and Cronch, 2007.

*Note: where, the red colour elements cannot be measered.

The liquid sample is pumped from a vial, via a peristaltic pump, into the nebulizer (Bazilio A and Weinrich J., 2012). Liquid droplets are formed on the tip of a needle, where they become nebulized due to argon gas flowing through a second needle perpendicular to the sample needle (Bazilio A and Weinrich J., 2012). A small amount of aerosol created is swept into the torch, but the majority of sample condenses on the walls of the nebulizer and is wasted to the drain (Bazilio A and Weinrich J., 2012).

Protocol for the Application of ICP-MS for the Detection of Heavy Metals in Plant/Soil/Sludge Sample (Bazilio A and Weinrich J., 2012)

In this section I am giving the general analysis techniques for the detection of heavy metals in the concerned samples through ICP-MS.

Instrument Startup and Daily Performance Check

1. Turn on gas (Argon).
2. Check the gas pressure of gas in the tank. It is Argon gas for the use. The delivery pressure should be at least 60psi.
3. Place the concerned samples of research in the beaker with Mili Q water.
4. Turn on the connected computer and then open the ELAN icon on the desktop.
5. File—Open workspace—Daily performance—Instrument tab—start (Plasma). The pressure of vacuum should be less than 10^5 torr.
6. The ready and plasma light on the instrument should be green.
7. Please wait 10-15 minutes for the plasma to warm up before performing day-to-day use.
8. Fill the beaker labelled daily performance (a quarter to a half) with Daily Performance Check solution (ELAN 6100 Setup Solution).
9. Switch the feed tube from the beaker of MiliQ water to the beaker with Daily Performance Solution. Analyze Sample (Start).
10. When the run is complete, a report will print. To view on screen select Rpt View. In this report: *(a)* Mg must be > 50,000; *(b)* In must be > 250,000; *(c)* Ur must be > 200,000; *(d)* Net Intensity mean of CeO should be 3 per cent (0.03); *(e)* Bkgd Intens. Mean should be 1.
11. If (d) and (e) are not satisfied, wait 5-15 minutes and run again.
12. Fill in values in the Log book (Populate all fields, including: your name and the date). Plmce the printed report in the Log and Daily Performance binder located next to the computer.

Preparing Standards and Samples

1. Standards should be prepared for a range of concentrations encompassing expected sample concentrations.

2. A minimum of 5mL of standard or sample should be used for each run.
3. Filter samples with a 0.45 μm filter.
4. 2 per cent by volume of nitric acid (HNO_3) should be added to samples and standards.
5. If testing for Bromide or Iodide, 0.1 per cent ammonium hydroxide (NHOH) should be added.

Creating a Method

1. Select Method Tab. File '! New '! Quantitative Analysis.
2. To select the analytes you wish to quantify: right click in the analyte column '! Select element from periodic table. You can select multiple isotopes of an element (Ctrl + Select).

   N.B. If measuring multiple Isotopes, change the names, *e.g.*, Br, Br1
3. The other fields will automatically populate after elements are selected.
4. Save the method. Use your initials and the date; may include elements analyzed.

Running Samples

1. Check pressure in gas tank, rinse solution level and waste collection container.
2. Sign Logbook.
3. Run daily performance check.
4. Connect sample tube to auto-sample tube.
5. Place sample in auto-sample try and create sample list.
6. Select samples to run in the sample list.
7. Click summary—summarize by analyte output to file—browse. Name the file to be created—save—OK. Buid Run list—Autostop.
8. Check that sample info is correct. Select analyze batch.
9. If prompted: Are you sure you want to use Auto stop? Then select Yes for this option.
10. Start sample run.
11. Remove your samples from the tray after run. Disconnect tubing from the peristaltic pump and leave lying flat for the purpose to prevent wear of the tubes.
12. To access data: C:/Elandata/Reportoutput.

Conclusion

In general, it is good practice for the user of the analytical data submitting samples for ICP-MS analysis to discuss the nature of the samples and the data quality required with the ICP-MS operator so that proper isotopic selection and/or sample preparation methods can be utilized to meet the end user's needs.

REFERENCES

Aceto M., Abollino O., Bruzzoniti MC., Mentasti E., Sarzanini C., Malandrino M. (2002). "Determination of Metals in Wine with Atomic Spectroscopy (flame AAS, GFAAS and ICPAES) ~ A Review". Food Additives and Contaminants, 19 (2): 126-33.

APHA. (1992). Standard Method for the Examination of Water and Waste Water. Amer. Public Health Assn., pp. 214-218, Academic Press, Washington D.C.

Bazilio A, Weinrich J. (2012). The Easy Guide to: Inductive Coupled Plasma Mass Spectrometry. pp. 2-11.

Chang ZM, Wu XH. (2005). Difference Comparison of three Alfalfa Varities Resistant to Cadmium Pollution. *Pratacult. Sci.* 22(12): 20-23.

Cieslinski G., Neilser GH., Hogue EJ. (1996). Effect of Soil Cadmium Applicat ion and pH on Growth and Cadmium Accumulation in Roots, Leaves and Fruit of Strawberry Plants. *Plant Soil,* 180: 267-271.

Davis RD. (1984). Cadmium – A Complex Environmental Problem: Cadmium in Sludge used as Fertilizer. Experiment, 40(2): 117-126.

Filek M., Zenbalab M., Hartikainen H., Miszalski Z., Komas A., Wietecka-Posluszny R., Walas P. (2009). Changes in Wheat Plastid Membrane Properties Induced by Cadmium and Selenium in Presence/Absence of 2, 4-dichlorophenoxyacetic acid. Plant Cell Tissue Organ Cult., 96: 19-28.

Foy C.D., Chaney R.L., White M.C. (1978). The Physiology of Metal Toxicity in Plants. *Ann. Rev. Plant Physiol.,* 29: 511-566.

Guo DF. (1994). Lead and Cadmium Source in Environment and the Harms on Human and Animal. *Environ. Sci. Prog.,* 12(3): 71-76.

Haung Mao~ Hieftje G. (1989). Simultaneous Measurement of Spatially Resolved Electron Temperatures, Electron Number Densities and Gas Temperatures by Laser Light Scattering from the ICP. Spectrochimica Acta Part B: Atomic Spectroscopy, 44 (8): 739-749.

Hieftje G. (1982). "Design and Construction of a Low Flow, LowPower Torch for Inductively Coupled Plasma Spectrometry". *Applied Spectroscopy,* 36 (6): 627-631.

Hieftje G. (2006). "Effect of the Plasma Operating Frequency on the Figures of Merit of an Inductively Coupled Plasma Time of Flight Mass Spectrometer. *J. Ana. Atomic Spectro.,* 21 (2): 160-167.

http://www.spectro.com/products/icpoesicpaesspectrometers

Jalil A., Selles F., Clark J.M. (1994). Effects of Cadmium on Growth and the uptake of Cadmium and other Elements by Durum Wheat. *Plant Nutr.* 17: 1839-1895.

Jiang Y., Liang W.J., Zhang Y.G., Xu Y.F. (2004). Research on Effects of Sewage Irrigation on Soil Heavy Metal Environmental Capacity and Rice Growth. *China Ecol. Agric. J.,* 12(3): 124-127.

Kastori R., Petrovic M., Petrovic N. (1992). Effects of Excess Lead, Cadmium, Copper and zinc on Water Relations in Sunflower. *Plant Nutr.,* 15: 2427- 2439.

Li F., Li MY., Pan XH, Xu YF. (2004). Biochemical and Physiological Characteristic in Seedlings Roots of different Rice Cultivars under low Phosphorous Stress. *Chinese J Rice Sci.,* 18(1): 48-52.

Mermet J.M. (2005). "Is it Still Possible, Necessary and Beneficial to Perform Research in ICP Atomic Emission Spectrometry". *J. Anal. At. Spectrom.,* 20: 11-16.

Phindsa R.S., Dhindsaa P.P., Thorpa TA. (1981). Leaf Senescence: Correlated with Increased Levels of Membrane Permeability and Lipid Peroxidation and Decreased Levels of Superoxide Dismutase and Catalase. *J. Exp. Bot.*, 32: p. 93.

Qin T.C., Ruan J., Wang LJ. (2000). Effects of Cadmium on Plant Photosynthesis. *Environ. Sci. Technol.*, 13: 33-35.

Richter C., Schweizer M. (1997). Oxidative Stress in Mitochondria. Cold Spring Harbor Laboratory Press, 34: 169-200.

Shah K., Kumar R.G., Verma S., Dubey RS. (2001). Effect of Cadmium on Lipid Peroxidation, Superoxide Anion Generation and Activities of Antioxidant Enzymes in Growing Rice Seedlings. *Plant Sci.*, 161(6): 1135-1144.

Shamsi I.H., Wei K., Zhang G.P., Jilani G.H., Hassan M.J. (2008). Interactive Effects of Cadmium and Aluminium on Growth and Antioxidative Enzymes in Soyabean. *Biol. Plant.* 52: 165-169.

Stefánsson A, Gunnarsson I., Giroud N. (2007). "New Methods for the Direct Determination of Dissolved Inorganic, Organic and Total Carbon in Natural Waters by Reagent Free Ion Chromatography and Inductively Coupled Plasma Atomic Emission Spectrometry". *Anal. Chim. Acta*, 582 (1): 69-74.

Stobart A.K., Griffiths WT. (1985). Effects of Cd^{2+} on the Biosynthesis of chlorophyll in Leaves of barley. *Physiol. Plant*, 63: 293-298.

Skoog D.A., Holler F.J., Crouch S.R. (2007). Principles of Instumental Analysis. Thomson Higher Education.

Thomas R. (2001). A Beginner's Guide to ICP-MS. Spectroscopy. 16(4): 38-42.

Uraaguchi S., Mori S., Kuramata M., Kawasaki A., Arora T., Ishikawa S. (2009). Root-to shoot Cd Translocation via the xylem is the major Process Determining Shoot and Grain Cadmium Accumulation in rice. *J. Exp. Bot.*, 60: 2677-2688.

Wang L., Zhou QX, Ding LL, Sun Y. (2008). Effect of Cadmium Toxicity on Nitrogen Metabolism in Leaves of *Solanum nigrum* L. as a Newly Found Cadmium hyperaccumulator. *Hazard. Mat.*, 154(1-3): 818-825.

Wang Z. (2000). Plant Physiology. China Agriculture Press. Beijing.

Yang J.F., Bu Y.S., Guo XY. (2005). Research on Effects of Soil Exogenous Cadmium and Lead Pollution on Rape Growth, *Shanxi Agri. Sci.*, 3: 26-28.

Zhang E.H., Zhang X.H., Wang H.Z. (2004). Adaptable Effects of Phosphorus Stress on different Genotypes of faba-bean. *Acta Ecol. Sinica.* 24(8): 1589-1593.

Zhang J., Shu W.S. (2006). Mechanisms of Heavy Metal Cadmium Tolerance in Plants. *J. Plant Physiol. Mol. Biol.* 32(1): 1-8.

Pages 126-140

HEAVY METALS AND METALLOIDS IN BIOSPHERE: *IMPACTS AND ASSESSMENT*
***Edited by* : Dr. Avnish Chauhan; Dr. Sandeep Gupta & Dr. Pawan Kumar Bharti**
***Edition* : 2017**
ISBN : 978-93-5056-860-6
***Published by* : Discovery Publishing House Pvt. Ltd., New Delhi (India)**

Applications of Chitosan Powder with in situ Synthesized nano ZnO Particles as an Antimicrobial Agent

Mujeeb Rahman P
K.Muraleedaran*
V.M Abdul Mujeeb

ABSTRACT

ZnO nanoparticles are immobilized on the chitosan matrix by an in situ sol-gel conversion of precursor molecules in a single step. Three different composites are prepared by varying the concentration of sodium hydroxide with same quantity of chitosan and zinc acetate dihydrate. The composites were characterised by: FT-IR, UV-Visible spectra and XRD. The observed decrease in the band width corresponding to –OH and –NH_2 group in the composites is ascribed to the reduction of hydrogen bond due to impregnation of ZnO groups. The direct evidence of the immobilization of nano-ZnO particles in the matrix was identified by SEM. The average particle size values obtained for the nanoparticles, using Debye-Scherrer equation from XRD, is in the range 10-18 nm. Optical studies proved that all the three composites studied have the same band gap energy (3.28 eV) in agreement with the reported values. We observed that the composites posses excellent antimicrobial activity against gram negative bacteria Escherichia coli (E.coli) and gram positive bacteria Staphylococcus aureus (S.aureus) than chitosan. Based on the above studies, the biocompatible, eco-friendly and low-cost composite powder could be applied in various fields as an antimicrobial agent.

Keywords: chitosan nanocomposites; antimicrobial activity; immobilization of nano ZnO particles.

Department of Chemistry, University of Calicut, Malappuram, Kerala - 673 635, India.

INTRODUCTION

Chitosan is the second-most plentiful natural polymer and has excessively studied in large number of applications [1] and the properties of chitosan can be tuned by changing its structure as well as adding nanoparticles to its polymer matrix [2]. In recent years much attention has been devoted to the hybrid materials of nanosized metal oxides and chitosan owing to their unique properties such as: photo catalysts, antimicrobial agents, etc. This hybridization could enhance the properties of each single component counterpart of composites. [3-4]. Since chitosan molecules contain a large number of reactive hydroxyl (–OH) and amino (–NH2) groups, they can act as a natural capping agent during the synthesis of nanoparticles [5]. Recent studies on chitosan nanocomposites - chitosan-CdS, chitosan-niobium (V) oxide and chitosan - cuprous oxide (p-type semiconductor) - reports their photocatalytic activities against organic dye molecules [6-10]. It has been reported that chitosan-nano ZnO composites act as sensors for DNA [11], cholesterol molecules [2], dye adsorption [12] and semi-conductor quantum dots [13]. Several authors have reported the antimicrobial properties of chitosan nano-silver and silver oxide composites [14-16]. Among the various inorganic metal compounds, ZnO is preferably used for the synthesis of chitosan - nanocomposite due to its unusual properties such as: wide band gap energy (3.37 eV) [17], high surface area, high catalytic efficiency, non-toxicity, chemical stability [2] antibacterial character, UV protection ability [18], etc.

Literatures survey reveal that, only a few reports are available on the hybrid of chitosan and nano ZnO composites and in all these pre-synthesized nano ZnO particles were used to develop the composites [2, 12, 19-21]. In the present work, a simple method for the fabrication of chitosan/nano-ZnO composite powder has been described. The nano ZnO particles were formed by in situ sol-gel conversion of precursor Zinc acetate dihydrate in the presence of NaOH. The highlights of this method include: the easiness of fabrication process, lower temperature requirement, in situ formation of nanoparticles, biodegradable and biocompatible polymer matrix to stabilize the nanoparticles. The utility of the composite powder was analysed for its antibacterial efficacy against Gram negative bacteria Escherichia coli (E.coli) and Gram positive bacteria Staphylococcus aureus (S.aureus).

It is a serious concern that several bacteria have developed antibiotic resistance against synthetic antibiotics [12], therefore, the design of efficient antibacterial agents are the need of hour. In recent years, there have been extensive investigations on the utilization of inorganic nanoparticles as antimicrobial agents. In view of this, the present work focused on the development of novel antibiotic composites containing chitosan and nano ZnO particles. The fabrication was aimed at the co-utilization of antibacterial properties of chitosan as well as nano zinc oxide particles [22]. It is already known that chitosan has inherent antimicrobial activity against gram negative and gram positive bacteria, but the exact mechanism of its antimicrobial activity is not clearly known. The ability of chitosan to inhibit or kill micro-organism can be tuned by varying its molecular weight, degree of deacetylation, temperature, pH and by immobilizing metal oxides in its matrix [23]. Owing to higher film forming property, chitosan and their various composites have been investigated as an antimicrobial packing material for preservation of food articles, vegetables and fruits [24]. The inherent antimicrobial activity of chitosan is believed to be due to the presence of the positively charged amino groups which interact with negatively charged cell membranes of pathogens, leading to the leakage of proteinaceous and other intracellular constituents and finally to the death of microorganism [25]. The sensitivity of any antibacterial film forming solution was determined by measuring the diameter of the inhibition zone and they are classified as: *(a)* not sensitive for diameters less than 8 mm; *(b)* sensitive for diameters of 9-14 mm; *(c)* very sensitive for diameters of 15-19 mm and *(d)* extremely sensitive for diameters larger than 20 mm [26].

The present work involves the fabrication of a novel, eco-friendly antimicrobial composite containing chitosan and ZnO nanoparticles by in situ sole – gel conversion. The objective of this work was to formulate a simple and cost effective bionanocomposite for the possible uses as an antimicrobial wound dressing materials, cotton fabrics and packing materials for food stuffs.

Experimental

Materials

Chitosan with 85 per cent degree of deacetylation was purchased from Sigma Aldrich Co. Ltd. (USA). Acetic acid, sodium hydroxide, and zinc acetate dihydrate were purchased from Merck (Germany). Mineral salt broth and nutrient agar are obtained from Himedia Chemicals (India). Escherichia coli (E. coli) and Staphylococcus aureus (S. aureus) were prepared at the microbiology laboratory, Department of Life Science, University of Calicut. Clinical sample of E. coli and S. aureus were obtained from Santhi hospital, Omessery, Calicut, India. Deionized water was used to prepare all the solutions. All the chemicals were of analytical grade reagents and used without further purification.

Preparation

Chitosan solution was prepared by dissolving 0.5 g of chitosan in 2 per cent acetic acid solution in room temperature. The solution was then filtered to remove undissolved particles and added 30 mL of 15 per cent zinc acetate dihydrate solution and shaken well. To this solution, 30 mL of 45 per cent sodium hydroxide solution was added slowly at a temperature of 70°C and the entire mixture was stirred at 70°C for 4 h. The white precipitate formed was allowed to settle by keeping the mixture for 24 h. The supernatant solution was discarded, the precipitate was rinsed with distilled water for several times to remove excess of NaOH present (if any), filtered and dried by keeping in an air oven maintained at a temperature of 50°C for 12 h. The white dried precipitate was powdered well in a mortar by using a pestle and this sample was designated as CN45. The above process was repeated with decreased concentration of sodium hydroxide, 30 and 15 per cent, the corresponding composites formed were designated as CN30 and CN15 respectively.

Characterization

The FTIR spectra of the samples were recorded in KBr pellets using Fourier Transform IR Spectrometer (Model: JASCO FTIR 4108). The absorption spectra of powder was recorded by using a UV-Visible spectrophotometer (Model: JASCO V-550) in the wavelength range of 200-800 nm. X-ray diffraction (XRD) patterns of composites were recorded with a X-ray diffractometer (Model: Rigaku Minifex 600) using Cu Kα radiation (kα = 0.15406 nm) at a scanning rate of 1° min^{-1}. The thermal stability and degradation behaviour of composites were assessed using a thermogravimetric analyzer (TG) (Model: TGA/DTA851e) under flowing air (at a flow rate of 60 µL min^{-1}) in the temperature range, 40 to 740°C at a heating rate of 10°C min^{-1}. The SEM images of chitosan and composites were recorded using a Field Emission Scanning Electron Microscope (Model: HITACHI SU–6600 FESEM).

Antibacterial Activities

The antimicrobial activity of chitosan and chitosan-based nanocomposite powders were evaluated by Agar well diffusion method. Gram-negative bacteria E. coli (MTCC 1687) and Gram-positive bacteria S. aureus (MTCC 737) were used as test organisms. Sterile NA plates were prepared and 0.1 µL of the inoculums of test organism was spread uniformly over it. Wells were prepared by using a sterile borer of diameter 6 mm and the samples of pure chitosan (C), CN15, CN30 and CN45 were added in each well separately. The plates were incubated at 35-37°C for 24 h, a period of time sufficient for the growth. The zone of inhibition of microbial growth around the well was measured in mm .The anti microbial efficacy of samples against clinical bacteria (E. coli and S. aureus) was evaluated by disc diffusion method. The anti microbial disc was prepared as described earlier [27]. Whatman No. 1 filter paper was cut into disc shape using a circular knife and autoclaved. This paper discs were soaked separately into 5 mL of 1 per cent acetic acid solution containing 0.05 g of C, CN45, CN30 and CN15 and dried at room temperature to adsorb the antimicrobes on the paper surface. Antibacterial properties of filter paper disc treated with bionanocomposites are measured by the inhibition zone method. The presence of any clear zone that formed around the disc on the plate medium was recorded as an indication of inhibition against the microbial species.

Results and Discussion

FTIR Spectroscopy

Fig. 7.1 shows the FTIR spectra of pure chitosan and chitosan-nano ZnO composites powder. The characteristic broad band at 3367 cm^{-1} observed in Fig. 7.1a is attributed to the stretching vibrations of $-NH_2$ group and –OH group of chitosan. The band at 2876 cm^{-1} is due to the asymmetric stretching vibration of –CH group and the bands at 1656 and 1588 cm^{-1} are designated to the stretching vibrations of C=O and the scissoring vibrations of $-NH_2$ of chitosan. The bands at 1150-1040 cm^{-1} is due to the stretching vibration of –C-O-C- of glycosidic linkage of the polymer [28].

The FTIR spectrum of ZnO composites (Fig. 7.1; b, c and d) are similar to that of pure chitosan but in contrast to Fig. 7.1a, the band corresponding to stretching vibrations of $-NH_2$, –OH, C=O, –C-O-C- and asymmetric stretching vibrations of –CH groups are shifted to lower wave number region indicating the strong interaction of these groups with ZnO particles. The decrease in the width of the band corresponding to –OH and $-NH_2$ group is ascribed to the reduction of hydrogen bond due to impregnation of ZnO groups. Moreover, the intense band at 470 cm^{-1} observed in Figs. 7.1b, c and d is ascribed to the stretching mode of Zn-O vibrations strongly supporting the presence of nanoparticles [29].

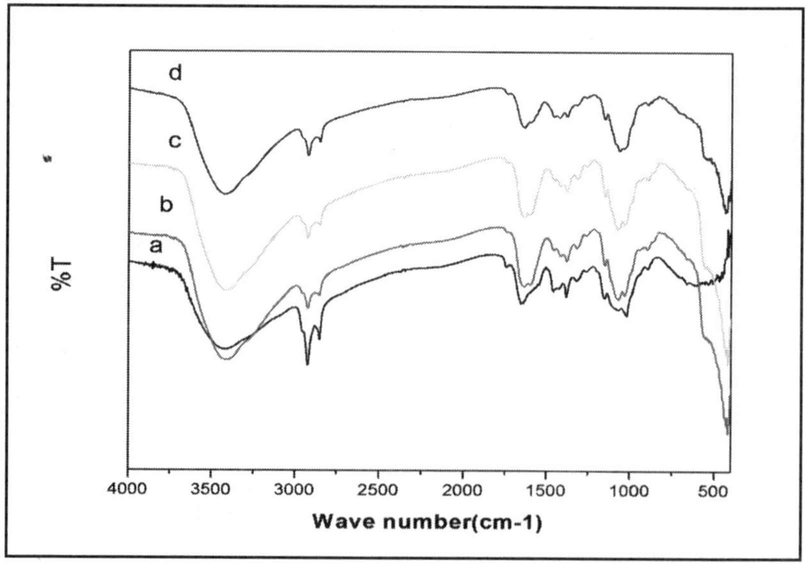

Fig. 7.1: **FTIR spectra of pure chitosan (a), CN 15 (b), CN 30(c), CN 45(d)**

XRD Analysis

Fig. 7.2 shows the XRD patterns of C and chitosan-nano ZnO composites powders. The typical peak of C at 19.9° (Fig. 7.2a) is not visible in chitosan nano –ZnO composites (Figs. 7.2b, 2c and 2d), which may be due the loss of semi-crystalline behaviour of chitosan in the presence of nanoparticles.

The major peaks at 31.78, 34.44, 36.27, 47.5, 56.56, 62.87 and 67.96° observed in Figs. 7.2 b, c and d of composites were assigned to diffraction from the planes (100), (002), (101), (102), (110), (103) and (201) respectively. And these results are consistent with the data base of (JCPDS No 36-1451) [30]. The XRD results revealed that the particles formed at the matrix are pure ZnO with hexagonal structure. From the XRD pattern it is observed that Figs. 7.2b and 2c, corresponding to CN15 and CN30, are exactly the same. The average size of particles (D) were calculated using Debye-Scherrer equation [31].

$$D = K\lambda / \beta \cos\theta \qquad (1)$$

where the value of K is equal to 0.89, λ is the wavelength of X-ray (1.54A°), β is the full width at half maximum and θ is the half of the diffraction angle, the values obtained for CN45 is 13.5 and for CN 30 and CN 15 is 18 nm.

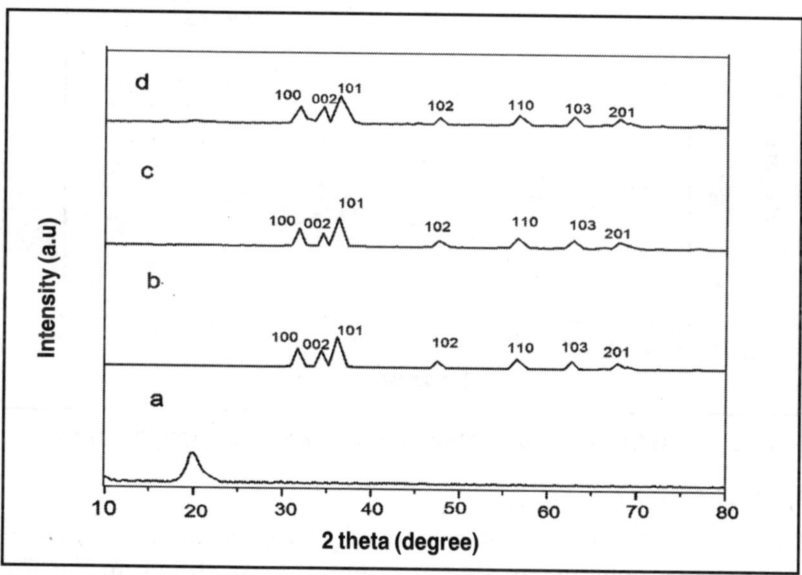

Fig. 7.2: **The XRD patterns of (a) pure chitosan powder (C) (b) CN15 (c) CN30 and (d) CN45**

Thermo Gravimetric Analysis

Thermo gravimetric analysis was used to characterise the thermal properties of chitosan and nano ZnO composites and is illustrated in Fig. 7.3. As shown in Fig. 7.3, pure chitosan (C) has different decomposition trend as compared to corresponding composite powder. However, the three composites: *(i)* CN15, *(ii)* CN30 and *(iii)* CN45, show the same decomposition trend. Pure chitosan polymer exhibited a two-step mass loss. The first stage of mass loss observed, up to 140°C, was attributed to the loss of hydrated water and the second stage of mass loss observed in between 290 and 500°C was due to the final degradation of the polymer [32]. However, the composites did not show considerable amount of mass loss below 150°C but in between 240-450°C they show significant mass loss due to the decomposition of polymer matrix [33]. The residual mass percentage of the pure chitosan (C) and composites (CN15, CN30 and CN45) at 750°C are respectively 20, 75, 72 and 70 per cent and the excess residual components indicate the presence of ZnO particles in the polymer matrix. The results also prove that irrespective of change in concentration of NaOH, the polymer matrix contain almost similar amount of ZnO particles and the curves are in agreement with the XRD analysis results.

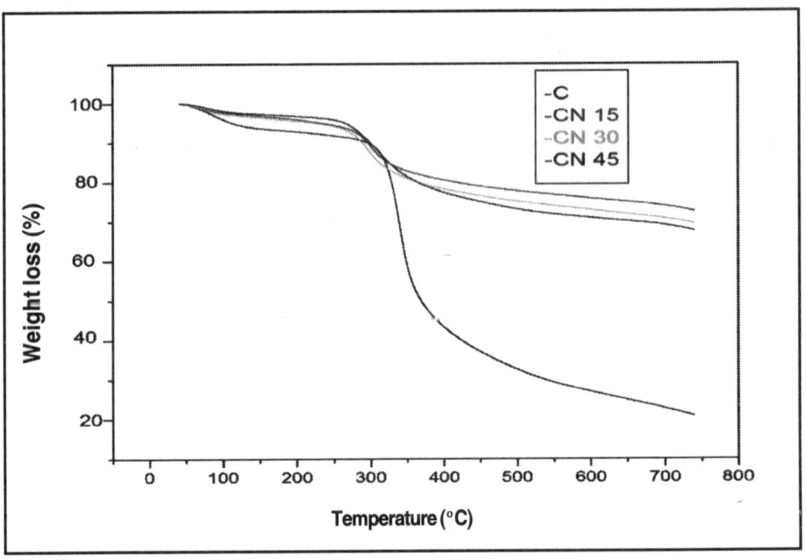

Fig. 7.3: **TGA curves of pure chitosan and nano-ZnO composite powders**

UV-Visible Spectral Analysis

The UV-Visible absorption spectra of pure chitosan and chitosan nano-ZnO composites powder are shown in Fig. 7.4. As shown in Fig. 7.4a, the absorption of pure chitosan powder is lower as compared to chitosan composites. The absorption peak of pure chitosan is lower than 300 nm due the absence of conjugated double bonds in the molecules. Compared to pure chitosan powder a sharp increase in absorbance below 380 nm is observed in Fig. 7.4b, c and d indicating the presence of nano zinc oxide particles in the chitosan matrix. The wave length corresponding to maximum absorbance was recorded at 348 nm for CN45 (b), at 335 nm for CN30 (c) and at 338 nm for CN15 (d) and these values is lower than that of the micro-crystalline ZnO (about 372 nm) [19]. It has been reported that UV-absorbance of ZnO nanoparticles is a size dependent property; when the size of nanoparticle is decreased, reduction in absorbance and blue shift into lower wavelength are observed [34]. Similarly due to the agglomeration of nanoparticles red shift in the wavelength is observed [35]. As shown in Fig. 7.4 the three composites show similar absorbance and their value of λ_{max} is almost close to each other supporting the XRD analysis results.

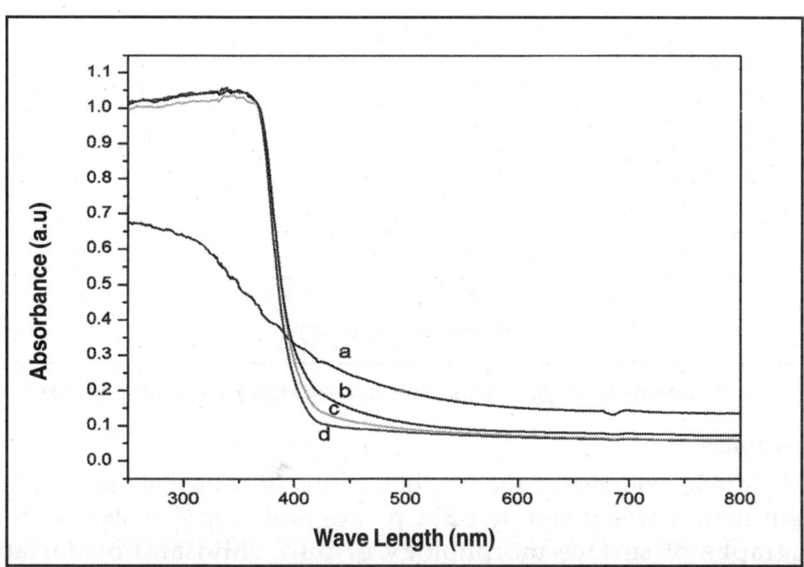

Fig. 7.4: UV-Visible absorbance spectra ; pure chitosan (a) CN 45 (b) CN 30 (c) and CN15(d)

Energy Band Gap of Chitosan–ZnO Nanoparticles

One of the major applications of semiconductor metal oxides or sulphides is their ability to function as photo catalyst. An ideal photo catalyst would have band gap energy in the visible region and long resistivity towards the photo corrosion reactions. The band gap energy of semi-conductor materials depend upon the size of particles. The structure and size of nano semiconductor particles can be tuned by varying the synthesis methods and reaction conditions, similarly photo corrosion can be reduced by dispersing the nanoparticles in the polymer matrix [36-38].

The band gap energy of chitosan-nanoZnO composites powder was measured from absorption spectra using the following equation [40]:

$$(\alpha h\gamma)^2 = E_D(h\gamma - E_g) \qquad (2)$$

where α is the optical absorption co-efficient, $h\gamma$ is the photon energy, E_g is the direct band gap and E_D is a constant. The Y intercept of the linear plot of $(\alpha h\gamma)^2$ *vs.* $h\gamma$ will give the value of direct band gap energy $(e._g)$. As shown in Fig. 7.5 it is interesting to note that nano ZnO particles in all the three composites studied has the same value of band gap energy (3.28eV), agrees very well with the reported values [39, 40].

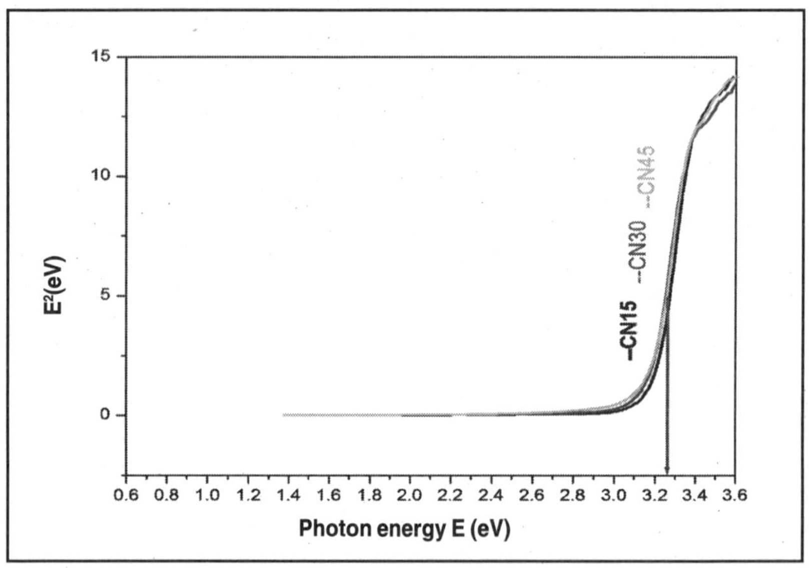

Fig. 7.5 **Energy band gap of three chitosan–ZnO nanocomposite powders**

SEM Analysis

The direct evidence of the immobilization of nano-ZnO particles in the chitosan matrix was given by SEM photograph. Fig. 7.6 shows the SEM photographs of surface morphology of pure chitosan powder and its composites CN45, CN30 and CN15. As shown in Fig. 7.6a, the surface of the chitosan was rather smooth. However, during the in situ formation of composite, the nano ZnO particles break the smooth surface of chitosan and are get impregnated over the matrix. SEM images shown in Figs. 7.6b-d clearly display the formation of nano ZnO particles, but the distribution of particles are varying when concentration of NaOH was changed. In CN45 (Fig. 7.6b) and CN15 (Fig. 7.6d) the agglomeration of rod like particles are taking place where as in CN30 (Fig. 7.6c) ZnO nano-rods are clearly seen with well defined boundaries.

Antimicrobial Properties

The antibacterial properties of composites were measured by Agar well diffusion method. The test was done against Gram negative bacteria (E. coli) and Gram positive bacteria (S. aureus). Figs. 7.7a and b exhibit the antimicrobial activity of pure chitosan (C), CN 45, CN 30 and CN 15 against E. coli and S.aureus respectively. The results of the activity of the pure chitosan and its composites against two pathogens E.coli and S.aureus were presented in Table 7.1. Figs 7.8a and b exhibit the antimicrobial activity of composites against clinical pathogens and Table 7.2 shows the results.

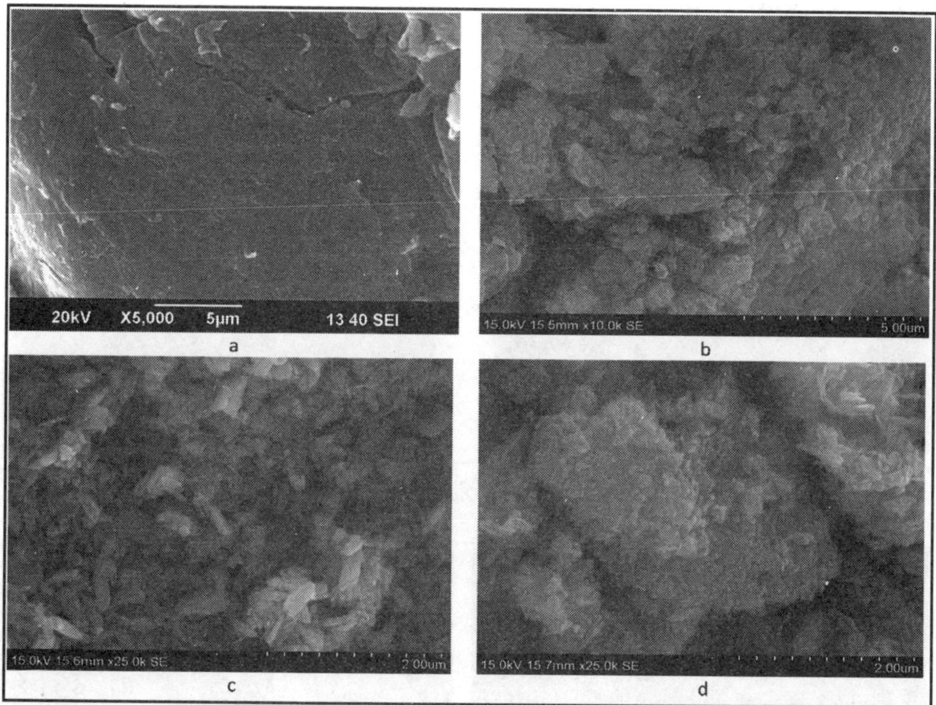

Fig. 7.6: **Scanning electron microscopy of pure chitosan C (a), CN 45 (b), CN 30 (c) and CN 15 (d)**

Table 7.1: Values of inhibition zone diameter of paper disc of E. coli and S. aureus

Sample	Inhibition Zone Diameter (mm)	
	E. coli	S. aureus
Control	0	0
Chitosan	7	5
CN15	13	10
CN30	12	11
CN45	15	12

Table 7.2: Values of inhibition zone diameter of paper disc

Sample	Inhibition Zone Diameter (mm)	
	E. coli	S. aureus
Control	0.0	0.0
Chitosan (pure)	7	5
CN 15	13	10
CN 30	12	11
CN 45	15	12

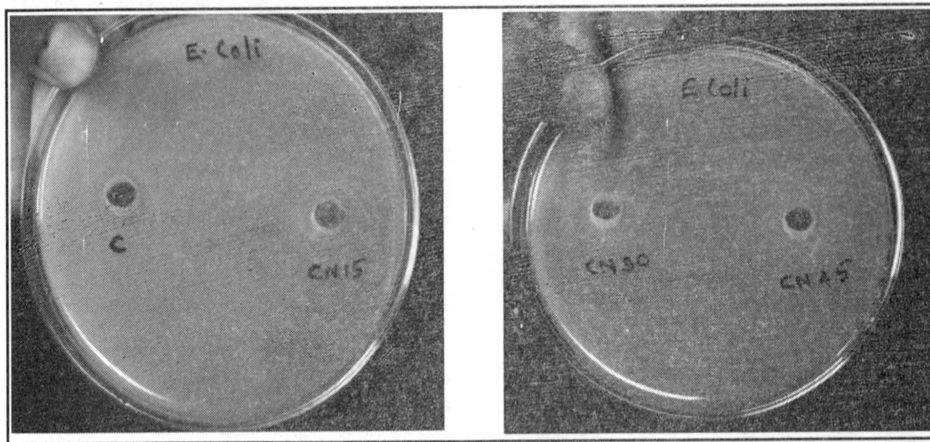

Fig. 7. 7a: **Anti microbial activity against E.coli - pure chitosan-(C), CN15, CN30 and CN 45**

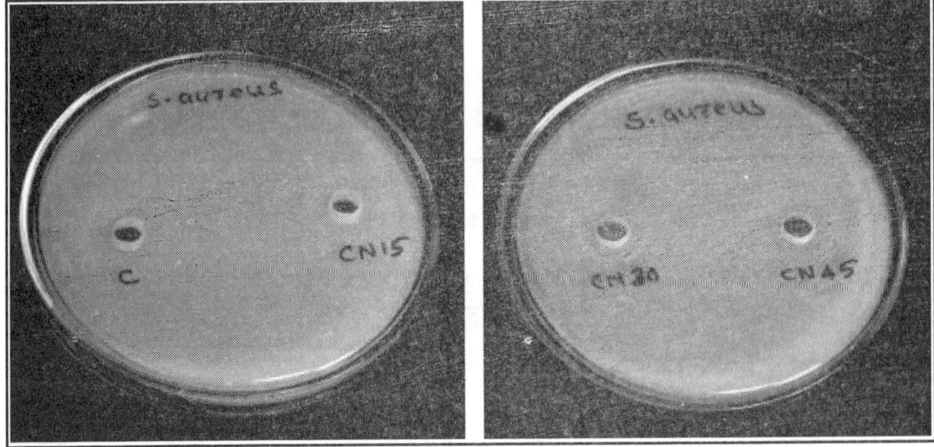

Fig. 7.7b: **Anti microbial activity against S.aureus pure chitosan-(C), CN15, CN30 and CN 45**

The data show that chitosan ZnO composite has enhanced antimicrobial activity as compared to pure chitosan, the augmentation in anti-microbial activity of composites in the presence of nano ZnO was due to the reactive oxygen species (ROS) produced by nano-ZnO particles. According to the observations reported in the literature, the ROS and Zn^{2+} ions attack the negatively charged bacterial cell wall and results the leakage of cell wall, finally the death of pathogens. The composites showed higher activity towards E.coli, compared to S.aureus, this may be due to the presence of a thick layer of peptide glycans in the cell wall of S.aureus [41]. Figures 7.7 and 7.8 also show that the composites are active against standard and clinical samples as well, but reduction of diameter in disc diffusion method may be due to lack of diffusion antimicrobes through the media.

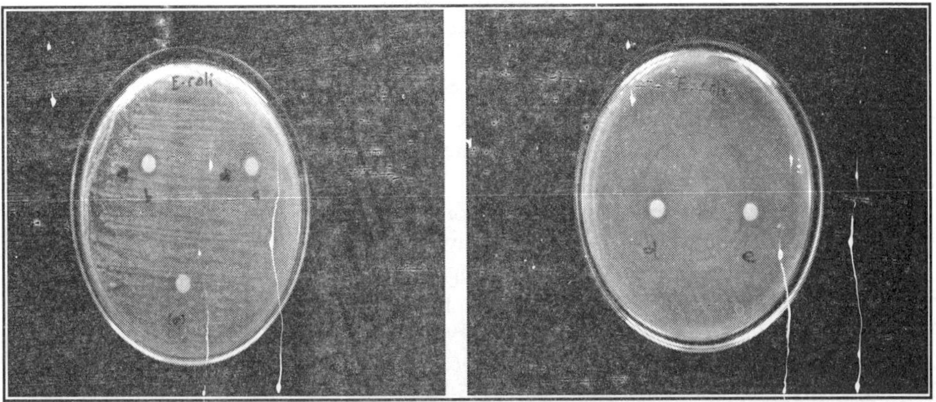

Fig. 7.8a: **Anti microbial activity against E.coli - controle (a) , pure chitosan-C(b), CN15 (c), CN30 (d) and CN 45(e)**

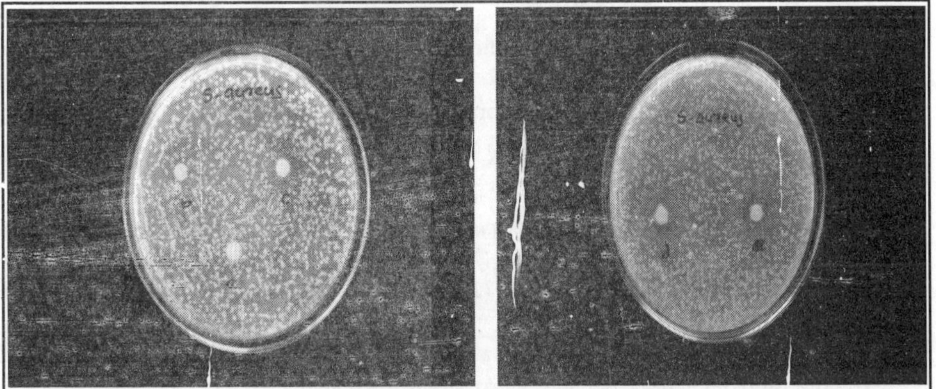

Fig. 7.8b: **Anti microbial activity against S.aureus - controle (a), pure chitosan -C(b), CN15 (c), CN30 (d) and CN 45(e)**

Conclusion

Chitosan/nano-ZnO composite powder was prepared through a simple and facile in situ method. The immobilization of nano ZnO on the chitosan matrix was endorsed by FTIR and UV-Visible spectrum. The thermal stability of the composite was examined by TG. The particle size and the structure of ZnO were determined by XRD analysis. The existence of particle and their sizes were determined from SEM photographs. Band gap energy of the composite was determined from UV-Visible spectral analysis. The antibacterial efficacy of composites against E.coli and S.aureus were tested using Zone inhibition method. It was proved that this composite has excellent antibacterial activity and could be used as natural anti-microbial agent and photo catalyst.

REFERENCES

1. Fereidoon Shahidi, Janak Kamil, Vidana Arachchi, You-Jin Jeon, Food Applications of Chitin and Chitosans, *Trends in Food Sci. Tech.* 10 (1999) 37-51.
2. R. Khan, A.Kaushik, P.R. Solanki, M.K. Pandey, A.A Ansari, B.D. Malhotra, Zinc Oxide Nanoparticles-chitosan Composite film for Cholesterol Biosensor, *Anal. Chem. Acta* 616(2008) 207-213.
3. Chayannan Petchthanasombat, Tinnakorn, Tiensing, Panya Sunintaboon, Synthesis of zinc Oxide – Encapsulated Poly (methyl methacrylate)-chitosan core – shell hybrid Particles and their Electro Chemical Property, *J. Colloid Interface Sci.* 369 (2012) 52-57.
4. Kanikireddy Vimala, Yallapu Murali Mohan, Kokkarachedu Varprasad, Nagireddy, Narayana Reddy, Sakey Ravindra, Neppalli Sudhakar Raju, Fabrication of curcumin encapsulated chitosan-PVA Silver Nanocomposite Films for Improved Antimicrobial Activity, *J. Biomet. Nanobiotech.* (2011) 55-64.
5. Manjusha Mathew, S. Sureshkumar, N. Sandhyarani, Synthesis and Characterization of Gold–Chitosan Nanocomposite and Application of Resultant Nanocomposite in Sensors, Colloids and Surfaces B: Biointerfaces 93 (2012) 143-147.
6. Ru Jianga, Huayue Zhu, Jun Yao, Yongqian Fu, Yujiang Guan, Chitosan Hydrogel Films as a Template for Mild Biosynthesis of CdS quantum dots with Highly Efficient Photo Catalytic Activity, *Appl. Surface Sci.* 258 (2012) 3513-3518.
7. Jiang Ru, Zhu Huayue, Li Xiaodong, Xiao Ling, Visible Light Photocatalytic Decolourization of C. I. Acid Red 66 by chitosan capped CdS Composite Banoparticles, *Chem. Eng. J.* 152 (2009) 537-542.
8. Huayue Zhu, Ru Jiang, Ling Xiao, Yuhua Chang, Yujiang Guan, Xiaodong Li, Guangming Zeng, Photo Catalytic Decolorization and Degradation of Congo Red on Innovative Crosslinked Chitosan/nano-CdS composite Catalyst under Visible Light Irradiation, *J. Hazard. Mat.* 169 (2009) 933-940.
9. Jocilene D. Torres, Elaine A. Faria, Jurandir R. SouzaDe, Alexandre G.S. Prado, Preparation of photoactive chitosan–niobium (V) Oxide Composites for Dye Degradation, *J. Photochem. Photobio. A: Chem.* 182 (2006) 202-206.
10. Jin-Yi Chen, Pei-Jiang Zhou, Jia-Lin Li, Studies on the Photocatalytic Performance of Cuprous Oxide/chitosan Nanocomposites Activated by Visible Light, *Carbohydr. Polym.* 72 (2008) 128-132.
11. Wei Zhang, Tao Yang, Da Ming, Kui Jiao, Electro Chemical Sensing DNA Immobilization and Hybridization based on Carbon Nanotubes/nano zinc oxide/ chitosan Composite Film, *Chin. Chem. Lett.* 19 (2008) 589-591.
12. Raziyeh Saehi, Mokhtar Arami, Niyas Mohammed Mahamoodi, Hajirm Bahrami, Shooka Khorramfar, Novel Biocompatible Composite (Chitosan-zinc oxide nanoparticles): Preparation, Characterization and dye Adsorption Properties, Colloids and Surface B: Biointerfaces 80 (2010) 86-93.
13. Eryun Yan, Cheng Wang, Shuhong Wang, Liguo sun, yuweiWang, Liquan Fan, Deqing Zhang, Synthesis and Charectrization of Fluorescent Chitosan-ZnO hybrid nanosheres, *Mat. Sci. Eng. B* 176(2011) 458-461.
14. Shirpa Tripathi, G.K. Mehrotra, P.K. Dutta, Chitosan-silver Oxide Nanocomposite Film: Preperation and Antimicrobial Activity, *Bull. Mater. Sci.* 34(2011) 29-35.
15. S. Honary, K. Ghajar, P. Khazaeli, P. Shalchian, Preparation, Characterization and Antibacterial Properties of Silver-chitosan Nanocomposites using different Molecular Weight Grades of Chitosan, *Tropical J. Pharmaceut. Res.* 10(2011)69-74.

16. Somanath Ghosh, Tasneem Kauser Ranebennur, H.N. Vasan, Study of Antimicrobial Efficacy of Hybrid Chitosan-Silver Nanoparticles for Prevention of Specific Biofilm and Water Purification, *Int. J. Carbohydr. Chem.* 1 (2011) 1-11. doi:10.1155/2011/693759.
17. Kimleang Khun, Zafar Hussain Ibupoto, Mohamad S. AlSalhi, Muhammad Atif, Anees A. Ansari, Magnus Willander, Fabrication of well-aligned ZnO nanorods using a Composite Seed Layer of ZnO Nanoparticles and Chitosan Polymer, Materials 6(2013) 4361-74.
18. A.El. Shafei, A. Abou-Okeil, ZnO-carboxymethyl Chitosan bionano-composite to Impart Antimicrobial and UV Protection for Cotton Fabric, *Carbohydr. Polym.* 83 (2013) 920-925.
19. Li-Hua Li, Jian-Cheng Deng, Hui-Ren Deng, Zi-Ling Liu, Lin Xin, Synthesis and Characterization of Chitosan/ZnO Nanoparticle Composite Membranes, Carbohydr. Res. 345(2010) 994-8.
20. Yan Wang, Qun Zhang, Chen-lu Zhang, Ping Li, Characterisation and Co-operative Antimicrobial Properties of Chitosan/nano-ZnO Composite Nanofibrous Membranes, *Food Chem.* 132 (2012) 419-27.
21. Yuvaraj Haldorai, Jae-Jin Shim, Chitosan-zinc Oxide Hybrid Composite, for Enhanced dye Degradation and Antibacterial Activity, *Composite Interfaces* 20(2013)365-377.
22. R. Rajendran, C. Balakumar, H.A. Mohammed Ahammed, S. Jayakumar, K. Vaideki, E.M. Rajesh, Use of zinc Oxide Nano Particles for Production of Antimicrobial Textiles, *Int. J. Eng. Sci. Technol.* 2(2010)202-208.
23. Y. Pranoto, S.K. Rakshit, V.M. Salokhe, Enhancing Antimicrobial Activity of Chitosan Films by Incorporating Garlic Oil, Potassium Sorbate and Nisin, LWT-Food Sci. Tech. 38 (2005) 859-65.
24. F. Devlieghere, A. Vermeulen, J. Debevere, Chitosan: Antimicrobial Activity, Interactions With Food Components and Applicability as a Coating on Fruit and Vegetables, *Food Microbio.* 21 (2004) 703-714.
25. I. Leceta, P. Guerrero, I. Ibarburu, M.T. Dueñas, K. de la Caba, Characterization and Antimicrobial Analysis of Chitosan-based Films, *J. Food Eng.* 116 (2013) 889-899.
26. M. Pereda, A.G. Ponce, N.E. Marcovich, R.A. Ruseckaite, J.F. Martucci, Chitosan-gelatin Composites and Bi-layer Films with Potential Antimicrobial Activity, *Food Hydrocolloids* 25 (2011) 1372-1381.
27. Asmaa Farouk, Shaaban Moussa, Mathias Ulbricht, Torsten Textor, ZnO Nanoparticles-Chitosan Composite as Antibacterial Finish for Textiles, *Int. J. Carbohydr. Chem.* 2012, Article ID 693629.
28. A. Pawlak, M. Mucha, Thermogravimetric and FTIR studies of Chitosan Blends, Thermochim. Acta 396 (2003) 153-166.
29. P. Bhadra, M.K. Mitra, G.C. Das, R. Dey, S. Mukherjee, Interaction of Chitosan Capped ZnO Nanorods with Escherichia Coli, *Materials Sci. Eng.* C 31(2011) 929-937.
30. Shahram Moradi Dehaghi, Bahar Rahmanifar, Ali Mashinchian Parviz, Aberoomand Azar, Removal of Permethrin Pesticide from Water by Chitosan–zinc Oxide Nanoparticles Composite as An Adsorbent. *J. Saudi Chem. Soc.* (2014). doi: 10.1016/j.jscs.2014.01.004.
31. T. Sheela, Y. Arthoba Nayaka, R.Viswanatha, S.Bavanna, T.G. Venkatesha, Kinetics and thermodynamic Studies on the Adsorption of Zn(ll), Cd (ll) and Hg(ll) Aqueous Solution using Zinc Oxide Nanoparticles, Powder Tech. 217(2012)163-170.

32. A.P. Martínez-Camacho, M.O. Cortez-Rocha, J.M. Ezquerra-Brauer, A.Z. Graciano-Verdugo, F. Rodriguez-Félix, M.M. Castillo-Ortega, M.S. Yépiz-Gómez, M. Plascencia-Jatomea, Chitosan Composite Films: Thermal, structural, mechanical and antifungal properties, Carbohydr. Polym. 82 (2010) 305-315.
33. Huayue Zhu, Ru Jiang, Yongqian Fu, Yujiang Guan, Jun Yao, Ling Xiao, Guangming Zeng, Effective Photocatalytic Decolorization of Methyl Orange Utilizing TiO2/ZnO/chitosan Nanocomposite Films under Simulated Solar Irradiation, Desalination 286 (2012) 41-48.
34. E.G. Goh, X. Xu, P.G. McCormick, Effect of Particle Size on the UV Absorbance of Zinc Oxide Nanoparticles, *Scripta Materialia* 78-79 (2014) 49-52.
35. Surabhi Siva Kumar, Putcha Venkateswarlu, Vanka Ranga Rao, Gollapalli Nageswara Rao, Synthesis, Characterization and Optical Properties of Zinc Oxide Nanoparticles, *Int. J. Nano Lett.* 2013, doi:10.1186/2228-5326-3-30.
36. Huayue Zhu, Ru Jiang, Yongqian Fu, Yujiang Guan, Jun Yao, Ling Xiao, Guangming Zeng, Effective Photocatalytic Decolorization of Methyl Orange Utilizing TiO2/ZnO/chitosan Nanocomposite Films under Simulated Solar Irradiation, *Desalination* 286 (2012) 41-48.
37. Nayereh Soltani, Elias Saion, W. Mahmood Mat Yunus, Maryam Erfani, Manizheh Navasery, Ghazaleh Bahmanrokh, Kadijeh Rezaee, Enhancement of Visible Light Photocatalytic Activity of ZnS and CdS Nanoparticles based on Organic and Inorganic Coating, *Appl. Surface Sci.* 290 (2014) 440-447.
38. Jiang Ru, Zhu Huayue, Li Xiaodong, Xiao Ling, Visible Light Photo catalytic Decolourization of C.I. Acid Red 66 by chitosan capped CdS composite Nanoparticles, *Chem. Eng. J.* 152 (2009) 537-542.
39. S. Anandhavelu, S. Thambidurai, Effect of zinc chloride and sodium hydroxide Concentration on the Optical Property of Chitosan-ZnO nanostructure Prepared in Chitin Deacetylation, *Mat. Chem. Phys.* 131 (2011) 449-454.
40. Jocilene D. Torres, Elaine A. Faria, Jurandir R. SouzaDe, Alexandre G.S. Prado, Preparation of Photoactive Chitosan–niobium (V) Oxide Composites for dye Degradation, *J. chem. Photobio. A: Chem.* 182 (2006) 202-206.
41. P.T. Sudheesh Kumar, Vinoth-Kumar Lakshmanan, T.V. Anilkumar, C. Ramya, P. Reshmi A.G. Unnikrishnan, Shantikumar V. Nair, R. Jayakumar, Flexible and Microporous Chitosan Hydrogel/Nano ZnO Composite Bandages for Wound Dressing: In Vitro and In Vivo Evaluation, ACS Appl. Mater. Interfaces 4(2012): 2618'29.

Pages 141-157

HEAVY METALS AND METALLOIDS IN BIOSPHERE: *IMPACTS AND ASSESSMENT*
***Edited by*: Dr. Avnish Chauhan; Dr. Sandeep Gupta & Dr. Pawan Kumar Bharti**
***Edition* : 2017**
ISBN : 978-93-5056-860-6
***Published by*: Discovery Publishing House Pvt. Ltd., New Delhi (India)**

Fluoride - Harmful or Beneficial

A Report on Fluoride in Rajasthan, India

Ranjeeta Soni

ABSTRACT

Fluoridation is a very common problem all over India but in Rajasthan it is up to threat level because excess of fluoride is available in drinking water. Rajasthan all 32 districts are suffered from Fluorosis diseases but 18 districts are fluoride prone areas. Fluoride is beneficial for health if the concentration of the fluoride ion (CF) in drinking water is less than 1.5 mg/L (WHO 1994). Various studies found many kinds of adverse effects of fluoride on human health. Fluoride when consumed in excess can cause several other kinds of manifestations like: dental, skeletal, and non-skeletal fluorosis. Dental fluorosis produces widespread brown stains on teeth and may cause pitting. Skeletal Fluorosis causes crippling and severe pain and stiffness of the backbone and joints (Bulusu and Nawlakhe, 1992). In non-skeltal fluorosis causes various disorders like: Neurological, Muscular, Allergic, Gastro-intestinal, and Urinary diseases. In For removal of excess of fluoride from drinking water many adsorbents are using from previous years but along with many demerits associated with these. But still we have not got perfect method.

Keywords: fluoride, drinking water, fluorosis, defluoridation, dental, skeletal, non-skeletal, health.

INTRODUCTION

Fluorine, the 13th most abundant element of the earth's crust, represents about 0.3g/kg of earth's crust. Its molecular weight is 19 and atomic number is 9. It occurs mainly in the form of chemical compounds such as: sodium fluoride

Department of Sciences, Jagannath University Chaksu, Jaipur, Rajasthan, India.

or hydrogen fluoride, which are present in minerals fluorspar fluorapatite, topaz and cryolite. The physicochemical properties of fluorides available in the form of sodium fluoride and hydrogen fluoride are given in Table. 8.1. In India, fluorite and topaz are widespread and contain a high percentage of fluoride. Fluoride pollution in the environment occurs through two channels, namely: natural and anthropogenic sources (Cengeloglu *et al.* 2002).

Fluoride is frequently encountered in minerals and in geochemical deposits and is generally released into subsoil water sources by slow natural degradation of fluorine contained in rocks. Fluorine is an important element for human beings, as it helps in growth and prevents the enamel of the teeth from dissolving under acidic conditions. Various dietary components influence the absorption of fluorides from gastrointestinal tract and the absorbed fluorides are distributed throughout the body. Drinking water and sea food are good sources of fluoride. Fluoride is beneficial to health if the concentration (CF) of the fluoride ion (F-) in drinking water is less than 1.5 mg/L (WHO 1994). A higher concentration causes serious health hazards. The disease caused manifests itself in three forms, namely: dental, skeletal, and non-skeletal fluorosis. Dental fluorosis produces widespread brown stains on teeth and may cause pitting (Bulusu and Nawlakhe, 1992). Skeletal fluorosis causes crippling and severe pain and stiffness of the backbone and joints (Bulusu and Nawlakhe, 1992). Even though extensive studies have been conducted, there seems to be no effective cure for these diseases. Therefore, it is desirable to drink water having a fluoride concentration less than certain value. Hence, drinking water with CF > 1.5 mg/L (1 mg/L in India) needs treatment (WHO 1994).

Table 81: Physicochemical properties of common forms of fluoride

Property	Sodium Fluoride (NaF)	Hydrogen Fluoride (HF)
Physical state	White, crystalline powder	Colour less liquid or gas with biting smell
Density (g/cm3)	2.56	–
Water solubility	42g/L at10°C	Readily soluble below 20°C
Acidity	–	Strong acid in liquid form; weak acid when dissolved in water

Source: Pranab Kumar Rakshit, 2004.

Fluoride in Water: An Overview

Throughout many parts of the world, high concentrations of fluoride occurring naturally in groundwater and coal have caused widespread fluorosis - a serious bone disease - among local populations. A range of everyday products, notably toothpaste and drinking water, the fluoride in small doses has no adverse effects on health to offset its proven benefits in preventing dental decay. But more and more scientists are now seriously questioning the benefits of fluoride, even in small amounts (UNICEF Report, 1980). Since some fluoride compounds in the earth's upper crust are soluble in water, fluoride is found in both surface waters and groundwater. In surface freshwater, however, fluoride concentrations are usually low - 0.01 ppm to 0.3 ppm.

In groundwater, the natural concentration of fluoride depends on the geological, chemical and physical characteristics of the aquifer, the porosity and acidity of the soil and rocks, the temperature, the action of other chemical elements, and the depth of wells. Because of the large number of variables, the fluoride concentrations in groundwater can range from well under 1 ppm to more than 35 ppm. In Kenya and South Africa, the levels can exceed 25 ppm. In India, concentration up to 38.5 ppm has been reported in drinking water (UNICEF).

Table 8.2: Permissible limit of fluoride in drinking water prescribed by various organizations

Name of the Organization	Desirable Limit (mg/L)
Bureau of Indian Standards (BIS)	0.6-1.2
Indian Council of Medical Research (ICMR)	1.0
The Committee on Public Health Engineering Manual and Code of Practice, Government of India	1.0
World Health Organization (International Standards for Drinking Water)	1.5

Basic facts about Fluoride

Fluoride exists fairly abundantly in the earth's crust and can enter groundwater by natural processes; the soil at the foot of mountains is particularly likely to be high in fluoride from the weathering and leaching of bedrock with high fluoride content.

According to 1984 guidelines published by the World Health Organization (WHO) fluoride is an effective agent for preventing dental caries if taken in 'optimal' amounts. But a single 'optimal' level for daily intake cannot be agreed because the nutritional status of individuals, which varies greatly, influences the rate at which fluoride is absorbed by the body. A diet poor in calcium, for example, increases the body's retention of fluoride.

Water is a major source of fluoride intake. WHO (1984, guidelines) suggested that, areas with a warm climate, the optimal fluoride concentration in drinking water should remain below 1 mg/liter (1ppm or part per million), while in cooler climates it could go up to 1.2 mg/liter. The differentiation derives from the fact that we perspire more in hot weather and consequently drink more water. The guideline value (permissible upper limit) for fluoride in drinking water was set at 1.5 mg/liter, considered a threshold where the benefit of resistance to tooth decay did not yet shade into a significant risk of dental fluorosis.

In many countries, fluoride is purposely added to the water supply, toothpaste and sometimes other products to promote dental health. It should be noted that fluoride is also found in some foodstuffs and in the air (mostly from production of phosphate fertilizers or burning of fluoride-containing fuels), so the amount of fluoride people actually ingest may be higher than assumed.

It has long been known that excessive fluoride intake carries serious toxic effects. But scientists are now debating whether fluoride confers any benefit at all.

Fluoride: Good or Bad for Health?

Fluoride was first used to fight dental cavities in the 1940s, its effectiveness defended on two grounds:

- Fluoride inhibits enzymes that breed acid-producing oral bacteria whose acid eats away tooth enamel. This observation is valid, but some scientists now believe that the harmful impact of fluoride on other useful enzymes far outweighs the beneficial effect on caries prevention.
- Fluoride ions bind with calcium ions, strengthening tooth enamel as it forms in children. Many researchers now consider this more of an assumption than fact, because of conflicting evidence from studies in India and several other countries over the past 10 to 15 years. Nevertheless, agreement is universal that excessive fluoride intake leads to loss of calcium from the tooth matrix, aggravating cavity formation throughout life rather than remedying it, and so causing dental fluorosis. Severe, chronic and cumulative overexposure can cause the incurable crippling of skeletal fluorosis (A. Tiwari *et al.* 2009).

Symptoms of Fluorosis

Dental fluorosis, which is characterised by discolored, blackened, mottled or chalky-white teeth, is a clear indication of overexposure to fluoride during childhood when the teeth were developing. These effects are not apparent if the teeth were already fully grown prior to the fluoride overexposure; therefore, the fact that an adult may show no signs of dental fluorosis does not necessarily mean that his or her fluoride intake is within the safety limit.

Chronic intake of excessive fluoride can lead to the severe and permanent bone and joint deformations of skeletal fluorosis. Early symptoms include sporadic pain and stiffness of joints: headache, stomach-ache and muscle weakness can also be warning signs. The next stage is osteosclerosis (hardening and calcifying of the bones), and finally the spine, major joints, muscles and nervous system are damaged.

Whether dental or skeletal, fluorosis is irreversible and no treatment exists. The only remedy is prevention, by keeping fluoride intake within safe limits.

Fluorosis Worldwide

The latest information shows that fluorosis is endemic in at least 25 countries across the globe (Fig. 8.1). The total number of people affected is not known, but a conservative estimate would number in the tens of millions. In 1993, 15 of India's 32 states were identified as endemic for fluorosis. In Mexico, 5 million people (about 6% of the population) are affected by fluoride in groundwater. Fluorosis is prevalent in some parts of central and western China and caused not only by drinking fluoride in groundwater but also by breathing airborne fluoride released from the burning of fluoride-laden coal. Worldwide, such instances of industrial fluorosis are on the rise (UNICEF).

Some governments are not yet fully aware of the fluoride problem or convinced of its adverse impact on their populations. Efforts are therefore needed to support more research on the subject and promote systematic policy responses by governments.

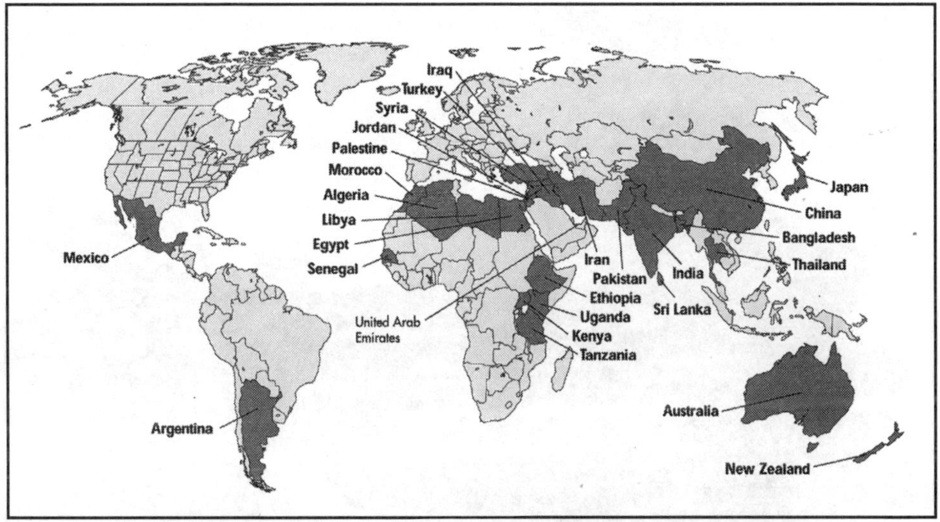

Fig. 8.1: **Endemic fluorosis in different countries of the World (UNICEF)**

Fluoride in India

India is among the many countries in the world, where fluoride contaminated ground water is creating health problems. Safe drinking water in rural areas of India is pre-dominantly dependent on groundwater sources, which are highly contaminated with fluoride. The concentrations in 17 States out of 32 are endemic for fluorosis being 1 to 48 mg/L. About 62 million people including 6 million children are affected with dental, skeletal and non-skeletal fluorosis.

This involves about 9000 villages affecting 30 million people (Nawlakhe and Paramasivam, 1993). It must be noted that the problem of excess fluoride in drinking water is of recent origin in most parts. Digging up of shallow aquifers for irrigation has resulted in declining levels of ground water. As a result, deeper aquifers are used, and the water in these aquifers contains a higher level of fluoride (Gupta and Sharma, 1995).

In India, the states of Andhra Pradesh, Bihar, Chhattisgarh, Haryana, Karnataka, Madhya Pradesh, Maharashtra, Orissa, Punjab, Rajasthan, Tamil Nadu, Uttar Pradesh and West Bengal are affected by fluoride contamination in water.

- *Worst affected*: Rajasthan and Gujarat in North India and Andhra in South India.
- *Moderately affected*: Punjab, Haryana, M.P. and Maharashtra.
- *Mildly affected*: T.N., W.B., U.P., Bihar and Assam.

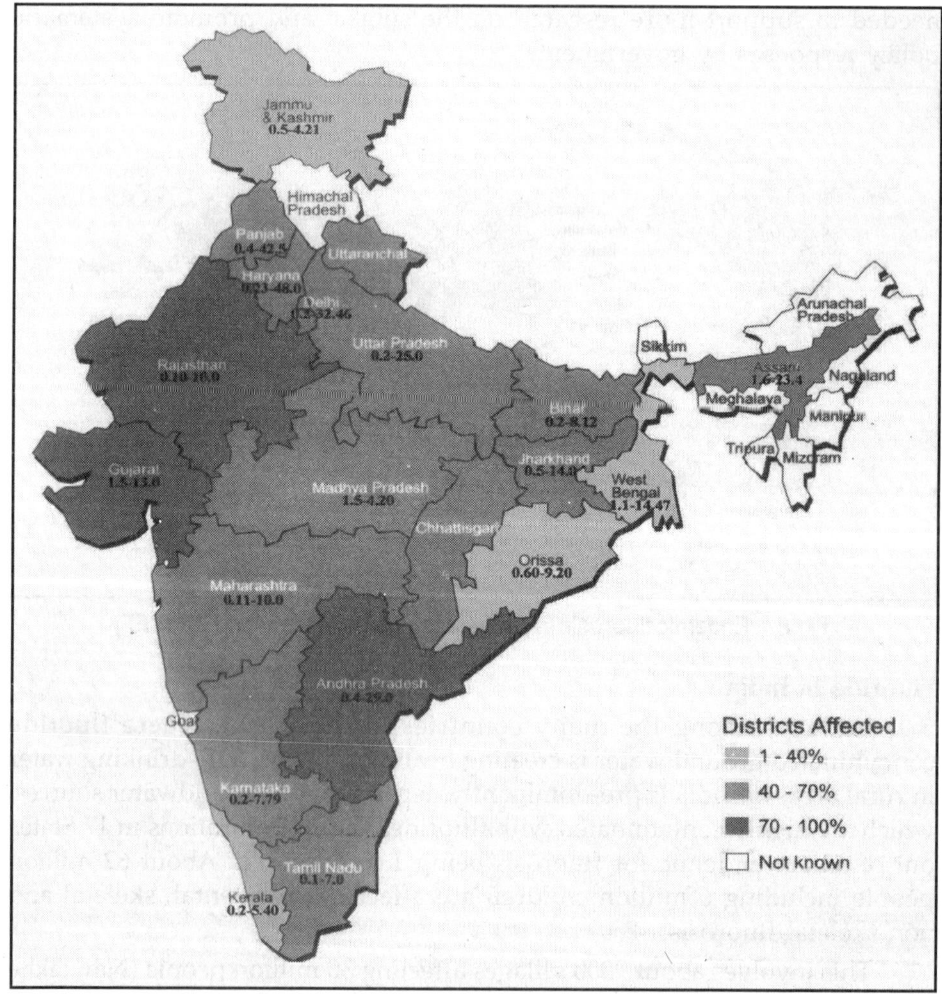

Fig. 8.2: **Fluoride affected states in India (UNICEF, New Delhi, 2001)**

Fluoride in Rajasthan

In Rajasthan the existence of fluorides was first detected in 1964 when a survey was under taken by state PHED in collaboration with NEERI on the basis of reports of some peculiar diseases. The concentration in ground water varied from as low as zero to 18.00ppm as maximum.

Fluorides make an entry in drinking water from indigenous rocks and ground water around the mica mines (Rajasthan has rich sources of mica). In the absence of perennial rivers, surface and canal system, groundwater remains the main source of drinking water. It contains 2 to 20 mg/L of fluoride. Fluoride is more common in ground water than in surface water. The main sources of fluoride in ground water are different fluoride bearing rocks. Fluoride ions are important in water supplies because of their peculiar characteristics. They cannot be tolerated in too low or too high concentration. A Fluoride concentration of approximately 0.5 mg/l to 1mg/l in drinking water effectively reduces dental caries or tooth decay without any harmful effects on health. Excess concentration of fluoride (more than 2 mg/l) causes dental fluorosis (disfigurement of the teeth) and harm to bony structures.

All the 32 districts of Rajasthan affected are from fluorosis. Nagour, Jaipur, Sikar, Jodhpur, Barmer, Ajmer, Sirohi, Jhunjhnu, Churu, Bikaner, Ganganagar districts have been declared as fluorosis prone areas. People in several districts in Rajasthan are consuming water with fluoride concentrations up to 24 mg/l. Rajasthan has more than 51 per cent of the affected villages in the country. The number of villages affected by fluoride has increased over time. In 1973, there were 1,871 villages with fluoride levels over 3mg/l. By 2001, this number had risen to 10,342 villages, an increase of more than five times. This makes Rajasthan the most severely affected state in India, with millions crippled as the result of consuming excessive amounts of fluoride (State Institute of Health and Family Welfare, Jaipur).

Various Health Impacts of Fluoride

Fluoride being an electronegative element and having a negative charge is attracted by positively charged ions like calcium (Ca^{++}). Bone and tooth having highest amount of calcium in the body attracts the maximum amount of fluoride and is deposited as Calcium Fluorapatite crystals. Intake of fluoride above 1.5 mg/L may lead to serious manifestations, which are described below:

Dental Fluorosis

Incidences of mottled teeth have been observed even with range of 0.7-1.5 mg F/l in drinking water. The minimal daily intake of fluoride that can cause very mild or mild fluorosis is estimated to be about 0.1 mg/kg body weight (P. Singh *et al.* 2011). Dental fluorosis is the loss of luster and shine of the dental enamel. The discoloration starts from white yellow, brown

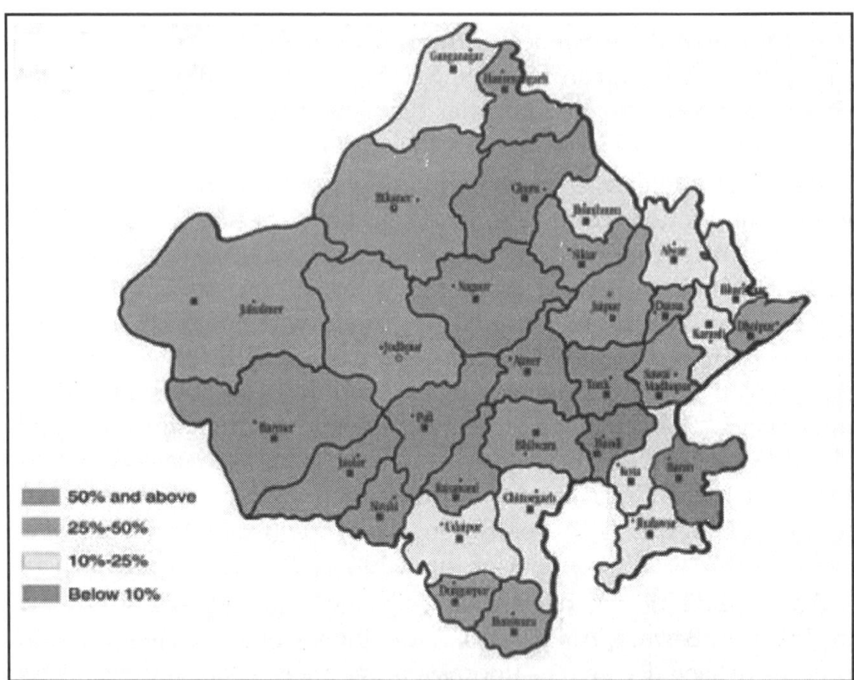

Fig. 8.3: **Fluoride affected districts in Rajasthan (2003)**

to black. (Discoloration is either as spots or horizontal streaks). Enamel matrix is laid down on incremental lines before and after birth. Hence dental fluorosis is invariably seen on horizontal lines or on bands on the surface of the teeth. Fluorosis is seen as mild, moderate and severe depending on the amount of fluoride ingested during the stages of formation of the teeth.

Teeth commonly affected by fluorosis are: central incisors, lateral incisors and the molars of the permanent dentition. It affects both the inner and the outer surfaces of teeth.

The symptoms of dental fluorosis are as given below:

1. Loss of teeth at early age.
2. Dullness of the teeth and loss of shine with developed white and yellow spots.
3. Discoloration of teeth, turning into brown and black streaks or spots on the enamel surface.
4. The teeth, once affected by dental fluorosis, cannot be reversed to normal. Only discolored teeth can be masked by the methods as prescribed below. Bleaching of teeth, Filling with high cure material and laminated veneering. Capping or crowning of teeth with metals like: chrome, cobalt, gold, porcelain and acrylic.

Skeletal Fluorosis

Excessive quantity of fluoride deposited in the skeleton, which is more in cancellous bone than cortical bone. Fluoride poisoning leads to severe pain associated with rigidity and restricted movements of cervical and lumber spine, knee and pelvic joints as well as shoulder joints. In severe cases of fluorosis, there is complete rigidity of the joints resulting in stiff spine described as 'bamboo spine', and immobile knee, pelvic and shoulder joints. Crippling deformity is associated with rigidity of joints and includes kyphosis, scoliosis, and flexion deformity of knee joints, paraplegia and quadriplegia. Skeletal fluorosis is an irreversible process as the dental fluorosis.

The symptoms of skeletal fluorosis are as given below:

1. Severe Pain in neck, back bone or joints.
2. Stiffness in the neck.
3. Rigidity in the hip region (pelvic girdle).
4. Construction of vertebral canal and inter vertebral forearm exerts pressure on nerves and blood vessels leading to paralysis and pain. The symptoms of dental and skeletal Fluorosis can easily view by following photographs:

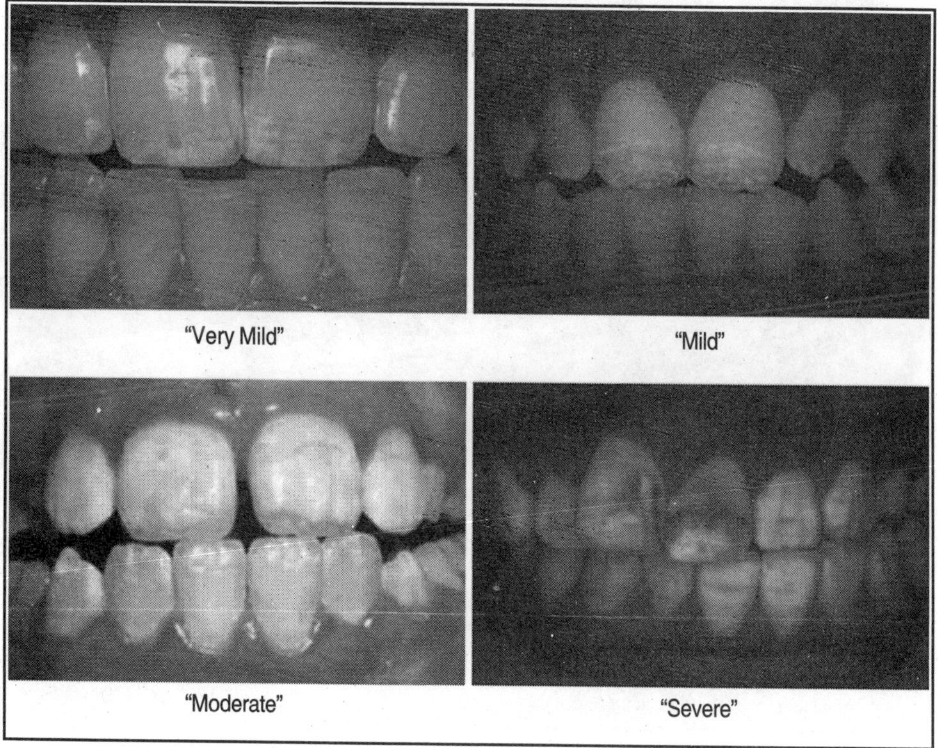

Fig. 8.4: **Dental Fluorosis**

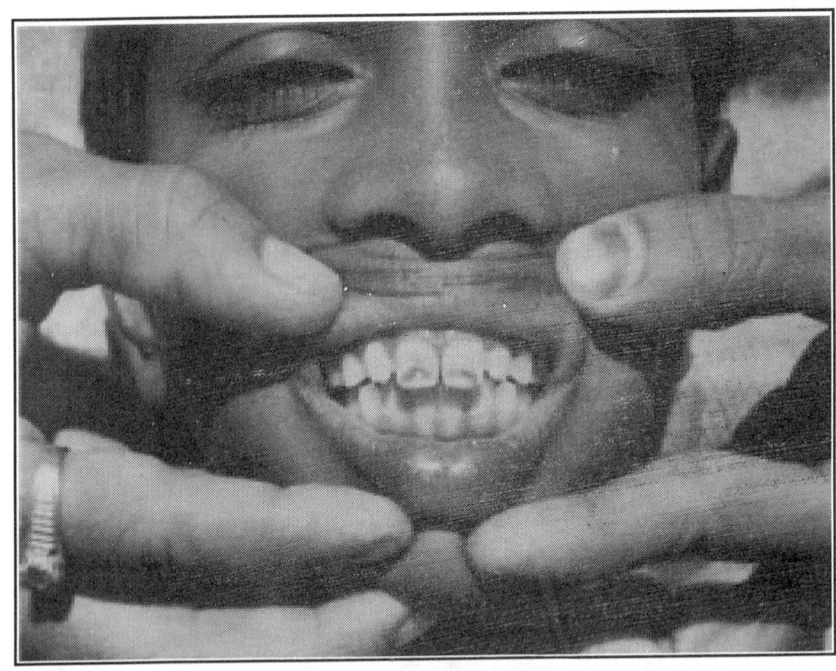

Fig. 8.5: **Dental Fluorosis**

Fig. 8.6: **Skeletal Fluorosis**

Fig. 8.7: **Skeletal Fluorosis**

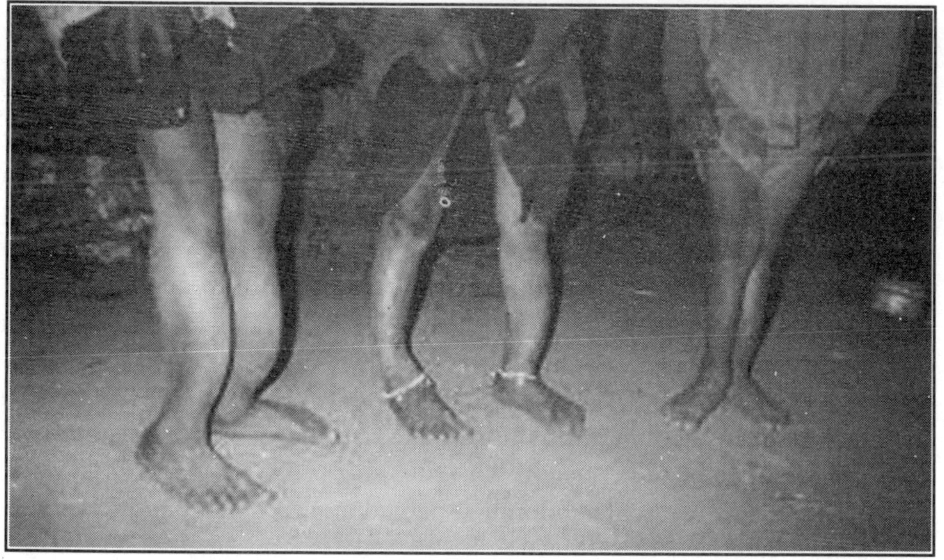

Fig. 8.8: **Skeletal Fluorosis**

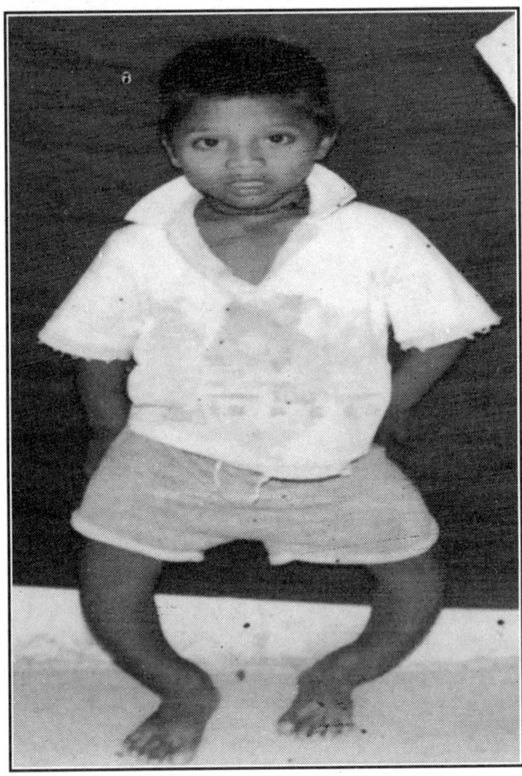

Fig. 8.9: **Skeletal Fluorosis**

Non-skeletal Fluorosis

This kind of fluorosis is often overlooked due to misconception that fluoride affects only bone and teeth. Fluoride when consumed in excess can cause several other kinds of manifestations.

- *Neurological:* Nervousness, depression, tingling sensation of fingers and toes, excessive thirst and tendency to urinate more frequently.
- *Muscular:* Muscle weakness, stiffness, pain in muscles and loss of muscle power.
- *Allergic:* Very painful skin rashes, which are perivascular inflammation prevalent in women and children, pinkish red or non-persistent oval shaped bluish - red spots on the skin.
- *Gastro-intestinal:* Acute abdominal pain, diarrhea, constipation, blood in stool tenderness in stomach.
- *Urinary tract:* Urine may be less in volume, red in colour and passed with itching and sensation.

Higher concentration of Fluoride can also damage a fetus, and adversely affect the IQ of children.

Table 8.3: Effects of fluoride concentration on human health

Concentration of Fluoride	Medium	Effects
1 ppm	Water	Dental caries reduction
2ppm or < 2ppm	Water	Mottled enamel (dental fluorosis)
8ppm	Water	10% osteosclerosis
20-80mg/day	Water or food	Crippling skeletal fluorosis
50ppm	Water or food	Thyroid changes
100ppm	Water or food	Growth retardation
125ppm	Water or food	Kidney changes
2.5-5.0ppm	Acute dose	Death

Drug induced Fluorosis

The prolonged use of drugs containing sodium fluoride is known to cause skeletal fluorosis. During 1982, two cases of drug induced skeletal fluorosis were reported from Switzerland. Patients of rheumatoid arthritis received uninterrupted and prolonged treatment with niflumic acid. The daily dose of drug administered was 3 capsules of 250 mg niflumic acid (Nifluril, UPSA Laboratories, France).

Fluoridated toothpastes and mouth rinses recommended for mouth hygiene may cause drug induced fluorosis, particularly if the user is exposed to high fluoride water consumption. The blood vessels in the oral mucosa and the sublingual blood vessel absorb fluoride from these preparations. The commercial mouth rinses are generally fluoridated preparations with very high fluoride content.

Industrial Fluorosis

Industrial fluorosis is a serious problem in the developed western and other industrialized countries. However, due to rapid industrialization in India, the problem of industrial fluorosis is reaching an alarming state and is compounding the problem of endemic, water and food borne fluorosis (Anurag Tewari and Ashutosh Dubey, 2009).

A number of industries use hydrofluoric acid and fluoride containing salts, in the different sections of an industry for one reason or other. The industries that use fluoride are:

1. Aluminum.
2. Steel.
3. Enamel.

4. Pottery.
5. Glass.
6. Bricks.
7. Phosphate Fertilizer.
8. Welding.
9. Refrigeration.
10. Rust Removal.
11. Oil Refinery.
12 Plastic.
13 Pharmaceutical.
14 Tooth paste.
15 Chemical Industries.
16 Automobile Industry etc.

Fluoride dust and fumes pollute the environment; inhaling the dust and fumes is as dangerous as consuming fluoride containing food, water or drugs.

Preventing Fluoride Poisoning

Fluoride poisoning can be prevented or minimized by using alternative water sources, by removing excessive fluoride from drinking water, and by improving the nutritional status of populations at risk.

Alternative Water Sources

Alternative water sources include surface water, rainwater, and low-fluoride groundwater.

- *Surface water:* Particular caution is required when opting for surface water, since it is often heavily contaminated with biological and chemical pollutants. Surface water should not be used for drinking without treatment and disinfection. Many water treatment technologies are available, but the most effective are usually too expensive and complex for application in poor communities. Simple and low-cost technologies, such as: sand filtration, ultraviolet water disinfection or chlorine water disinfection, are adequate in some but not all cases. Community capacity is an essential factor in ensuring successful utilization of these technologies. Water chlorination at household level is widely used only in emergencies.
- *Rainwater:* Rainwater is usually a much cleaner water source and may provide a low-cost simple solution. The problem, however, is limited storage capacity in communities or households. Large storage reservoirs are needed because annual rainfall is extremely uneven in tropical and subtropical regions. Such reservoirs are expensive to build and require large amounts of space.

- *Low-fluoride groundwater:* Fluoride content can vary greatly in wells in the same area, depending on the geological structure of the aquifer and the depth at which water is drawn. Deepening tube wells or sinking new wells in another site may solve the problem. The fact that fluoride is unevenly distributed in groundwater, both vertically and horizontally, means that every well has to be tested individually for fluoride in areas endemic for fluorosis, extrapolating sample tubewell tests to a larger area does not provide an accurate picture.
- *Changing the dietary habits:* People living in high fluoride zone can make certain changes in their diet, it may help them to keep away the problem of fluorosis. Vitamin C inhibits the progress of fluorosis (P. Singh *et al.* 2011). Thus people should be directed to add items like: amla, lemon, oranges, tomato, sprouted cereals/pulses and dhainya leaves in their food. Clinical data indicate that adequate calcium intake is clearly associated with a reduced risk of dental fluorosis. So it is recommended to consume calcium rich food in endemic zones. It includes: milk, yoghurt, leafy vegetables, drumstick leaves and sesame seed. Foods containing anti-oxidants help in preventing fluorosis. These foods include garlic, ginger, carrot, papaya, pumpkin white onion and green leafy vegetables. Vitamin E also has a prophylactic role. Its sources include: whole grain cereals, vegetable oils, green vegetables and dried beans. Avoid the use of Tobacco and beetle nut.

These do not remove Fluoride:

- *Boiling water:* This will concentrate the fluoride rather than reduce it.
- *Freezing water:* Freezing water does not affect the concentration of fluoride.

Steps to reduce Fluoride

- Avoid fluoride supplements.

Fluoride Rich Food Substances

- Black tea and Lemon tea (tea with milk is safe).
- Black rock salt (kala namak).
- Black rock salt lased pickles.
- Garam masala, salty snacks.
- Chaat and Chaat masala.
- Canned fruit juices.
- Cannel fish.
- Fluoride contaminated drinking water.
- Chewing of tobacco.
- Supari (arccanut).
- Hajmola and other Churan containing rock salt.

Fluoride Rich Dental Products

- Fluoridated toothpaste.
- Mouth rinse.
- Varnish.
- Sodium fluoride tablets (for treatment of Osteoporosis) (UNICEF).

Conclusion

After the study of various research papers it has been observe that many diseases and health problems have been generated due to the excess intake of fluoride in the drinking water. Source of drinking water in rajasthan is ground water, is based on Fluoride poisoning can be prevented or minimized by using alternative water sources, by removing excessive fluoride from drinking water, and by improving the nutritional status of populations at risk. Some governments are not yet fully aware of the fluoride problem or convinced of its adverse impact on their populations. Efforts are therefore needed to support more research on the subject and promote systematic policy responses by government.

REFERENCES

1. Agarwal V., Vaish A.K. and Vaish P., Ground Water Quality: Focus on Fluoride and Fluorosis in Rajasthan. Current Science, 1997, Vol. 73, No. 99. pp. 743-746.
2. A Report on Fluorosis by State Institute of Health and Family Welfare, Jaipur (SIHFW), 2008.
3. A.K. Susheela, Sound Planning and Implementation of Fluoride and Fluorosis Mitigation Programme in an Endemic Village, Proceedings: International Workshop on Fluoride in Drinking Water: Strategies, Management and Mitigation, Bhopal, 2001, p. 1-12.
4. A.K. Vaish and P. Vaish, A Case Study of Fluorosis Mitigation in Dungarpur District, Rajasthan, India, 3rd International Workshop on Fluorosis Prevention and Defluoridation of Water 1997. p. 97-104.
5. A.N. Deshmukh, P.M. Wadaskar, and D.B. Malpe, Fluorine in Environment: A Review Gondwana Geol. Mag., 1995, 9: 1-20.
6. Booklet on International Workshop on fluoride in Drinking Water, Strategies, Management and Mitigation, Public Health Engineering Department, Governent of Madhya Pradesh, Bhopal (22-24 January, 2001), 27p.
7. Choubisa, S.L., Fluoride Distribution and Fluorosis in some Villages of Banswara District of Rajasthan, *Ind. J. Environ. Health* 39 (4) 1997, 281-288.
8. Defluoridation of Drinking Water: Efficacy and Need Anurag Tewari*, Ashutosh Dubey A. Tewari *et al. Journal of Chemical and Pharmaceutical Research 2009*, 1 (1):31-37.
9. Prevention and Control of Fluorosis in India, Rajiv Gandhi National Drinking Water, Mission 1993.
10. Rani, Bina, Fluoride and Fluorosis in Rajasthan: An Overview, A Project Report [IGNOU], 2006.

11. RGNDWM, Prevention and Control of Fluorosis in India. Health Aspects, Ministry of Rural Development, CGO Complex, 1993.
12. SARITA, Severity of Fluoride Pollution in Drinking Water of the Rural Sector of Dungarpur district of Rajasthan, Final Project Report, 1995104 pp.
13. Susheela, A.K., Fluorosis Management Programme in India Current Science, 1990, 77, 1250.

Pages 158-175

HEAVY METALS AND METALLOIDS IN BIOSPHERE: *IMPACTS AND ASSESSMENT*
Edited by **: Dr. Avnish Chauhan; Dr. Sandeep Gupta & Dr. Pawan Kumar Bharti**
Edition **: 2017**
ISBN : 978-93-5056-860-6
Published by **: Discovery Publishing House Pvt. Ltd., New Delhi (India)**

Assessment on Defluoridation in Water using Chemical Method

Batch Study and Optimization by Response Surface Methodology (RSM) and Artificial Neural Network (ANN)

Swapnila Roy

ABSTRACT

The present study is focused on de-fluoridation in water using calcium chloride ($CaCl_2$) in acidic medium and the different process parameters are optimized using four parameters Response Surface Methodology (RSM) and Artificial Neural Network (ANN). ANN is the mathematical model which is the weighted sum of all input variables via connections and computes its own output value through output variables. In RSM a central composite design (CCD) with the help of Design Expert Software is applied to study the interactions of different process parameters. The optimum conditions are obtained by statistical investigation such as: strength of $CaCl_2$ solution 2M, volume of phosphoric acid (H_3PO_4) 12 ml, reaction temperature 323 K; reaction time 8 minutes. Under the optimized conditions, fluoride removal efficiency is obtained as 99.983 per cent. So it can be concluded that the present investigation provides valuable insights for designing and establishing a wastewater treatment unit.

Keywords: fluoride removal, calcium chloride, phosphoric acid, response surface methodology, artificial neural network, desirability function.

INTRODUCTION

Fluorine is the most electronegative element in the periodic table. The only oxidation state exhibited byfluorine is -1. The ready acceptance of an electron is the reason of the strong oxidizing nature of fluorine. It oxidizes

Department of Chemical Engineering, Jadavpur University, Kolkata, India.

the halide ions in solution or even in solid phase. Anomalous behaviour of fluorine is due to its small size, highest electronegativity, low F-F bond dissociation enthalpy. Most of the reactions of fluorine are exothermic due to its small and strong bond formed by it with other elements.

Fluoride (F^-) is the naturally occurring ion which is mostly found in water. In water it is found in the range of concentration 0.1 ppm to 10 ppm. While groundwater passes through the earth and come in contact to the fluoride compounds, fluoride is dissolved .The deeper the water flow, more the fluoride concentration will be there [1,2,3,4]. Fluoridation in water is defined as the dosing of fluoride waste products from industry in supplied municipal water to get fluoride concentration of approximately one part in a million by weight. Under treated conditions hexa-fluorosilicate is added to fluoridate water, which is 100 per cent dissociated to form fluoride ion. So, water fluoridation is the controlled addition of fluoride to a public water supply. Fluoride is a persistent bio-accumulator. Fluoride has serious side effects, affecting almost every organ in the body and does not reduce tooth decay [5]. The decline in tooth cavities is same in fluoridated and non-fluoridated countries. Fluoride chemically interferes with the hydroxylation of proline. Too much exposure of fluoride disrupts the synthesis of collagen. It results the breakdown of collagen in bone, muscle, skin, cartilage, lungs, kidney [6,7]. The prolonged intake of fluoride contaminated water causes the stiffing of bones and joints. As fluoride has affinity towards calcium, it stores in bones, results mottling of teeth and outward bending of legs from knees. Fluorine gas, which is released in the industry, is very dangerous because it can cause death at very high concentrations and at low concentrations it causes eye and nose irritations.

According to WHO 1984 and Indian standard drinking water specification 1991, the maximum permissible limit of fluoride in drinking water is 1.5 ppm and highest desirable limit is 1.0 ppm [8]. It is practically observed that low calcium and high bicarbonate alkalinity are favorable conditions for high fluoride content in groundwater [9,10]. Fluoride concentrations above 1.5 ppm in drinking water cause dental fluorosis and much higher concentration skeletal fluorosis. Low concentration (approximately 0.5 ppm) provides protection against dental caries. India is among the 23 nations around the globe where health problems occur due to the consumption of fluoride contamination water and the extent of fluoride contamination in water varies from 1.0 to 400 mg/l. In India, 20 million people are severely affected by fluorosis and 40 million people are exposed to risk of endemic fluorosis.

A response surface methodology (RSM) is a set of design of experiments (DOE) which helps to optimize the response [11,12]. This methodology is used to refine models after determining important factors using factorial designs. Response surface methods mainly involves 3 steps:

1. Calculating the coefficients by statistically conducting experiments.
2. To achieve the best operating conditions from maximum or minimum response.
3. Number of responses to be optimized at the same time and desirability function also used in the final step.

Artificial neural network (ANN) is very effective mathematical methods suitable for modeling of different procedures in practical applications. In case of operational models ANN is used because this network is involved with high level of non-linearities, large number of parameters and missing information. ANN is extensively used in different field such as: control systems, optimization and decision making [13]. So this is more beneficial fact. It is experimentally proved that requirement of experiments in ANN is more than RSM to develop a proper mathematical model. But practically ANN can act very well with relatively less data which are statistically well distributed in the input domain. Therefore, experimental data of RSM is very effective to build a reliable model of ANN.

In the present study four different parameters such as: strength of calcium chloride, volume of H_3PO_4, reaction time and temperature are known as input variables (process parameters). Total 25 experiments were carried out to estimate the interaction effects of the four input variables on fluoride removal efficiency (output variable).

Materials and Methodology

Preparation of Synthetic Fluoride Solutions

Sodium fluoride (Merck, Germany) is used in this study. Stock fluoride ion solution (1000 mg L^{-1}) was prepared by dissolving accurately weighed quantity in double-distilled water. Experimental fluoride solution of different concentrations were prepared by diluting the stock solution with suitable volume of double-distilled water.

Preparation of Different Strength of Calcium Chloride ($CaCl_2$) Solution

Here calcium chloride dehydrate (Merck) is used in this study. 1000 ml of 1 M calcium chloride stock solution is prepared by weighing 147.02 g of $CaCl_2.2H_2O$ (Molecular weight = 147). Then it is dissolved in distilled water. Similarly other different strength of $CaCl_2$ solution are prepared by weighing accurate quantity of $CaCl_2.2H_2O$ and dissolving in double-distilled water according to the required volume.

Experimental

Batch Experiments

For batch experiments, 100 mlfluoride solutions of concentration 50 mgL^{-1} were taken in 250 mL PTFE conical flasks. The particular weighed amount of adsorbent was added to each solution. Then the flasks were agitated at 150 rpm in an incubator shaker at different temperatures. The effects of reaction time (10,15, 25,30, 40,45,50 and 60 min), reactant dose (0.2,0.5, 0.75,1 ,1.5 g/ 100 ml) and temperature (303, 308,313,320, 323,328 and 333 K) were evaluated during the batch studies.

Experimental Setup

Experiments were conducted in temperature controlled incubator shaker (INNOVA 4430, New Brunswick Scientific, Canada). Temperature fluctuations in the reactor were negligible. After shaking for particular time intervals those samples were collected from the flasks for analysis of fluoride concentration in the solution. The residual amount of fluoride ineachconical flask was estimated by using ion-meter (Thermo Scientific Orion ion-meter, USA).

Fluoride Concentration Determination

The change in fluoride (F^-) concentration due to chemical reaction is determined by Orion ion-meter according to Standard Methods [14]. 10 ml sample is placed in 100 ml beaker and 1ml of TISAB III solution is added to the beaker to maintain pH 5-5.5 and to eliminate the interference effect of complexions [15]. The total volume should be sufficient to immerse the electrode and permit the use of the stirrer. Fluoride concentrations of the samples are taken directly from the ion-meter.

Percentage of fluoride removal efficiency is calculated with a standard RSM design (CCD) and 20 experiments were carried out. The per cent removal (%) of fluoride is determined by using the following equation:

$$R(\%) = \frac{C_i - C_0}{C_i} \times 100 \qquad (1)$$

Where C_i is the initial fluoride concentration (mg L^{-1}) and C_0 is the final fluoride concentration in solution (mg L^{-1}).

Optimization using Central Composite Design (CCD)

The main objective of this study is to determine the optimum set of operational variables of the removal of fluoride solution by applying a standard RSM design which is called the CCD. RSM is a statistical method which can optimize the complicated chemical process. So the number of experimental trials are increased to get proper chemical equilibrium or in other words optimum response. But RSM reduces the number of experimental trials. A standard RSM design is used to identify the relationship between the response variable (% removal) and the process variables (strength of $CaCl_2$, volume of nitric acid, reaction time, reaction temperature). By CCD analysis high range prediction is possible with in and outside the design range. The experimental range of the selected process variables with their units and notation is given in Table 9.1. The response *i.e.,* output variable is expressed as a function of the independent variables.

Table 9.1: Experimental range and levels of independent variables

Sl. No.	Variable	Unit	Notation	Range and Levels (coded)				
				$-\alpha$	-1	0	+1	$+\alpha$
1.	Strength of $CaCl_2$	Molar	A	0.5	1	1.5	2	2.5
2.	Volume of H_3PO_4	ml	B	3	6	9	12	15
3.	Reaction time	min	C	3.5	5	6.5	8	9.5
4.	Reaction temperature	K	D	308	313	318	323	328

Statistical Analysis

In order to maintain quality assurance, the precision, accuracy, repeatability and reproducibility of the obtained experimental data, all experiments are performed thrice, and the mean values are expressed in data analysis. The calculated relative standard deviations within ± 2 per cent.

Results and Discussion

Batch Chemical Studies

Batch chemical studies are carried out using 100 ml solution of fluoride in a PTFE conical flask with constant shaking using an incubator shaker in temperature controlled condition. The following operating conditions such as: initial concentration, volume of H3PO4, reaction time and strength of $CaCl_2$.

Interaction Effect of Process Parameters

Effect of Concentration

It is illustrated from (Fig. 9.1) batch experiments that with increasing concentration of fluoride solution, de-fluoridation efficiency increases gradually. This phenomena can be explained that within the experimental range (20-500 mg L^{-1}) of concentration of fluoride solution results in larger amount of precipitated calcium fluoride (CaF_2). As a result de-fluoridation efficiency increases. In this case, the optimum concentration of fluoride solution is 50 mgL^{-1}.

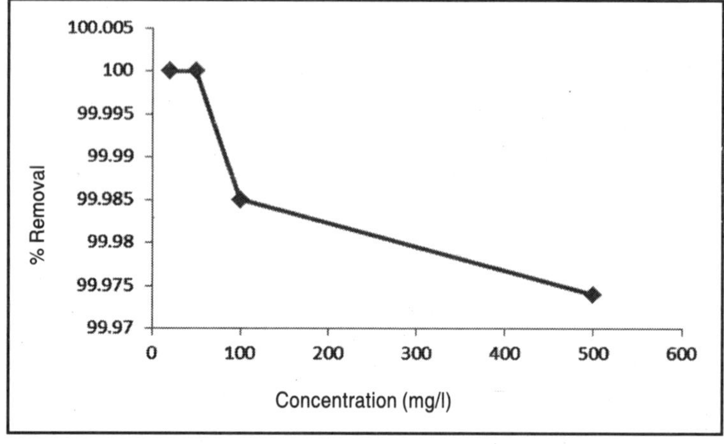

Fig. 9.1: **Effect of initial concentration of fluoride on de-fluoridation by $CaCl_2$**

Effect of pH of Solution

It is observed (Fig. 9.2) that with decreasing pH at particular temperature, percentage removal efficiency increases. In this chemical study if the pH of medium increases at particular temperature, the fluoride removal efficiency decreases. The reason is that if acidity in medium increases, most of the fluoride ions are precipitated as CaF_2, but if acidity in medium decreases the fluoride ions increases in solution, which results decrease in removal efficiency. In this experimental study, the optimum pH determined as 2.00, at which maximum de-fluoridation efficiency is achieved.

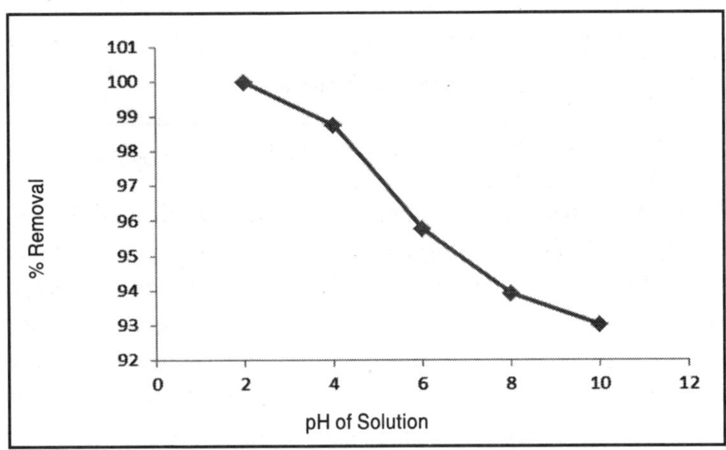

Fig. 9.2: **Effect of pH on de-fluoridation by $CaCl_2$**

Effect of Reaction Time

It is observed (Fig. 9.3) from the experimental results that on increasing the contact time at particular temperature, de-fluoridation efficiency increases. As the reaction time increases, chemically the precipitated form of fluoride (CaF_2) accumulated gradually. But after certain point (40 min), de-fluoridation efficiency decreases. This was because of most of fluoride ions are precipitated, so saturation point is achieved. After that dissolved fluoride ions are increasing, which results in decreasing de-fluoridation efficiency.

Effect of Strength of $CaCl_2$ Solution

It is observed (figure not given) that with increasing the strength of $CaCl_2$ solution, the percentage removal of fluoride increases in solution upto a certain point. With increasing the strength of $CaCl_2$ solution, Ca^{2+} and Cl^- ions increases quantitatively, consequently in the fluoride solution those ions are increasing in the specified volume. As $CaCl_2$ has higher solubility, solower ratio of $CaCl_2$ to solution is required. But at certain point (2 M) the chemical reaction attained the saturation point. Chemically, most of the reactant molecules are reacted (CaF_2 precipitated), so in soluble form fluoride ions are not available remarkably. After that point Ca^{2+} and Cl^- ions increases but as the reaction has attained at saturated point, the removal efficiency is constant.

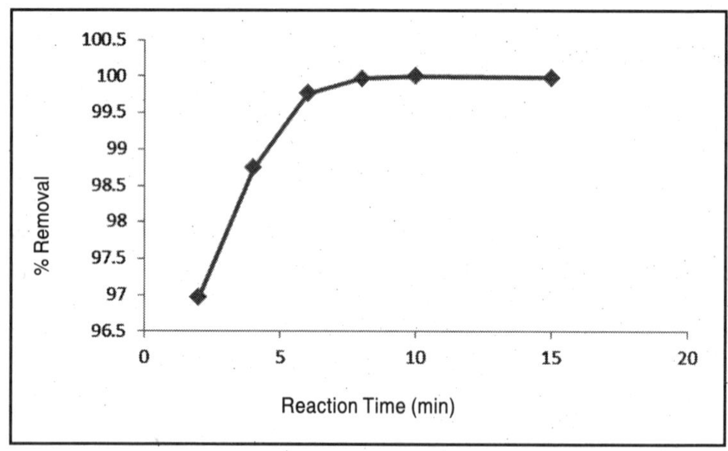

Fig. 9.3: **Effect of reaction time on de-fluoridation by $CaCl_2$**

Chemical Effect of different Parameters on Fluoride Removal

Precipitation of the fluoride species into a chemically stable form is the most effective form of the removal of fluoride from waste water [16,17,18].

- Fluorides of alkali metals have low solubility. Among the alkali metal fluorides, CaF_2 is least soluble in water. So removal of fluoride from waste water by converting it into CaF_2 has become the most widely used method for treatment. $CaCl_2$ has higher solubility, so the lower ratio of additive to solution is required. It is cost effective and it has better control pH of the treated solution.
- The effect of pH of treated solution is the important factor to reach chemical equilibrium. The reaction with $CaCl_2$ is more complex, as shown by equations (1) and (2) given below:

  $NaF + H_3PO_4 = Na_3PO_4 + 3\ HF$ .... (2)

  $2HF + CaCl_2 = CaF_2\ (ppt) + 2\ HCl$ .... (3)

  In order to drive the reaction to the right side, and remove more of the soluble fluoride, the low pH of the solution is required. That is why H_3PO_4 is required. In case of H_2SO_4,99 per cent solution is precipitated as $CaSO_4$, which interferes in the equilibrium system. In case of HCl, HNO_3, the pH of the solution is not as low as for fluoride removal system required. So H3PO4 is the proper choice for fluoride removal.
- Reaction time is the significant factor to attain the reaction equilibrium in the proper time. As the reaction time increases, the ionic interaction within the reactant molecules increases proportionally. According to the Le-chatelier's principle, all the chemical reactions are reversible in nature. It can be used to predict the effect of a change in conditions on a chemical equilibrium. So the reaction proceed towards the right side of the equilibrium to get precipitated as CaF_2. If the reaction equilibrium is

achieved in the particular time then by the effect of any extraneous factors it has tendency to further proceed to the left side of reaction equilibrium.

- Reaction temperature is the important driving force to get the reaction in the equilibrium state within a short time. After particular temperature most of the reactant molecules reached in the activated energy state. In the activated energy state the highest number of molecules are interacted and consequently equilibrium drives to the right hand side. As a result fluoride concentration decreases in the soluble form, increases in the precipitated form which enhances the removal efficiency in the system.

Estimation of Response Surface for Maximum Fluoride Removal

The response variable is expressed as a function of the process variables which is statistically called second order multiple regression model:

$$\% \text{ Removal} = \beta_0 + \sum_{i=1}^{k} \beta i\, xi + \sum_{i=1}^{k} \beta ii\, xi2 + \sum_{i=1} \sum_{j=i+1} \beta ijxixj + \varepsilon \quad \text{.......................} (4)$$

where, β_0 is the constant coefficient, β_i, β_{ii} and β_{ij} are the coefficients for the linear, quadratic and interaction effect, x_i and x_j are the design variables and ε is the error.

A total of 25 experiments are conducted in triplicate according to the CCD matrix in Table 9.2 and the average values are utilised in data analysis. The experimental data are analyzed by Design Expert Software. The interaction among the different independent variables and their corresponding effect on the response are studied by analyzing the response surface and contour plots.

Table 9.2: CCD for four independent variables along with the observed response

Run No.	A: Strength of $CaCl_2$ (M)	B: Volume of H_3PO_4 (ml)	C: Reaction Time (min)	D: Reaction Temperature (K)	% Removal of Fluoride
1	2	3	4	5	6
1	0.5	9	6.5	318 K	99.956
2	1.5	9	6.5	318 K	99.959
3	1.5	3	6.5	318 K	99.911
4	1.5	9	9.5	318 K	99.964
5	1.5	9	3.5	318 K	99.956
6	1.5	15	6.5	318 K	99.976
7	2.5	9	6.5	318 K	99.965
8	1.0	6	8	313 K	99.956
9	2.0	6	5	313 K	99.953
10	2.0	12	8	313 K	99.971

Contd...

1	2	3	4	5	6
11	1.0	12	5	313 K	99.968
12	1.0	12	8	313 K	99.972
13	2.0	6	8	313 K	99.953
14	1.0	6	5	313 K	99.949
15	2.0	12	5	313 K	99.972
16	1.0	12	8	323 K	99.979
17	1.0	6	8	323 K	99.96
18	1.0	12	5	323 K	99.917
19	2.0	12	5	323 K	99.981
20	2.0	12	8	323 K	99.983
21	2.0	6	5	323 K	99.964
22	2.0	6	8	323 K	99.962
23	1.0	6	5	323 K	99.958
24	1.5	9	6.5	328 K	99. 952
25	1.5	9	6.5	308 K	99.973

In this case response surface quadratic model shows that the interaction effects of strength of $CaCl_2$, volume of H_3PO_4, reaction time and temperature are significant. Also, the square effect of above process variables are significant. In order to study the interaction among the different independent variables and their corresponding effect on the response, response surface plots are drawn. A contour plot is a graphical representation of a three dimensional response surface as a function of two independent variables, keeping all other variables constant. These plots are helpful in understanding both the main and interaction effects of the independent variables on the response.

The response variable which is expressed as a function of independent variables defined in multiple regression model (Eq. 4), developed by the software is expressed in the form of different numerical factors in equation (5) given below:

$$\begin{aligned}\%\ \text{Removal} = &+99.77927-0.090417*A+8.47222E\text{-}004*B-0.030009*C+0.012075*D \\ &+7.04167E\text{-}003*AB-2.50000E\text{-}004*AC+7.50000E\text{-}005*AD+8.47222E\text{-}004*BC \\ &-4.37500E\text{-}004*BD+2.25000E\text{-}004*CD+9.45833E\text{-}003*A^2+2.76620E\text{-}004*B^2 \\ &+8.84259E\text{-}004*C^2-8.04167E\text{-}0058*D^2 \quad (5)\end{aligned}$$

In this case B, C, D, AB, BC, BD, A2, B2, C2, D2 are significant model terms. The goodness of fit of the modelis verified by the correlation coefficient (R^2) between the experimental and model predicted values of the response variable [19] (Fig. 9.4). Statistically R^2 value of 0.9771 indicates that the model is statistically significant. The predicted correlation coefficient (predicted R^2 0.9316) also shows good agreement with the adjusted correlation coefficient (adjusted $R^2$0.9557). A coefficient of variance (3.577×10^{-3}) indicates reliability of the data obtained by performing 25 experiments. Overall, the applicability of the model is used to predict the percentage removal of fluoride in solution within the limits of the experimental factors.

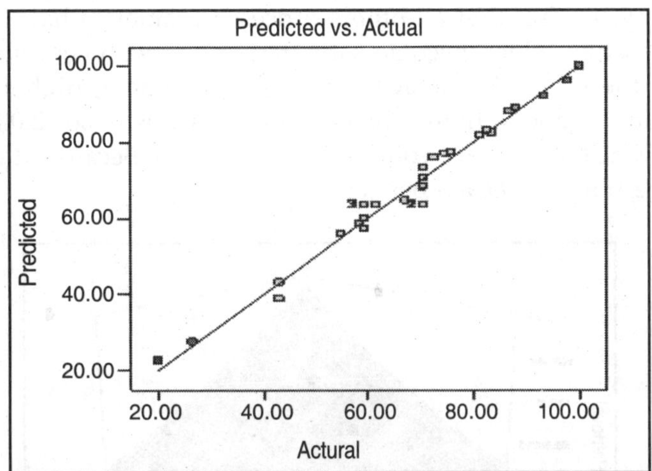

Fig. 9.4: **The graph showing predicted removal % vs actual removal % of fluoride**

Interaction Effect

Effect of Reaction time and Strength of $CaCl_2$

Within the experimental range, the response function, *i.e.*, percentage of removal increases not proportionally as there are also other function such as: volume of phosphoric acid and reaction temperature. These two factors (temperature and volume of acid) interfere in this chemical reaction. On the contrary, the fluoride content decreases in solution with increasing reaction time. In the Fig. 9.5 the optimum point is (2.00,8.00), where the strength of $CaCl_2$ is 2 M and reaction time is 8 min. Because at this point the optimum response is 99.983 per cent.

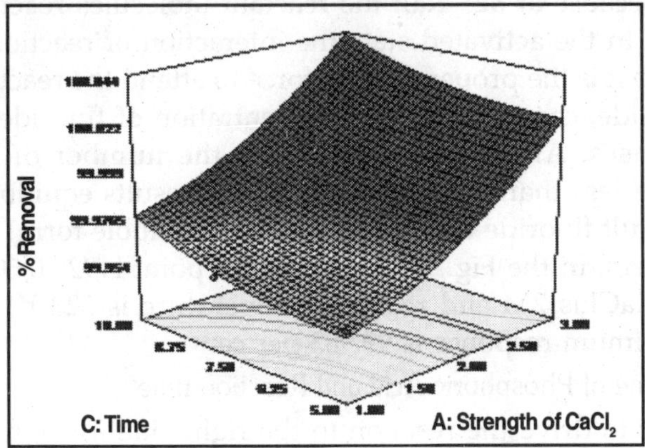

Fig. 9.5: **RSM plot showing interaction effect of strength of CaCl2 and reaction time**

Effect of Volume of Phosphoric Acid and Strength of $CaCl_2$

From Fig. 9.6, it is observed that the response function *i.e.,* percentage removal increases, with increasing the strength of $CaCl_2$ and volume of phosphoric acid within the experimental range. Such behaviour can be explained by the fact that all others process parameters have capability of chemical reaction which become saturated at a certain concentration. With increasing the strength of $CaCl_2$ and volume of acid, higher response is observed. In the above figure the optimum point is (2.00,12.00), where the strength of $CaCl_2$ is 2 M and volume of acid is 12 ml. Because at this point the optimum response is 99.983 per cent.

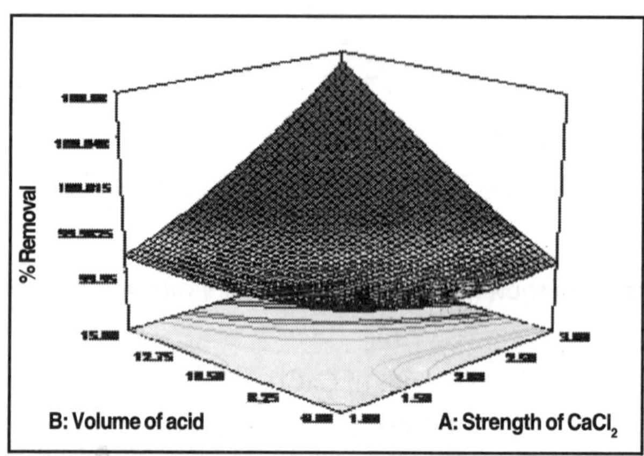

Fig. 9.6: **RSM plot showing interaction effect of strength of $CaCl_2$ and volume of acid**

Effect of Strength of $CaCl_2$ and Reaction Temperature

Within the experimental range, the response function, *i.e.,* percentage of removal increases not regularly as there are also other function such as: volume of acid and reaction time (Fig. 9.7). At 323K response function is maximum. Because at 323 Kall the reactant molecules reached at activated energy state. In the activated state the interaction of reaction molecules are maximum. So it is the proper driving force to attend the reaction equilibrium in the right side, consequently the concentration of fluoride (in the soluble form) decreases. After that temperature the number of non-interacted molecules are less than the first stage, which results equilibrium to the left side. As a result fluoride concentration (in the soluble form) increases in the removal system. In the Fig. 9.7 the optimum point is (2.00,50.00), where the strength of $CaCl_2$is 2M and reaction temperature is 323 K. Because at this point the optimum response is 99.983 per cent.

Effect of Volume of Phosphoric Acid and Reaction time

In order to drive the reaction to the right side for removal of fluoride in soluble form, reaction time and pH of the solution, *i.e.,* volume of

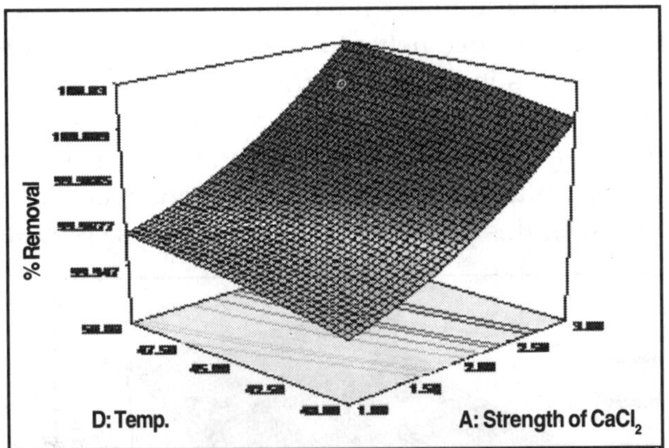

Fig. 9.7: **RSM plot showing interaction effect of strength of $CaCl_2$ and reaction temperature**

phosphoric acid are the significant factors. If the volume of acid increases, consequently, lower pH of solution effectively drive the reaction to the right side, as well as higher reaction time indicates the higher the time of ionic interaction resulting the decreasing fluoride concentration (soluble form) in the system. So these two factors affected proportionally to the fluoride removal system. In Fig. 9.8 the optimum point is (12.00,8.00), where the volume of acid is 12 ml and reaction time is 8 min. Because at this point the optimum response is 99.983 per cent.

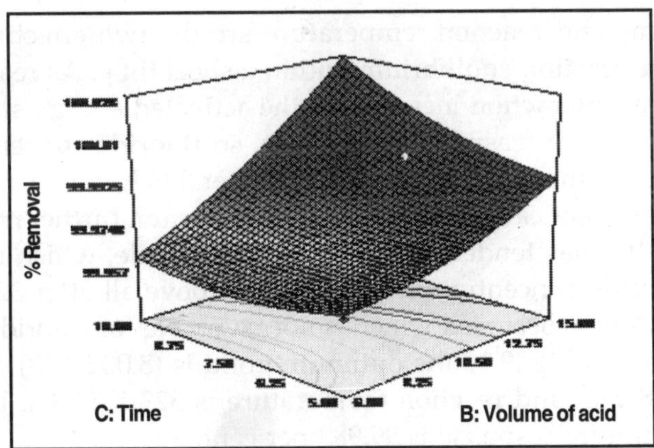

Fig. 9.8: **RSM plot showing interaction effect of volume of acid and reaction time**

Effect of Volume of Phosphoric Acid and Reaction Temperature

With increasing the volume of nitric acid, per cent removal of fluoride in solution increases. At 323 K(50°C) the optimum response function is shown maximum. Because at this temperature graphically activation energy is the highest, so at that point the number interaction of molecules is maximum. Consequently, this driving force helps to attain the reaction equilibrium in the right side, which results in decreasing fluoride concentration in solution. But after 323 K(50°C), the ionic interaction decreases which results increasing fluoride concentration in solution. In Fig. 9.9 the optimum point is (12.00,50.00), where the volume of nitric acid is 12 ml and reaction temperature is 323 K(50°C). Because at this point the optimum response is 99.983 per cent.

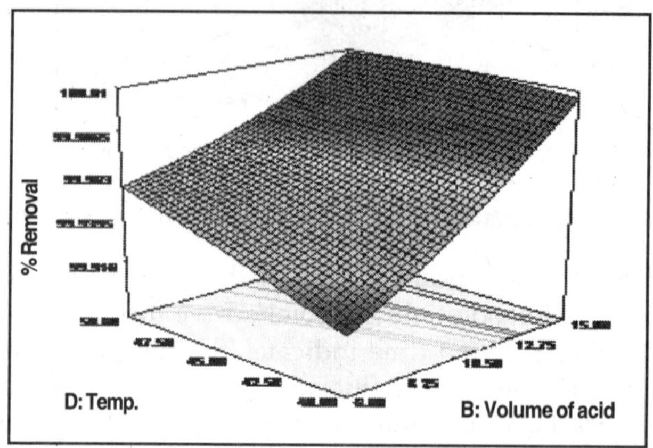

Fig. 9.9: **RSM plot showing interaction effect of volume of acid and reaction temperature**

Effect of Reaction Time and Reaction Temperature

Reaction time and reaction temperature are the two effective driving force to attain the reaction equilibrium within a short time. As reaction time increases, the ionic interaction increases in the activated energy state, which helps the reaction to be feasible at right side, so fluoride concentration in solution decreases in the removal system. But after 323 K (50°C), most of the reactive molecules chemically interacted and equilibrium further not proceed to the right side but has tendency to proceed at left side, which results the increment of fluoride concentration in solution. Above all after 323 K(50°C) the opposite incident is occurred which is not favorable for fluoride removal system in solution. In Fig. 9.10 the optimum point is (8.00,50.00), where the reaction time is 8 min and reaction temperature is 323 K(50°C). Because at this point the optimum response is 99.983 per cent.

Desirability Function

From the optimization results using central composite design, it is observed that the optimized functions are: strength of CaCl-$_2$ 2 M, volume of H_3PO_4 12 ml, reaction temperature 323 K; reaction time 8 minutes, which are expressed as desirability ramps.

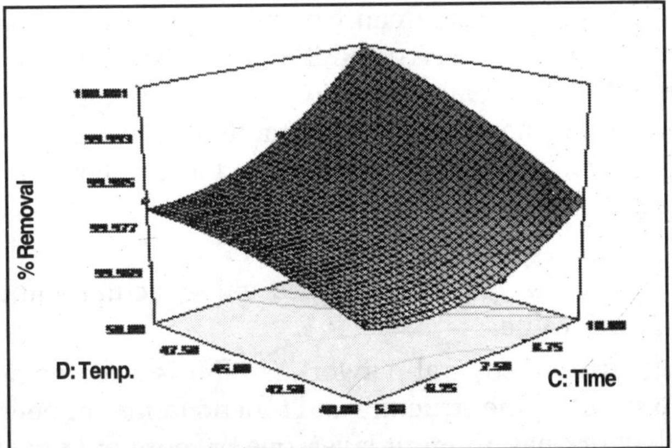

Fig. 9.10: **RSM plot showing interaction effect of reaction temperature and reaction time**

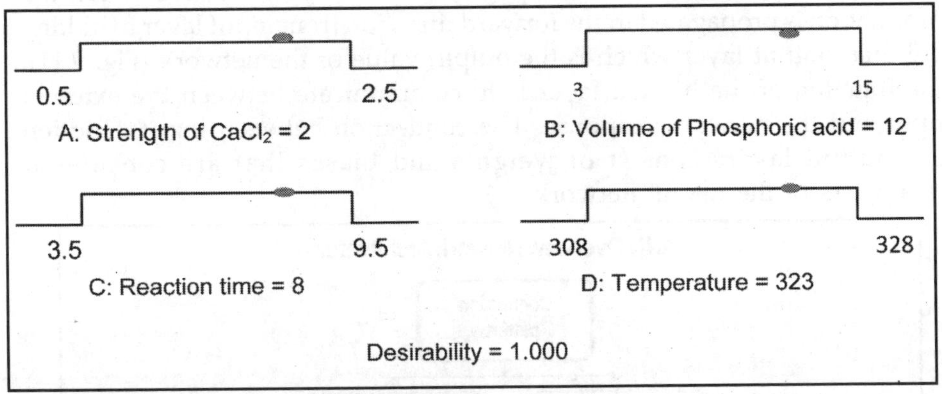

Confirmatory Experiments

To support the optimized data given by numerical modeling confirmatory experiments are conducted with the parameters as suggested by the model (strength of $CaCl_2$ solution 2M; volume of H3PO4 12 ml, reaction temperature 323 K; reaction time 8 minutes). These are found to be optimum condition for maximum fluoride removal. The corresponding removal efficiency in optimum condition is found 99.983 per cent experimentally and theoretically it is 100 per cent and the error observed is 0.017 per cent which is very low. The removal efficiency of the techniques (RSM and ANN) is performed in this study. The predicted responses achieved from RSM and ANN are compared with the actual values.

Optimisation using Artificial Neural Network (ANN)

- *Artificial Neural Network (ANN):* ANN is the mathematical software which is used in this study for simulation. The input variables are concentration of calcium chloride, reaction time, reaction temperature and volume of concentrated nitric acid. The corresponding fluoride removal efficiency is used as a target. The performance of the ANNs is statistically computed by the root mean squared error (RMSE), the coefficient of determination (R^2) and the absolute average deviation (AAD). All experimental variables and response are normalized between 0 and 1 due to higher homogeneous results. The normalization equation applied is as follow:

$$y_n = \frac{y_a - y_{min}}{y_{max} - y_{min}}$$

where y_n, y_a, y_{min}, y_{max} are normalized value, actual value, minimum value, and maximum value.

In generally artificial neural network (ANN) is a mathematical model which is used to simulate the structure and functionalities of neural networks [20]. A neural network has an input layer, one or more hidden layer, and an output layer. The objective of a neural network is to calculate output values from input values by its own propagation. In the feed forward ANN, the information is propagated in the forward direction from input layer to hidden and then output layer which is the output value of the network (Fig. 9.11). The function of the hidden layer is to communicate between the external input and the network response. The connection between inputs, hidden and output layers consist of weights and biases that are considered parameters of the neural network.

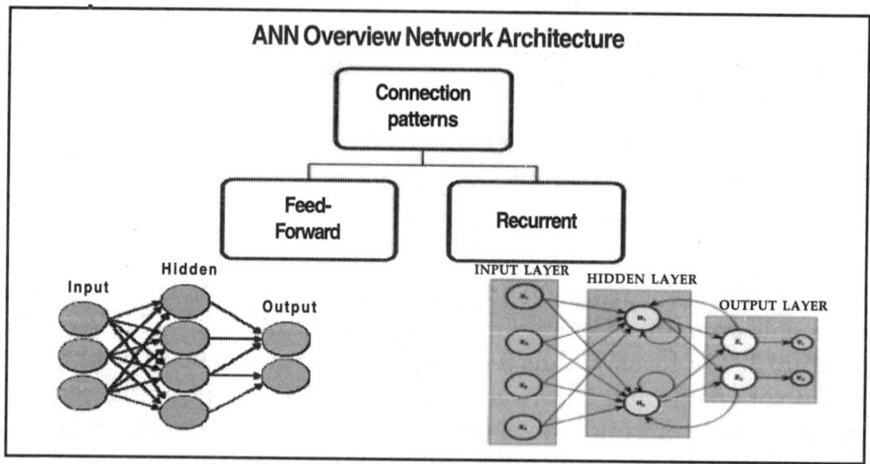

Fig. 9.11: **ANN Overview**

In this present study, output vs targets is graphically plotted (Fig. 9.12) and theoretical removal vs experimental removal is plotted. (Fig. 9.13).

Conclusion

The objective of the present study is to investigate the combined effect of various process parameters on chemical removal of fluoride using response surface methodology. ACCD is used to study the effect ofstrength of $CaCl_2$,

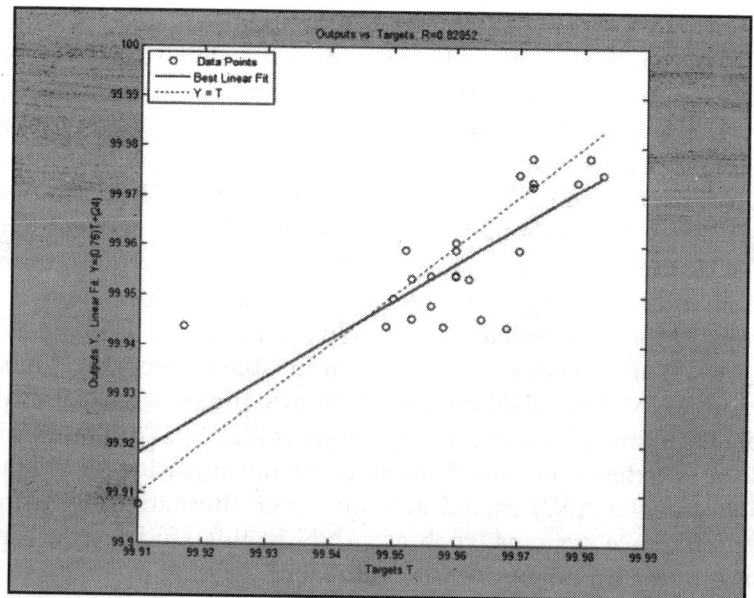

Fig. 9.12: **The plot showing Output variables Vs Target**

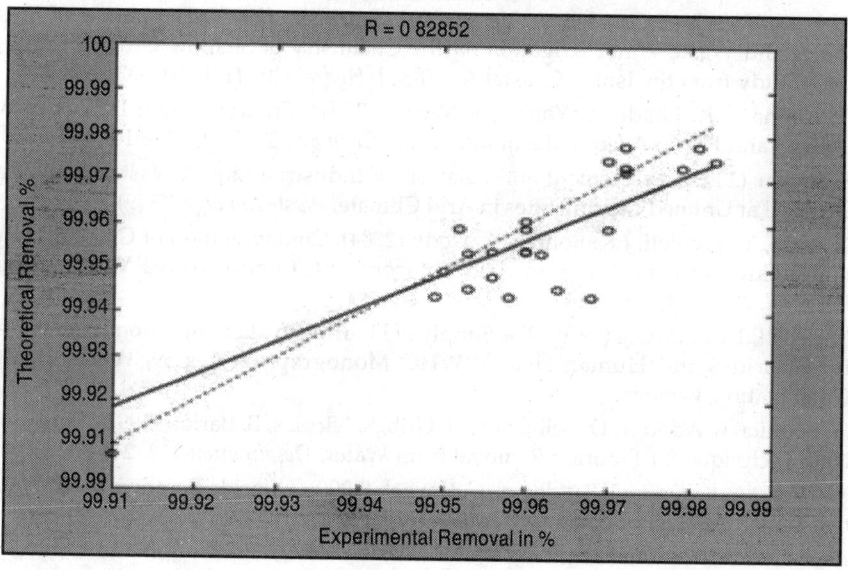

Fig. 9.13: **The plot showing Theoretical removal Vs Experimental removal**

volume of phosphoric acid, reaction time and reaction temperature. An empirical quadratic model equation is developed for the chemically removal process [21]. The experimental values are found to be in good agreement with the values predicted by the model. The interaction effect of the experimental parameters is established by response surface plots. It was observed that strength of calcium chloride solution, volume of H_3PO_4, reaction time, and reaction temperature significantly affected the fluoride removal efficiency. The level of the four variables, strength of $CaCl_2$ solution 2M; volume of H_3PO_4 12 ml, reaction temperature 323 K; reaction time 8 minutes are found to be optimum for maximum fluoride removal. The corresponding removal efficiency in optimum conditions is found 99.983 per cent. Overall, it can be said that the application of RSM is an effective approach for optimization and modelling of the fluoride removal process. The root mean square error (RMSE), coefficient of determination (R^2) and absolute average deviation (AAD) are used together to obtain reliable mathematical model of the RSM and ANN. The ANN model has higher predictive capability than RSM model with limited number of experiments [22]. So it can be concluded that as RSM is extensively used method for optimization of chemo defluoridation, but the ANN model may be better alternative. By using the artificial intelligence systems, such as: ANN in this study, an acceptable performance in the modeling for the removal of fluoride is achieved.

REFERENCES

1 A. Kass, Y.Yechieli Gavrieli, A. Vengosh, A. Starinsky (2005). The Impact of Fresh Water and Waste Water Irrigation on the Chemistry of Shallow Groundwater: A Case Study from the Israeli Coastal Aquifer, *J. Hydrol.* 300 (1-4), 314-331.

2. C. Amina, L.K. Lhadi, A. Younsi, J. Murdy (2004). Environmental Impact of An Urban Land Fill on A Coastal Aquifer, *J. Afr. Earth Sci.* 39 (3-5), 509-516.

3. F. Anwar (2003). Assessment and Analysis of Industrial Liquid Waste and Sludge Disposal at Unlined Landfill Sites in Arid Climate, *Waste Manage.* 23 (9), 817-824.

4. O. Oren, Y. Yechieli, J.K. Bohlke, A. Dody (2004). Contamination of Ground Water under Cultivated Fields in an Arid Environment, Central Arava Valley, Israel, *J. Hydrol.* 290 (3/4), 312-328.

5. M.C. Bell, T.G. Ludwig (1970). The Supply of Fluoride to Man: Ingestion From Water, In: Fluorides and Human Health, WHO Monograph Series 59, World Health Organization, Geneva.

6. H. Lounici, L. Addour, D. Belhocine, H. Grib, S. Nicolas, B. Bariou (1997). Study of a New Technique for Fluoride Removal from Water, *Desalination* 114, 241-251.

7. M. Hichour, F. Persin, J. Sandeaux, C. Gavach (2000). Fluoride Removal From Water by Donnan Analysis, Sep. *Purif. Technol.* 18, 1-11.

8. Rajiv Gandhi National Drinking Water Mission (1993). Prevention and Control of Fluorosis in India.

9. K.R. Bulusu, B.N. Pathak (1980). Discussion on Water Defluoridation with Activated Alumina, *J. Environ. Eng. Div.* 106 (2), 466-469.

10. J.O. Hem (1959). Study and Interpretation of Chemical Characteristics of Natural Water, U.G. Geological Survey Water Supply Paper, p. 1473.

11. U.K. Garg, M.P. Kaur, D. Sud and V.K. Garg (2009). Removal of Hexavalent Chromium from Aqueous Solution by Adsorptionon Treated Sugarcane bagasse using Response Surface Methodological Approach, *Desalination*, 249,475-479.

12. M. Jain, V.K. Garg and K. Kadrivelu (2011). Investigation of Cr(VI) Adsorption onto Chemically treated *Helianthus annus*: Optimizationusing Response Surface Methodology, Bioresour. *Technol.*, 102, 600-605.
13. D. Bas and I.H. Boyaci (2007). "Modeling and Optimization II: Comparison of Estimation Capabilities of Response Surface Methodology with Artificial Neural Networks in a Biochemical Reaction," *Journal of Food Engineering*, Vol. 78, No. 3, pp. 846-854.
14. APHA, AWWA, WEF (2010). Standard Methods for Examination of Water and Waste Water. 22nd ed. Washington: American Public Health Association; 2012. 1360 pp. ISBN978-087553-013-0.
15. G. Alagumuthu; M. Rajan. *Chem. Eng. J.*, 158, 451-457.
16. Nawlakhe W.G., Paramasivam R. (1993). Defluorination of Potable Water by Nalgonda Technique. *Current Science*; 65(10): 743-8.
17. Azbar N., Turkman A (2000). Defluorination in Drinking Waters. Water Science Technology; 42(1-2):403-7.
18. Reardon EI, Wang YX (2000). A Limestone Reactor for Fluoride Removal from Waste Waters. *Environ. Science Technology*; 34:3247-53.
19. Hamsaveni D.R., Prapulla S.G., Divakar S. (2001). Response Surface Methodological Approach for the Synthesis of Isobutyl Butyrate. Process Biochem 36:1103-1109.
20. W. Lou and S. Nakai (2001). "Application of Artificial Neural Networks for Predicting the Thermal Inactivation of Bacteria: A Combined Effect of Temperature, pH and Water Activity," *Food Research International*, Vol. 34, No. 7, pp. 573-591.
21. Amini M., Younesi H., Bahramifar N., Lorestani AAZ., Ghorbani F., Daneshi A., Sharifzadeh M. (2008). Application of Response Surface Methodology for Optimization of Lead Biosorption in an Aqueous Solution by Aspergillusniger. *J. Hazard Mater* 54:694-702.
22. M. Basri, R.R. Zaliha, A. Ebrahimpour, A.B. Salleh, E.R. Gunawan and M.B. Abdul-Rahman (2007). "Comparison of Estimation Capabilities of Response Surface Methodology (RSM) with Artificial Neural Network (ANN) in Lipase-Catalyzed Synthesis of Palm-Based Wax Ester," *BMC Bio-technology*, Vol. 7, pp. 53-63.

Index

*****